Since My Last Confession

Also by Scott Pomfret

(with Scott Whittier)

nonfiction

Q Guide to Wine and Cocktails

fiction

E-Male
Hot Sauce
Nick of Time
Nothing Personal
Razor Burn
Spare Parts
Surf 'n' Turf

Since My Last Confession

a gay catholic memoir

Scott Pomfret

Arcade Publishing ✠ New York

FIRST EDITION

Title page illustration by Dennis Cox / iStockphoto

Some names, identifying characteristics, topics of discussion, and the timing of events have been changed to protect confidentiality.

Library of Congress Cataloging-in-Publication Data

Pomfret, Scott.
  Since my last confession : a gay Catholic memoir / Scott Pomfret. —1st ed.
    p. cm.
  ISBN 978-1-55970-869-2 (alk. paper)
  1. Catholic gay men—Massachusetts—Boston—Biography. 2. Catholic gay men—Religious life. 3. Homosexuality—Religious aspects—Catholic Church. I. Title.

  BX4705.P65256A3 2008
  282.086'642—dc22   2008006943

Published in the United States by Arcade Publishing, Inc., New York
Distributed by Hachette Book Group USA

Visit our Web site at www.arcadepub.com
Visit Scott Pomfret's Web site at www.ScottPomfret.com
Visit the book's Web site at www.SinceMyLastConfession.com
Visit the book's official confessional at ConfessYourSinsHere.blogspot.com

10 9 8 7 6 5 4 3 2 1

Designed by James Jayo

EB

PRINTED IN THE UNITED STATES OF AMERICA

Contents

Dramatis Personae

Friars

Francis the Franciscan Friar	head of lay ministry committee
Father Bear-Daddy	the Shrine's holy terror
Father Abraham	lector trainer
Father Myron McCormick	benevolent "Let the People Vote" priest

Diocesan priests and Jesuits

Picasso	painter/GLBT Spirituality Group member
Father McSlutty	promiscuous priest
Father Butterballino	struggled with gay marriage directives
Father Pamplemousse	married Rory and Jezebel
Walter Cuenin	testified against amendment banning gay marriage
Father John Sullivan	Courage chaplain
Richard Lewandowski	testified against amendment banning gay marriage
Thomas Carroll	testified against amendment banning gay marriage
James Keenan	testified against amendment banning gay marriage

Lay ministers

Mary Flanagan	fellow lay minister (a Hale Mary)
Mary Flaherty	fellow lay minister (a Hale Mary)
Mary Fleming	fellow lay minister (a Hale Mary)
Cosby	competitive eucharistic minister
Her Highness	competitive eucharistic minister

Other Shrine-goers

Chewbacca	wheelchair-bound saint
Witchy Widow	Ye Olde Piety Show participant
Haunted Man	conversationalist with souls in purgatory

G-L Spirituality Group members

Mama Bear	co-leader of G-L Spirituality Group
Job	long-suffering group member
Abacus	group member with accountant's soul
Thelma and Louise	fierce lesbian couple
Ward and June	straight couple with wayward gay son
Sherwin	group member with especially strong prayer life
Alphaba	skeptical lesbian member with caustic manner
Magoo	self-described sissy-boy
The Landscaper	self-loathing member on the prowl for dates
Martina	boyish lesbian with necklace like rock candy
Angela	lesbian from Castro Parish

Family and friends

Scott Whittier	boyfriend
Bruce	brother
Mikaela	godchild and Bruce's daughter
Gram	Scott's grandmother
Dick	Gram's ex-husband
Clare	Dick's new wife
Rory	Scott's brother
Jezebel	Rory's wife
Tim	college friend
Erin	college friend

Right-wing nutjobs

Bill the Breviary	threatening man with breviary
Ruben Israel	antigay protestor
Mr. Sodomy	antigay protestor
Pastor Bob	antigay protestor
Gerry D'Avolio	former Massachusetts Catholic Conference staff
Daniel Avila	Massachusetts Catholic Conference staff
Ed Saunders	Massachusetts Catholic Conference staff

Courage members

Dan	contact person for Boston Courage
Ewald	man with creases in his jeans
Ben	nerdy Courage newbie
Demetrius	long-term Courage member

Legislators

Marian Walsh
Paul Kujawski
Paul Loscocco
Christine Canavan

Archdiocesan folk

Seán O'Malley	cardinal
Richard Erickson	vicar general
Robert Kickham (Father Kick-Me)	secretary to Seán Cardinal O'Malley
Daniel Hennessey	vocations director
Richard Lennon	former vicar general

Vatican folk

Pope Benedict XVI	B16, the Rat, Joseph Cardinal Ratzinger
Pope John Paul II	J2P2
Bernard Cardinal Law	former cardinal of the Archdiocese of Boston
Gabriele Amorth	chief exorcist

Other

Michael	my first date in Boston
Tony Cinnabonini	coworker who signed petition against gay marriage
Captain Handsome	my favorite airline pilot
Sarah Butler	Vatican apologist regarding ordination of women
Seamus O'Dooley	client at Saint Anthony Shrine legal center
Marianne Duddy	Executive Director, DignityUSA
Holly Gunner	lobbyist for marriage equality
Joan of Arc & Clare of Assisi	lesbian couple in Fr. Butterballino's parish

Author's Note

am the wrong person to write this book. I've met hundreds of Catholics far better suited to the task. They walk old ladies across the street, and visit the sick, and clothe the naked, and bury abandoned babies, and adopt ailing children with birth defects from Cambodian crack houses, and experience rainbow stigmata.

Me? Not so much. I am not pretty enough for prime time, a bad godfather, a worse boyfriend, and — according to said boyfriend, who is reading over my shoulder as I type — a really poor sugar daddy. Worst of all, I am impious, irreverent, and a shade profane.

But let me prevail on your good graces: please view my irreverence and impiety with charity. This is not an attack on the Church. It's an invitation to laugh.

As the nun said to the schoolboy, "Sister's doing it because she loves you." Then she whacked him on the knuckles with a wooden ruler ten sharp times.

Prologue

hadda we want?" cried the motorcycle dyke through her megaphone.

"Equal rights!" shouted the crowd.

"When do we want 'em?" she yelled. She was wearing a stars-and-stripes scarf, a leather vest pierced with gay pride pins, baggy pants, and impossibly small shoes that made her look as if she would topple any second.

"*Now!*" we shouted.

A man shouldered his way behind me and my boyfriend. His "Sodomy: It's to Die For" sign cast a long shadow.

"Whadda we want?" the motorcycle dyke yelled.

In perfect time, we responded, "Civ-il rights!"

"Bleeding rectums!" shouted Mr. Sodomy.

"What do we want?" she cried again.

We yelled: "Gay marriage!"

"Kaposi's sarcoma!" yelled Mr. Sodomy.

And so it went. The dyke called, and Mr. Sodomy and the progay crowd responded in harmony. Not your typical religious call-and-response, for sure, but it had its own charms.

"What do we want?"

Us: "True equality!"

Him: "Syphilis!"

"What do we want?!"

Us: "Safe families!"

Him: "AIDS!"

Trying to drown out Mr. Sodomy, I shouted louder and louder until my voice broke like a pimpled teen's. A full morning at the protest had worn my vocal cords raw. A young Haitian woman next to me tore a hole in a package of throat lozenges. She shook a single golden lozenge out into her pink palm and unwrapped it with agonizing deliberation. She plucked out the candy and discarded the wrapper, not on the ground — I had hoped for an opportunity for some Earth Day–based moral superiority — but in the public waste receptacle. She placed the lozenge on her shockingly pink tongue. As it moved around in her mouth, the lozenge clicked against her teeth. Her placid expression reflected its triple-strength soothing action. My heart filled with envy.

"What do we want?" the motorcycle dyke shouted.

A throat lozenge, I thought wistfully.

It was February 11, 2004. Three months after the highest court of Massachusetts had legalized gay marriage, the legislature had convened yet another in a series of constitutional conventions. The proposed amendments included proposals for longer legislative terms, biennial instead of yearly budgets, a process for appointing House or Senate members if a terrorist attack led to massive vacancies in the legislature — and, of course, a ban on same-sex marriage.

Crowds gathered between the State House and the Boston Common, where the Minutemen had assembled in April 1775 on the way to Lexington and Concord at the start of the Revolutionary War. (Until 1817, the Common was also the forum for public hangings.) Nothing separated opposing points of view. White-collared female Episcopalian priests surrounded a clean-cut Christian youth holding a sign that read "I Want to Marry My Dog"; a dozen apocalyptic preachers straight out of Flannery O'Connor bellowed among cops on horseback and queer youth with pink hair playing hooky from high school; lesbian mothers tripped friend and foe alike with double-wide strollers; curious passersby procrastinated on their way to work; and duck boats full of passengers screamed "quack, quack" as the driver intoned something about the Revolution.

On the Common, vendors hawked everything imaginable: silk scarves and sweatshirts; sausages and statues of the Founding Fathers, JFK, and rogue mayor James Michael Curley; fake Louis Vuitton bags, pirated CDs, books with covers torn off, and a thousand other counterfeits. An empty flatbed truck boomed techno music. A contingent of twenty-somethings wearing T-shirts that proclaimed them "queerspawn" marched up from the Common with arms proudly linked. Three drag queen slatterns clung to the wrought iron gates of the State House and chain-smoked.

Not far from us, a man who identified himself to a reporter as "Pastor Bob" loudly proclaimed his hatred for the sin of homosexuality. He said, however, that he loved the homosexuals themselves.

When someone yelled, "Hypocrite!" Pastor Bob responded: "Would I be standing here with a sign like this if I didn't love you?"

The sign read, "Homosexuals Are Possessed by Demons."

All morning long, the Haitian woman and her companions had said their prayers. During one lull, they sang a French hymn that took my breath away. When Mr. Sodomy came on the scene, they rolled their eyes and shuffled away from him. There was something endearingly immediate in the sisters' reverence. They seemed open to the possibility of a miracle, right here, this day, on this crowded street among the jostling demonstrators. Not that they were *expecting* a miracle, mind you. It seemed obvious they would go home, make dinner, and kiss their husbands good night no matter how the day ended. But if a miracle had happened on the double yellow line down the middle of Beacon Street, these Haitian sisters would not have been caught by surprise.

Stealing a page from the religious playbook, the motorcycle dyke started a new chant: "Love thy neighbor."

"Love thy neighbor! Love thy neighbor!" we repeated.

The Haitian women were also chanting a religious phrase I could not make out. It had a similar beat, and gradually we got in sync with each other.

The woman with the lozenges glanced at me and smiled. My voice broke. The Haitian woman held out her bag. Gratefully, I accepted the lozenge she shook out on my palm.

"I have an extra bottle of water, if you want it," I shouted over the din.

She declined, smiling again.

As I popped the lozenge — oh, sweet *Jesus*, it was pure ecstasy — I reflected that, under other circumstances, I could have prayed with this woman. My father, who went to Catholic high school, had taught us the *Notre Père*. Wouldn't it have been a kick for me and the Haitian to say it together in French?

Maybe afterward she and I might have discussed *les choses françaises* or American stuff. Perhaps we would have talked of the lives of the saints. I might have asked her how different Haiti was from, say, St. Maarten, where my boyfriend and I had recently vacationed. I might have asked her how long she had been in the United States and what had brought her here. I might have tried to understand where she was coming from.

And maybe I'd have had the courage to pose the question that had been plaguing me all morning: *How in God's name could a refugee who presumably came to America for its freedoms and opportunities wish to deny freedoms and opportunities to others by amending the constitution to forbid gay marriage?!*

These conversations went unhad. Reporters skirted the crowd; cameras zoomed in on our faces. My boyfriend and I exchanged a long, slow kiss for the camera. We rarely resist the opportunity for gratuitous public whoring.

But the cameramen were looking for the money shot. They were looking for conflict. They rushed off to Ruben Israel, who had traveled from Los Angeles to participate in the protest. He was parading in a sandwich board. One side said "God Abhors You." The other said "The Wages of Sin Is Death." He accused almost everyone he saw of being a sodomite or an abomination.

"This is what I do," Israel explained to a reporter. "My job is to be as blunt as their sin." If my sin were as blunt as he suspected, I would be a porn star.

To demonstrate his point, Israel explained to a gay anarchist with three tats and a ring through his lower lip that he was going to die of AIDS. The anarchist turned purple with fury. Toe to toe with Israel, he spewed a torrent of abuse. Cops drifted toward the conflict more slowly than the television cameras.

Scott and I stayed put. The organizers of the rally had repeatedly instructed us to be on our best behavior. They said, "Don't engage with the other side." (I'm sure the organizers had issued an official secular indulgence for throat-lozenge engagements.)

As the convention got underway, we abandoned the street. Security in the State House was as tight as an airport: all bags and jackets were X-rayed, signs and bumper stickers confiscated, and the metal-detecting wand liberally used. Once we passed security, we heeded the protest coordinators' call for volunteers to help out in the Great Hall on the third floor, directly outside the joint legislative chamber, where the Constitutional Convention was taking place.

The Great Hall, a massive, rectangular room, stood two stories high, with a balcony skirting the second story. Revolutionary war murals covered the walls. The floors were marble. Velvet ropes separated the public from the heavy, dark doors with opaque oval windows that marked the entrance to the legislative chambers. Media filled the no-man's-land between the doors and the demonstrators.

Marriage opponents and marriage supporters jammed side by side, jockeying for space. Any time a television camera panned, the crowd surged toward the lens. I battled for position against a trench-coated man with a neatly knotted tie and bloodshot eyes. From time to time, jackbooted troopers waded among the protestors, plucked the belligerent from the crowd, and hustled them out.

Gay marriage supporters launched into "America the Beautiful." Locked arm in arm, we were boisterous, jubilant, happy, a long line of singing queens. In the 1950s, we might have been gathered around a piano in some unmarked dismal dive, singing show tunes. But instead, the year was 2004, and we stood in a brightly lit Great Hall under the public eye of the cameras. We sang "Shine a Light on Me" and the "Star-Spangled Banner" and "God Bless America" and "Yankee Doodle Dandy" and "You're a Grand Old Flag." We tried a chorus from "We Shall Overcome," but it proved too dirgelike for this exuberant crowd.

Energy never flagged; in fact, if anything we got louder, and by five o'clock, virtually all the marriage equality opponents had climbed aboard their buses and gone home. Gay marriage supporters had free rein in the Great Hall. We probably sang the national anthem two hundred times, until almost everybody was hoarse. The two-hundred-year-old chandeliers shook and danced, and some miracle worker produced a case of lemon throat lozenges at 10:00 P.M. to keep us going through midnight.

Soothed again, I thought: *We, too, have saints on our side.*

When the final votes were tallied, we had won. The legislature had deferred consideration of the amendment to a future date. (We later lost, of course, when the amendment finally came to a vote. In 2005, we won again, when the amendment was defeated without much fuss. Then we lost in 2007 again. And won again, too. But we'll get to all that later.)

At work the next day, my receptionist said, "Hey! I saw you on TV! On the news!" I grinned the silly grin of the instantly, undeservedly famous, but I couldn't say anything. It took six days before my voice recovered. During that time, it was prone to sudden, disconcerting midsentence adolescent pitch changes and a rasp that sounded as if I had chain-smoked four cartons of Lucky Strikes. In women, such a low rasp can be sexy in a come-hither way. In me, it sounded as if I were minutes away from having my larynx removed and talking for the rest of my life through one of those creepy electronic devices you hold to your throat.

Within days of the protest, an e-mail appeared in my in-box from my pastor at Saint Anthony Shrine. Perhaps Francis, the Franciscan friar, had also seen the evening news. I was "busted," as we used to say in seventh-grade social studies class when the teacher caught us wadding up spit balls.

Instead, the e-mail was an invitation to become a member of the Lay Ministry Committee (LMC) at Saint Anthony's. The LMC organized and trained 150 volunteers for various roles assisting the priests at Mass: lectors, acolytes, eucharistic ministers, ushers, and the ad hoc ministries. For those who are lapsed or otherwise un-Catholic, please consult the handy Catholic vocabulary sidebar.

Handy Catholic Vocabulary Alert!

Q. Who are all those presumptuous nonpriests puttering around the pews — and what's their purpose?

- Lector: Person who climbs up into a device on the chancel called an ambo (a lectern, podium, or pulpit) to proclaim the non-Gospel Bible readings during Mass.

- Acolyte: Person who brings the chalice, water and wine, and host (i.e., communion, Eucharist, or "those little wafery crackers Catholics eat") to the priest, helps him wash his hands, and clears away the dirty dishes after the meal.
- Eucharistic minister: Person who distributes the host to the other parishioners during Mass. Such a person is also known as an "extraordinary minister."
- Usher: If you can't figure this one out, put down this book and back away slowly.
- Ad hoc ministers: People who do everything else, such as rubbing ashes into foreheads on Ash Wednesday.

Think of the church as a cloth-napkin restaurant. The priest is the chef. The acolyte is the holy busboy. The eucharistic minister is the one who says, "I'm Wanda, and I'll be your server today." The usher is the maître d'. The lector is like the guy with a violin who serenades your table so you can't get a word in edgewise to your date without paying the violinist handsomely.

At the time of Father Francis's e-mail, I had been a lector at Saint Anthony's for five years, but my involvement in the parish was minimal: I attended an initial theological training and a practicum that made me eligible to read at Mass, receiving a little medallion to mark my passing grade from lector school. Every Friday, I proclaimed a single reading at the Friday-noon mass. Before the service, I greeted the priest and chatted with my fellow servers, and then vanished for another week. We never discussed my life outside the parish. It was almost as if I didn't have one.

But I did. I had a life with my boyfriend, Scott Whittier. Scott and I shared a condo in Boston's South End, a gayborhood subsequently renamed Strollersville to reflect the double-wide, space-age, high-tech, all-terrain urban assault strollers of the infant class and their yuppie parents. Not that I have a problem with straight people. Some of my favorite blood relatives are straight. But the strollers cause problems when I have to make my way across four double-wides to secure my bloody Mary.

Scott and I also ran a business writing Harlequin-style romance novels for gay men. Dozens of our erotic short stories appeared in *PlayGuy*, *Honcho,* and *Indulge*, and anthologies of the year's best porn reprinted many of them:

> You have a hundred hands, and your fingertips stink of ass.
> His butt's a loaf of bread you want to drive your thumbs
> into and tear open to let the hot, fresh-baked steam escape.

Sodomy is a fact of my life. As an attorney, I had even been cocounsel in a lawsuit challenging the constitutionality of the antisodomy laws of Massachusetts — and won a ruling from the Supreme Judicial Court that they could not be enforced in private. And now Francis the Franciscan Friar was asking me to assume a more visible leadership position over the volunteers at Saint Anthony Shrine.

I didn't want to embarrass Father Francis or the Shrine. I had no wish to interfere with the religious experience of parishioners who might be distracted by recognizing my face from TV — or my name from my pornography or my legal briefs, for that matter. And I assumed in turn that the Shrine wouldn't want me if it knew who I was. One side of my life deliberately didn't engage the other.

Francis the Franciscan Friar and I scheduled a meeting for the following week. At the appointed time, the creaky elevator took me to the priests' quarters. Taking an elevator — even a rickety, uninspected elevator — felt like an unnecessary express toward my doom. *If I have to walk the plank,* I thought indignantly, *I should be allowed to trudge under my own power.* I squeaked out a few Hail Marys as a prophylactic against any divinely ordained mechanical difficulties.

The priests' quarters only added to my discomfort. The air was stale. Sounds were hushed. The furniture was blocky, solid, and simple. Saints lurked in every nook and cranny. Pithy biblical quotations nagged from every bulletin board. It felt as if I were back in junior high, trudging to confession with a conscience heavy with looking at other boys' penises, self-abuse, and lying to my mother.

Francis the Franciscan Friar had a thick head of prematurely white hair, skin so ruddy it looked freshly scrubbed, and a slow, patient voice that sounded as if it would outlast every human folly. He was wearing a black shirt and pants and a Roman collar. I had never before seen him without his brown Franciscan robes, macramé sash, and tire sandals. To be honest, it was a letdown. If I were going to be chastised for my antics on Beacon Hill and for my perfidious homosexual lifestyle, and assigned a hundred thousand more non-elevator-related Hail Marys, I wanted the punishment to come from on high. Father Francis's civvies made me feel as if I were talking to an equal.

A dish of horehound candies lay on the table between us. There was little small talk; my vocal cords were still too raw. Instead, I hoarsely explained my willingness to participate on the LMC and take a leadership role at the Shrine. I told him I understood the higher-visibility role and that the friars would be counting on me in new ways. But, I warned, there were things Father Francis should know before he formally made the offer to bring me aboard.

I took a deep breath and quashed an impulse to cross myself. Like many Catholics, I have a sound track that automatically plays in my head for moments like this: *Oh my God, I am heartily sorry for having offended Thee. . . .*

In a rush of words, I confessed that I was gay and had a public role in the same-sex marriage debate. I explained television, the Haitian woman, throat lozenges, Mr. Sodomy, and the evening news. I explained my reluctance to interfere with others' worship. I talked until my vocal cords again gave way.

Then it was Father Francis's turn. I told myself to be on my best behavior. *Don't engage with the other side, no matter what offensive things came out of his mouth.*

Father Francis slid the dish of horehound candies my way. "The friars here at St. Anthony's are opposed to the Church's teaching. We think it is inhumane," he said.

"But-but-but . . . " I spluttered, thinking, *What about abomination? What about the pope? What about eternal damnation? What would happen if Archbishop O'Malley paid a visit to the Shrine and heard a happy porn-writing sodomite proclaim the Word? What about the likelihood that as soon as Father Francis handed me the keys to the Shrine, I would rub my palms together, cackle maniacally, declare, "It's mine, all mine," and immediately put my radical, life-denying homosexual agenda into place?*

Father Francis forestalled my skepticism. He continued, "People have asked us why we friars don't speak out against gay marriage. This is why. We believe the grace of marriage comes from the commitment, not from who the persons entering the marriage are."

I was stunned. What Father Francis was saying could have been motorcycle-dyke-megaphone-chant material. With slogans like that, he could have joined us out on the front lines, jostling with Haitians and warding off Mr. Sodomy and Pastor Bob. Who says there are no miracles anymore?

I helped myself to a horehound candy. I was immediately soothed.

Francis the Franciscan Friar stuck out his hand. "Now that we've got that out of the way," he said, "welcome to the Lay Ministry Committee. When can you start?"

Since My Last Confession

I

The Tunnel Builders

The existence of different currents of thought seems necessary if an excessive conformism is to be avoided. . . . The Christian message is universal. It addresses itself therefore to very different people. It is to be expected that there would be diverse approaches. This implies plurality.

— Joseph Cardinal Ratzinger, now Pope Benedict XVI

Mrs. American Gothic

RAM WAS WORRIED we were all going straight to hell. She didn't say it aloud. She rarely mentioned the error of our ways. In fact, Gram was almost *too* gracious with her hospitality. Because our ultimate destiny was the fiery pits, Gram determined that we should have a few fond memories of earthly life to sustain us through eternity. Hence the steady supply of fresh-baked whoopee pies and generous servings of Grape-Nuts pudding.

The first time my boyfriend Scott invited me to Gram's "camp" in rural Maine, we arrived after midnight. I slept through the whole three-hour ride. When I woke, it was as if Boston had returned to its pastoral beginnings: cows on the Common, towering maples, and a winding, unpaved road to her house.

Gram and her then-husband Dick built the camp themselves in 1963 on the shore of Thompson Lake. What Dick didn't know about plumbing and carpentry, he taught himself. Gram had had a railing put on the back porch and replaced the outhouse with a leaching field, but forty years later, the roof had never leaked and the walls were holding strong, and God bless indestructible kitchen linoleum.

The camp was no more than eight hundred square feet, painted brick red and shaded by a dozen evergreens that dropped needles and pitch relentlessly on the picnic tables below. Reed baskets hung from the roof beams, and every shelf teemed with bric-a-brac that Gram had collected over the years — pottery owls, granite inchworms, brass sailboats, and even a pewter mug that had belonged to Gram's grandmother and might have been in the family for centuries. It was a world of Mary Kay cosmetics, plastic violets, and a kitchen window bird feeder designed for a hummingbird whose buzzing wings made me want to steal Gram's badminton racquet and swat it like a mosquito.

That first night, I expected Mrs. American Gothic to answer the door. In fact, Gram was wearing a bathrobe and slippers, but her finger was tucked into a Bible, which she had nested in a book cover knit from spare yarn. The bottle of Palmolive by the sink and the air freshener canister in the bathroom wore matching knit dresses.

Leviticus or Paul, I thought. No doubt about it. *You've got to put on a good show when the sodomites come to visit.*

Gram folded away her Bible, kissed her grandson, and extended her hand toward me with the dignity of royalty.

"You are welcome. You are welcome." She articulated the words with perfect elocution and appeared as sincere as the friars of Saint Anthony Shrine. She pointed the way to her queen-size bed. "Never mind me. I can sleep on the bunk bed."

Scott was delighted, but I took a temporary vow of chastity. Aside from the innate wrongness of scoring between your grandmother's sheets, the interior walls reached only two-thirds of the way to the ceiling, and Gram's bed squeaked. Weeks later, I learned she was stone-deaf. My attempt to have sex without actually moving a muscle had been a useless precaution.

My squeamishness proved otherwise silly. Saturday morning, I emerged from the bedroom in my swim trunks, shirtless, with a towel slung over my shoulder. Gram darted toward me with surprising alacrity for an octogenarian. I dodged, but she thrust her face against my chest and nuzzled my chest hair.

"Gram!" Scott scolded. "Men have been killed for less than that. Get away from my fur!"

Gram released me, chuckling uproariously, not the least bit embarrassed. She had the same taste in men as her grandson. She was an old-school Yankee with snow-white hair, but she had a swimmer's body and big breasts, and her grandchildren traded rumors they'd heard about the wild days of the Swingin' Sixties.

Gram and I got along for the most part. She never held it against me that I shave my head and have a four-inch scar on my left cheek, which makes me look like a serial killer. (As a joke, one of my law-firm colleagues once gave our interns snapshots of Ted Bundy, Charles Manson, Jeffrey Dahmer, and me. He invited the interns to pick out the lawyer from the group. Ted Bundy was the near unanimous choice.)

Gram *did* suspect that a city boy like me would be unable to distinguish loons from ducks, and she watched me like a hawk out of fear that I'd use the undrinkable tap water for the morning coffee. But our main point of contention concerned strawberries. She favored refrigeration. I do not. I set newly purchased strawberries on the windowsill. She whisked them to the refrigerator while doing housework. I liberated them from the fridge before noon, but they were back in the crisper by cocktail hour. Even when I hid the strawberries in our Honda's glove compartment, Gram somehow sniffed them out. We never directly engaged one another. We didn't defend our positions; our differences were irreconcilable. In time, we put competing strawberry concoctions on the table and judged our righteousness solely by whose dessert had the smallest slice left after Scott's relatives had eaten their fill.

Scott and his grandmother were startlingly alike in personality and looks. Both were unnaturally slim, with pale skin that tanned olive. Each had blue eyes and a hooked nose, and neither had patience for the presence of other cooks in their respective kitchens. They were fiercely competitive at cards, obsessed over Scrabble, and played marathon games of cribbage. They were too much alike for either to get away with the rampant cheating they both saw as just another part of the game. Both were vain about their age and their figures and would as soon be seen in public without hair product as appear naked on national television.

Though Gram clearly viewed my unwillingness to play cribbage ad nauseam as a character flaw, she never once suggested that our homosexuality was a problem. This had not always been the case. When Scott first moved to Boston and came home on summer weekends talking about his then-boyfriend, Gram cornered him one afternoon. She made Bible noises. Stern with moral righteousness, she said, "I'd be disappointed to have to tell people my grandson was like that."

Scott had been Gram's favorite until that time, but the exchange broke the bond between them and replaced it with suspicion and mistrust. Scott didn't go back to camp for years.

"Leave it in Boston," Scott's father said approvingly.

No Skin off Gram's Ass

Sodomy was not the only — or even a primary — reason Gram believed that her grandchildren were going to hell. A confirmed Protestant, Gram viewed Catholicism with the lip-curling disgust many profess to have when they see two men kiss. To her, it was a spooky combination of paganism, mysticism, sexual deviance, and funny costumes. Growing up, she firmly believed that a tunnel ran between the priests' rectory and the nuns' quarters, through which the priests passed nightly for unlimited sexual orgies. She believed the priests reported their unholy machinations over a telephone hotline to Rome. Of course, it didn't help that Gram's ex-husband had been wooed away by a "French Canadian Catholic harlot" named Clare. Clare was a sweetheart. She always gave me lottery scratch cards for Christmas stocking stuffers that never failed to win.

Clare aside, Gram's anti-Catholicism was purely theoretical, born from observations on the idolatrous worship of Mary and the saints and the absurdity of putting a man between you and God when it came time to confess your sins. It was no skin off Gram's ass what all those Mary-worshipping tunnel builders did in their spare time. With the exception of Clare, Gram could live and let live.

That is, until Scott's brother Rory became a crossover.[†] His crossing over was strictly religious, though. Raised, like Scott, to be a Protestant, he converted to Catholicism in order to marry his girlfriend. (Let's call her Jezebel. Gram did.)

Having a gay grandson must have been a trial, but Rory's conversion made Scott and me seem positively saintly. With the ferocity of a purebred, the normally stoic Yankee retreated to her kitchen muttering about idolatry and popes, wondering what she had done to have her grandson betray her and turn his back on God and family. Her habit of having an afternoon margarita in a mason jar only threw fuel on the fire.

Gram, Rory, Jezebel, Scott, and I were sipping summer wine. The day was clear and blue, the lake calm. We discussed loon sightings and supper plans and in-season fruits. Without warning, the conversation spiraled into condemnations and defenses of Catholic principle and practice.

Gram was my first up-close and personal experience of anti-Catholic sentiment. In eastern Massachusetts, where the immigrant Irish, Italians, French Canadians, and Portuguese had long since overwhelmed and mongrelized the *Mayflower* Protestants, you couldn't swing a cat without knocking down a parish priest. Everybody was Catholic. Those few who weren't knew Catholics, and no one talked about the tunnel.

Scott, who has no interest in religion, rolled his eyes and slipped away to discuss boob jobs with his cousin. Rory, Jezebel, and I defended Catholic doctrine as best we could, but wished we had a simple primer to help Gram understand, if not get over, her prejudices. We imagined it would look something like this:

---

† *Crossover* is a derogatory term for a gay man who had sex with women before coming out. A *purebred*, on the other hand, has only had sexual experiences with men. Purebreds typically feel superior to their brethren who have crossed over.

A Catholic Catechism

Q. Is there really a tunnel between the rectory and the nunnery?
A. Yes. But 60 percent of priests are gay, so the traffic is typically for tea parties or the next diocesan fashion show.

Q. Why do priests wear dresses when they say Mass?
A. See above. And it's called a "cassock."

Q. How do you know the pope is infallible?
A. Because he said so in 1870.

Q. Was he infallible before that?
A. No. God flipped a switch, and it was so. Amen.

Q. What's up with the bread and wine?
A. We believe it becomes the body and blood of Christ during Mass.

Q. Why?
A. The pope said so. And he's infallible.

Q. But isn't that cannibalism?
A. (*Shrug.*) Tastes like chicken.

Q. What up with Mary-worship?
A. We don't *worship* Mary. We just think she's extra special — "blessed amongst women," as we say — so we build monuments to her, see her image in drainpipes, and accept that she appears to small peasant girls centuries after she was whisked bodily into heaven. And we ask her to pull strings on our behalf with the Almighty.

Q. Sounds a little corrupt. Can't you get by on your own merits?
A. Hell, no. We're guilty, serious sinners, bad people — the worst.

Q. How do you know that?
A. Our moms told us so.

Q. Are your moms infallible, too?
A. Dude, don't talk about my mom.

Scott's father also bellowed about his proposed daughter-in-law's wearing of the religious pants. Scott's mother gently questioned why her own faith wasn't good enough. Even I looked down on Rory's crossing over since, religiously speaking, I was a purebred.

Rory made matters worse by embracing a very bold and rule-bound form of Catholicism. He became all-Catholic all the time. He presented his mother with an array of photos of statues of saints. He wore a crucifix and foisted unwanted graces on his family's table. He and Jezebel mentored Catholic youth groups and chattered incessantly about their parish priest and how religious people in America were brutally oppressed.

Then they announced that they were abstaining from sex until their wedding day. Never mind that (A) they had been living together for six months and (B) they had already done the nasty.

Their vow led to particularly animated conversations over the fire pit at Gram's camp, as Scott tried to understand what precisely they could do during this period and what was *verboten*.

"Intercourse?"

"Out."

"Blow jobs?"

"Out."

"Manual stimulation outside the clothing?"

"In."

"Direct manual stimulation?"

"Out."

"Kissing?"

"In."

"Let me get this straight," Scott finally said. "You're not going to have sex for *six months*?"

"Worse," I interjected. "Masturbation is out, too." I turned to the happily engaged couple. "Right, guys?"

Rory and Jezebel nodded wistfully.

"So no orgasms at all," I said. "Zip. Zero."

Scott and his cousins gasped, but Rory offered a correction. "Um. On the manual stimulation over the clothing point? *That* could theoretically lead to orgasm."

Then he blushed. He was obviously speaking from (messy) experience.

The Naughty Altar Boy

Scott's religious skepticism didn't limit itself to the convoluted rules
guiding Rory's premarital sexual practice. Growing up, he had been
the kind of out-there atheist who lost no opportunity to confront the
faithful with his aggressive unbelief. Long before Rory crossed over,
Scott's most caustic disdain had fallen upon Catholicism. Based on his
experience with a string of naughty Catholic boyfriends, Scott viewed
Catholicism as an ill-deserved get-out-of-jail-free card. As he understood the Church's basic tenets, Catholics could do anything, no matter
how venal, depraved, and contrary to his wishes, so long as they said
sorry. Confession was an oral permit to go and sin some more. "You
guys let yourselves off too easy," he complained.

When it came to religion, he and I agreed on exactly one thing: the
five-foot cherry wood church pew we found on eBay. It was going to
look fabulous in our living room. We ignored the look of sheer horror
on the face of a designer friend when he heard what we proposed to
add to our decor.

"That's the one!" Scott insisted.

The pew was the platonic ideal of pew-ness: stark, spare, uncomfortable, and upright. Just staring at the thumbnail images made me
start mumbling Hail Marys. It was so hard that it made sodomy seem
infinitely less like a pain in the ass.

According to the seller, the pew came from the wreckage of a defunct church north of Albany, New York. It was only five feet, end to
end, so I imagined a quaint, intimate chapel with a neatly mowed lawn
set against a backdrop of oak trees and blue sky. I imagined a congregation hardly more than a dozen strong, where the pastor was as
familiar with each parishioner's sins as his own. I imagined a congregation so small that perhaps they had been wiped out all at once in
a tragic *E. coli* accident at the church fair by some contaminated spa-
nakopita prepared by the (now deceased) choir master.

And all so that God's plan could be fulfilled, and the pew could find a new home in the distant Boston gayborhood where it would become a member of our family. Oh, the humanity! Nothing opens an Irish Catholic pocketbook faster than a potent combination of melodrama and tragedy — imaginary or otherwise.

My only misgiving? It was Protestant. Scott, a Protestant-by-birth boyfriend, I could tolerate. A Protestant pew in my living room, on the other hand, seemed positively heretical. Channeling a million Irish mothers before me, I said, "I gotta find a nice Catholic one." If Gram could have her religious bigotry, I was damn sure going to get my share.

Scott went across the street to get another bottle of wine. I tried eBay searches for "pew catholic," "pew saint," "pew holy," and "pew our mother of perpetual motion." The search results yielded enough loot from sacristies nationwide to stock the home dungeon of any pedophile with a Catholic high school girl fantasy. But the resale market for readily identifiable Catholic pews was astonishingly limited. Few Catholic churches had given up the ghost. In the decades-long death match among flavors of Christianity, Catholics had edged out the Protestants, at least in terms of online pew availability. Thank the Good Lord for His small Graces.

The nearest authentically Catholic pew for sale was in Albuquerque. It was ten feet long and three thousand miles away. Fueled by an $8 pinot noir, Scott and I furiously debated the pews' relative merits.

Four glasses into the evening, Scott hit rhetorical pay dirt. He clicked a link to reveal the Catholic pew's $500 shipping price tag. My theological misgivings evaporated instantly.

"Bring on the Protestant pew," I said in defeat. There was only so much tragedy a good Catholic boy could afford.

While the auction ran its course, Scott and I took measurements and rearranged living room furniture as if we were bringing a little pink bundle of joy home from the maternity ward. We discussed bidding strategies, confessed eBay sins we had committed in the past, and watched the prized pew like hawks.

Sip of wine. Refresh the browser. Check pillow fabrics. Refresh the browser. Sip of wine. Take a pee. Refresh the browser.

We were toasting our imminent victory when Satan himself — screen name: SnuggleMonkey — appeared in the auction's final moments. SnuggleMonkey bid a few dollars more. We bid. SnuggleMonkey raised the stakes. Back and forth it went, until I wanted to throttle SnuggleMonkey and leave the corpse to be devoured by sand mites.

The seconds ticked down. We stared at the screen, awaiting the e-mail that would herald our victory or loss.

"You bid too low —" I accused.

"Shh!" Scott shot back.

While we squabbled over our final bid on the pew, and the division of labor, financial responsibility, and, ultimately, love in our relationship, the auction ended.

The dream pew was ours! Eat your heart out, SnuggleMonkey!

Now full of frisky conciliation, Scott slipped Sade into the CD player and nudged me in the ribs.

"When we get the pew," he said, "I'll play the naughty altar boy if you want to be the evil priest."

At last! I thought. We were finally getting to the raucous debauchery to which the religious right had promised the gay lifestyle led.

II

Follow the Smudges

I could not disavow words like "thanksgiving" or "host" or "communion bread."
They have an undying tremor and draw, like water far down.

— Seamus Heaney

Catch the Devil by His Tail

 N MY HOMETOWN OUTSIDE BOSTON, the good kids went to parochial schools. They wore crisp white shirts, blue plaid skirts, and striped ties, and their parents inevitably wore smug, morally superior expressions. It was common knowledge that the parochial school kids would be assumed into heaven like the Virgin Mary.

I was a public school Catholic. Therefore I was doomed. Optimists made advance reservations for a long stay in purgatory. The rest of us resigned ourselves to the express train to hell — decades before Gram ever had a say in it.

Realizing our moral inferiority, we public school Catholics took the only road left to us: we tormented the parochial school kids for their silly uniforms. From this experience I learned a principle that has served me well in life: If you cannot beat them in virtue, pull off your wickedness with more style.

My parents, God bless them, tried to redeem us. My siblings and I were sent weekly to CCD — Continuing Catholic Development —

where we scribbled dirty words in the margins of shiny new texts full of uplifting stories.

Summers saw us packed off to Catholic camp, where we learned that if another camper jumped in the air to avoid a low throw in dodgeball, a second ball launched right after the first and aimed at the dodger's ankles would cause him to flip upside down in a spectacular and potentially bloody wreck. From time to time, I was required to make a rote confession. Forgive me, Father, for I have sinned. It has been six months since my last confession. Since then, I have raped my mother, plundered a village, called my brother a fag, and taken the name of Gloria Gaynor in vain. Amen.

Anything more devout then purely ordinary Sunday churchgoing, however, attracted family-wide consternation. When my older brother suddenly took to attending Mass on a daily basis, our parents worried that it would go on his permanent record and keep him out of Harvard Law. The prospect of a hyper-pious blood relative nosing into my affairs for the rest of my life worried me.

Fortunately, my brother soon discovered liquor and girls. His churchgoing gave way to breaking into neighbors' houses to make long-distance phone calls to his girlfriend and piloting our parents' tank-sized 1972 Fleetwood limousine across the grassy median of local roundabouts. He showed no further signs of sanctity. Indeed, quite the contrary. He became a lawyer.

Despite our lukewarm piety, we had a real, genetic connection to the sterner pre-Vatican II Church — the Church of the Tridentine Mass in Latin, public condemnations of self-abuse, and knuckle-whacking nuns who forced my left-handed father to convert to right-handedness. My mother was Irish, born and raised. And in the 1970s, her native land had not yet embraced the world of folk masses, macramé guitar straps, and music directors with a passing physical resemblance to Jesus Christ.

On one early trip to the motherland, my grandfather dragged us to a nine-hundred-year-old stone chapel that was pure postcard Ireland. Celtic crosses lay uprooted on the front lawn, and gravestones had worn smooth with rain. It was a long drive from Dublin, so when the car finally stopped, my siblings and I shot across the churchyard, chasing each other, laughing and screaming.

My grandfather — a brilliant, beloved, erudite figure of endless dignity — sternly herded us together. We were breathless and giddy and trying to make each other laugh. We didn't yet know it was wrong to be happy on holy ground.

"There's a legend about this church," my grandfather said.

"A legend?" my brother asked, taking the bait.

"If you run three times counterclockwise around this church, they say the devil himself will appear and take your soul."

My brothers and I stared in awe at the dark, hoary structure. As my grandfather no doubt anticipated, we behaved for the rest of the afternoon. But as the hours wore on, a naughty excitement infected my awe. The devil was so close, and the soul so easily lost! One small slip, and damnation was mine. *Maybe I could run around just two and a half times and then stop*, I thought. *Maybe I could go close enough to see just a glimpse of his hooves, his tail. No more, I swear.*

The lesson I took back to the States was this: church is a place of confrontation. It's where good and evil meet. Choices are stark and immediate; the boundary is thin. Every moment ticked with spiritual tinder. One small spark might cause an inferno of consequences. At any moment, I imagined, I might be annihilated.

Heady stuff for a six-year-old. Personal responsibility weighed on my shoulders. I understood that I had a direct hand in the outcome: *my* acts and *my* prayers could make all the difference in terms of salvation. And not just my own failings, but the failings of others that I failed to prevent, faults I failed to detect, correct, or scold. Forget to mention my beloved grandfather in my bedtime prayers? Next thing I knew, he had highly metastatic colon cancer.

My hometown parish had no hoary legends. Saint John the Evangelist, a thoroughly modern church, airy and bright, smelled of incense and candle wax. The lectionary, a book of daily readings, was heavy as a stone tablet. The pews were full. The music was, in retrospect, awful. Familiar brass bells marked the start of Mass and the various blessings. The parishioners' signs of the cross were like the wings of a thousand butterflies. I was baptized at Saint John's. I was confirmed at Saint John's. I attended weekly mass at Saint John's until I left for college. My brother was married at Saint John's. My first godson was baptized there. I still have both my baptism certificate and my First Communion card.

The spiritual hotspot, the locus of the confrontation, was up front — where the priest was, where the tabernacle and the book were, where wine changed to blood, and flatbreads became flesh, and the priest murmured sweet nothings to Jesus under his breath. The altar.

Where the Hell Am I? A Guide to Church Geography

For those who have been absent a while, finding your way around a Catholic church presents a challenge. Here's a handy guide:

- Narthex: The vestibule of the church — typically as far as sinful folk dare to go, and a handy place for priests to dispose of unwanted literature sent from the local bishop.
- Nave: The center aisle and surrounding pews, where you can best see and be seen.
- Chancel: Area at the front of the church where the altar is, typically raised a few inches to show that the priest is a much better person than you can ever hope to be.
- Altar: Eucharistic dinner table located in the chancel, or sanctuary.
- Reredos: Fancy backdrop behind an altar, often of stained glass.
- Tabernacle: An ornate bank safe for storing consecrated hosts under lock and key. Typically located within shouting distance of the altar, so eucharistic ministers don't have to wear their hiking boots to Mass.
- Pulpit, lectern, and ambo: Names for the podium from which priests and lay ministers proclaim the Gospels and other readings.

- Sacristy: Priest's dressing room. Don't disturb the starlets before they go on stage. Typically located adjacent to the chancel.
- Ambulatory: Hall between sacristy and sanctuary; not a great place to pick up tricks.
- Transept: For churches with a cross-shaped floor plan, the part to which Jesus's arms would have been nailed.

Just a few years after Vatican II, when I was four or five, a low rail along the chancel separated us from the altar. Parishioners kneeled on one side of the rail. The priest and altar boy moved in tandem on the other. They worked their way along the railing from the far left of the church to the far right and back again. The altar boy placed the brass plate beneath the communicant, and the priest held up a host that looked as big as the moon.

The recipient crossed herself and returned to her pew. She did not touch the host with her soiled fingers. She did not chew. She swallowed whole, and Enforcement Nuns stood sentinel for telltale movements of the jaw. Someone new took her place and waited patiently for the priest and altar boy to make their way back from the other side of the sanctuary.

The altar itself was forbidden territory. Only a few holies could breathe the rarefied air. From the altar came words like *dire* and *grave* and *mortal* that made it seem as if a thundercloud loomed above your head twenty-four seven. From the altar flowed a whole series of rules that could be broken, rules I had not known existed, but of which the parochial school kids were no doubt fully aware. I never imagined I might someday be called to speak from the altar. I never imagined myself as a priest. That, too, was reserved for parochial school kids.

Ultimately, that sense of personal responsibility and all that scolding made me feel that whatever I did, I couldn't possibly do right. Sure, we Catholics sound off about confession and reconciliation, but the Irish-blooded among us know certain sins lie beyond forgiveness. Hardcore priests still tell us we're going to hell. The gentler ones assure us that God can forgive us, but because we are Irish, and we are full of sin, and our sin is colossal, we side with the hardcore priests: He *could*, but He *wouldn't*. Best to take communion and hightail it out before lightning strikes.

Psychologists call this phenomenon "learned helplessness." In a famous experiment, they put a dog in a cage with a partially electrified floor. A buzzer sounded before a shock was delivered. The dog learned to move from the electrified part of the cage to the nonelectrified part after hearing the buzzer sound. In the second phase of the experiment, the entire floor was electrified, so the dog could not escape the shock. When the buzzer sounded, it cowered helplessly. This behavior persisted even when half the cage was de-electrified. In other words, the dog still cowered even when it had a chance to save itself. That's how I felt at the altar.

On a dark New England evening, a single streetlight shone down from the roof of Saint John's. In the back seat of my mother's car, I played shadow games. Up front, my mother was interrogating my older brother about the words of the Hail Mary and the Our Father, on which the kids in my brother's CCD class were scheduled to be tested.

My brother didn't need her help. But to me, the prayers seemed fantastically long, truly biblical. Wars took place and people died and eons passed before my brother finally reached the end. "Amen," we all said. That someday I, too, would be forced to endure the trial my brother had faced paralyzed me. There were only so many grandfathers I could afford to lose.

Years later, after a long absence from churchgoing, I returned. Not only the Our Father and Hail Mary, but also great big chunks of the liturgy, had stuck in my brain. I stumbled only where gender-neutral language had crept in since I was a kid.

Marking Territory

Irish-American guys are dogs. It's not simply the learned helplessness, but the primordial instinct that compels us to mark our territory when we move to a new place:

- Find a bar.
- Find a church.
- Get laid.

Shortly after I graduated from law school and moved to Boston, I jumped to bullet point three. "Michael" was a couple of years younger than I. His online picture showed him wearing a black leather coat. He lived in a lovely Victorian brownstone that I suspected he could not afford on his own, but my gay vocabulary didn't yet contain the phrase *sugar daddy*.

I had prepared for the awkward, husky-voiced, precoital conversation ("So . . . what do you like to do?") between arrival and lust. I had packed condoms in my backpack. I had even bothered to shower and shave. But the first naughty thing Michael did to me was to mention his hearty dislike for the writings of Christian philosopher C. S. Lewis.

Needless to say, this opening gambit startled me. But because I had written via e-mail that I was "game for anything," I played along. Michael thought I was humoring him. To him, my responses sounded like disingenuous intellectual foreplay, the sort of dubious behavior you would expect from a public-school boy insufficiently versed in spiritual matters. An honest, God-fearing parochial school boy would have gone straight to the sex without pussyfooting around.

Pushing aside a zigzag fold of fresh condom wrappers, I plucked a copy of *The Problem of Pain* from my backpack. By His grace alone, and without any knowledge of Michael's religious predilections, Lewis's explanation for why a good God permits humanity to suffer just happened to be among my current stack of to-be-read books.

Michael's eyes lit up like a slot machine: jackpot! My interest in Lewis was — ironically — a definite turn-on. Unfortunately, mutual mental masturbation was the day's high point. After some awkward and unsatisfying physical fumbling, we gave up getting it on and lay around naked in Michael's bed talking about his desire to convert to Catholicism, who might be the perfect mentor, and what local parishes might embrace gay men.

Michael, a journalist, had nominated the Jesuit Urban Center at the Church of the Immaculate Conception as the "Best Non-Bar Venue to Pick Up Gay Men" for *Boston* magazine's Best of Boston annual picks. Known for its gay-friendliness and a theology focused on social justice, Immaculate Conception hosted an after-Mass doughnut social every Sunday, where, according to Michael, you could score if you'd been unlucky Saturday night.

A day or two later, Michael e-mailed me. Among other things, he described his coming-out. The first time Michael had walked into a room full of gay men, the burden of his self-consciousness had fallen away from him, and the air seemed to change colors.

"Not I," I wrote back. "No way. Gay men make me acutely self-conscious. When in a room of heteros, I go thankfully ignored. With gay men, my thoughts race, my gaze flickers, and I am acutely conscious of not wearing this year's 'it' shoes. Or last year's. Or any year's."

When I finally forced myself to attend Mass at the Jesuit Urban Center, I understood immediately why the Church of the Immaculate Conception attracted the aesthetically supercharged. The church was a hundred-fifty-year-old soaring edifice of white New Hampshire marble, its architecture precisely calculated to produce shocked dogs and cowering jellies. It had no permanent pews; the entire floor of the sanctuary was open. Were you to feel especially butch, you could have held a game of touch football between the holy water font and the altar.

The palpable gayness of the place knocked me off my feet. It felt as if my skin was sloughing off in great waves. A cluster of Scottie dogs was tied to the railing outside the front door. The seats were brimming with sophisticated men thin as a pair of folding spectacles. Bearded bears served as acolytes. Rainbow banners streamed from the ceiling. The preferred sign of peace was a same-sex kiss.

It made me panic. And it was hard to concentrate on worship while counting gay men like sheep before bedtime. I ran out without taking advantage of a single cruller.

Doing My Religious Business

Blame my beloved, erudite grandfather. When it comes to religion, my tastes run to the Gothic, not the gay — hence the pew, *The Problem of*

Pain, the learned helplessness, and the atheist boyfriend. Modernized biblical language and Unitarian ecumenism leave me cold and unsatisfied. Give me hoary nineteenth-century cathedrals, goblins and gargoyles, Latin benedictions, heavy arches, hidden naves, and unforgiving priests wearing white stoles decorated with the five wounds of Christ smiting the faithful. Therein lies the good stuff. I'm talking spiritual nipple clamps and an electrified floor.

As frequently happens in relationships and religion, fantasy gives way to convenience. Rather than locate the ecclesiastical dungeon of my dreams, I settled on Saint Anthony Shrine as my church of choice.

I found the Shrine the old-fashioned way: on Ash Wednesday, 1999, I followed a trail of forehead smudges. They were streaming from a dull, Cold War–era building that had no bell or steeple. A bank and the Boston Stock Exchange anchored one end of the block. A CVS Pharmacy and a Macy's guarded the other. Stuck in the middle, the Shrine, too, looked like another place of commerce. A half-dozen glass department-store doors listed its hours, as if the friars might someday hold a white sale on altar linens.

Even the two-story hammered-bronze crucifix over the front door seemed circumspect, as if Christ's final agony was just a minor discomfort. Only when approached from the subway entrance across the street did the crucifix take on a menacing aspect, as if you had wrongfully escaped from hell, and Jesus was going to extend a hammered-bronze leg and boot you back where you belonged.

Saint Anthony Shrine is known as the Worker's Chapel, because its downtown location is accessible to thousands who sneak out from their day jobs. The Shrine's two sanctuaries alternately crank out masses every half hour, twelve hours a day, seven days a week. Statues of Saint Anthony of Padua, Saint Clare, and the Holy Virgin receive nonstop devotion, and there's a steady traffic in votive candles. Outside the ground floor chapel, a great silver font contained enough holy water to drown a cat.

On that particular Ash Wednesday, at least sixteen people were dispensing ashes from various corners of the sanctuary. A group of Franciscan friars was gossiping in the lobby. If you ignored their habits — brown robes and knotted belts — they were indistinguishable from a gaggle of old gay men at a P-town cocktail party, effeminate and affectionate, though the teasing wasn't sexual.

Next to the Franciscans stood a display case holding dolls — nuns, Franciscans, popes — made by one of the friars. A hand-lettered sign above the case read "Not for Sale." Rumor had it that the dolls' outfits were religiously correct down to the very undergarments.

A Franciscan Fashion Show

Q. What is good Father McButterpants wearing under his habit?

A. A priest celebrating Mass does not just throw on a dress like some Appalachian hussy who just finished kissing Daddy. Here are a few sartorial essentials for a well-stocked sacristy:

- Alb: A white full-length slip often seen peeking out provocatively beneath Father McButterpants's chasuble. Basically, it's a camisole secured at the waist with a girdle. (Brides aren't the only ones who don't want to look fat at the altar.)
- Amice: A liturgical bib. If Leviticus hadn't outlawed eating shellfish, it would serve well at a lobster feed or clambake.
- Cassock: A religious hoodie. A close fitting ankle-length garment with or without a mantle (or "burnoose"), depending on your level of fabulous. Also, a dirty anagram. Gram always did love word games.
- Chasuble: Capelike outer garment for gay superheroes. Its color changes every liturgical season.
- Cincture: A liturgical belt, generally white to signify purity and chastity. Take a deep breath before tightening to emphasize that wasp-sized waist.
- Cope: A full cape worn by liturgical superheroes such as Super Transsubstantiator and his sidekick, Homilist Man.
- Crosier: The shepherd's crook bishops carry to yank misbehaving priests from their parishes. Historically, clerics used it

as a weapon as well as an aid in hiking the grand marble stair-
cases of their Episcopal palaces.
- Mitre: A bishop's triangular hat, from the Greek word for
turban. (Think Joan Crawford.)
- Stole: A liturgical boa.
- Surplice: Another liturgical undergarment, but it may be
worn without overgarments à la Cindy Lauper or Superman.

Banners over the Shrine's front doors announced, "All are welcome," and the friars damn well meant it. While I awaited my turn
with the ashes, I cynically classified the Ash Wednesday crowd into
categories:

- good Catholics
- bad cops
- daily communicants
- chronic masturbators
- the homeless
- the drunk
- lapsed Catholics returning briefly to remind themselves of
all they hate
- priests
- old Irish guys drawing disability and state pensions
- Vietnamese women who run T-shirt stands outside the
church and consider themselves children of God, even if
they do sometimes cheat the tourists
- skeptical twenty-something paralegals in low-rise jeans
and tight belly shirts who never put out on the first date
- Shrine security
- back-row lurkers
- the confessing
- the confessed
- the certifiably crazy

And then there was me. The homosexual. The *lone* homosexual. Aside from the friars, of course, but priests don't count.

My childhood fear of the altar took hold. I sat as far back and to the side as possible, so that neither God nor anyone else would notice me. It was not so much that I felt out of place, or acutely conscious of my sins. Rather, I felt like some rare bird, some impossible hybrid, some fucking lunatic.

For the next few months, I used Saint Anthony Shrine like a religious version of an X-rated theater. I slipped in, did my religious business anonymously, and slipped out again. Maybe I was ashamed of these private acts, but they gave me a short-lived, lukewarm satisfaction, like peeing down your pant leg after struggling for hours to hold back a weak bladder.

During this time, I made every effort to avoid the matter of the Church's attitude toward homosexuals. *Homo who? Shut up, and give me another communion wafer*.

Deals with God and Boyfriend

Compared to picking a Protestant pew, picking up a Protestant boyfriend was no sweat. Acquiring boyfriends had never been a problem for me. I've had dozens, mostly brief, and frequently overlapping. *Mea culpa. Forgive me, Father, for I have sinned. . . .*

I met Scott at a Catholic Charities event for disabled children. A child on crutches was making her way toward the front of the room. She stumbled. Scott and I jumped out from opposite sides of the aisle and caught her before she fell. We took one look into one another's eyes, and romance caught fire. We dropped the child and flew into one another's arms. Now, along with Rory and Jezebel, we live in chastity and are saving ourselves for marriage.

If your suspicious, filthy mind is thinking this tale is a figment of my deepest imagination or something I prepared for my mother's benefit, you can stop thinking that right now.

You are absolutely correct.

Truth is, I met Scott on gay night at a dance club called Manray. It was the Feast of the Epiphany in the liturgical calendar, which Scott loves to point out; he views himself as *my* epiphany! Scott was twenty-six years old, impossibly slender, with dark spiky hair and blue-gray eyes. His T-shirt hugged his pecs like a second skin. After boosting my courage with a couple of vodka tonics, I slipped up next to him. I pretended to survey the dance floor as I inched closer, until I could have taken Scott's pulse with my elbow. From time to time, I stared at the side of his head until he looked at me. Then I looked away. Forty-five minutes of this courtship technique left me with a back cramp, a full bladder, and a bald patch on my forearm from frantic "casual" brushing against his skin.

In that moment of extremis, I made the following deal with God: *God, if this hot guy is still at the rail when I come back from the men's room, I'll take it as Your will. I'll ask him to dance.*

When I returned, the space at the rail was empty. My heart fell. Apparently, God's will was for me to go home alone and masturbate.

Despondent, I turned to the bar for a little solace. And there he was.

"Hey," I said.

"Hey."

"What's your name?"

"Scott."

"Hey! Me, too! Buy you a drink?"

"Sure, vodka tonic."

"Hey! Me, too." *Oh, my God, we had so much in common! God obviously meant for us to be together!* "Wanna dance?"

"Sure."

I was on a roll. "Wanna come home with me?"

He shrugged. "Why not?"

Amen, I thought. Thy will be done.

Scott and I started dating, which complicated my religious life. We had a bit of a scheduling conflict. The problem was the Sabbath. God chose Sunday for its celebration, unless, of course, you are Jewish or Muslim. Unfortunately, in our gayborhood, Sunday is for brunch. Communion wine hasn't got a chance against a bloody Mary in a pint glass at our local gay sports bar, Fritz. Yes, that's right: gay sports bar. Not an oxymoron. They exist.

Now, God appreciates a good bloody Mary, too, so He and I reached a mutually acceptable compromise — a covenant, if you will. Friday became my Sabbath; specifically, the noon mass at Saint Anthony Shrine. I kept it holy. And honored my mother and my father and my pint-sized bloody Mary, and all those other commandments.

Having reached this covenant with the Almighty, I felt guilty. So I made one last gratuitous concession — as God no doubt knew I would. Omniscience is a boon at the bargaining table. My concession was this: I'd take added responsibility for the liturgy on that Friday Sabbath of mine. I agreed to serve as a lector at Saint Anthony's.

"Lay ministry?" Scott said. "That sounds hot!"

"It has nothing to do with getting laid."

"Oh." He frowned. "Whoa! Wait. You're going to do this during working hours?"

"Yes."

"I don't want this religion business to interfere with my long-term plan to sit home and eat bonbons," he warned, shaking his finger at me. "Go easy on it. How are you going to get a job as general counsel of a hedge fund and start supporting me in the manner to which I could easily become accustomed?"

"Half hour, once a week," I promised. "No sweat. It won't affect worklife."

"Well, OK, I guess that's not so bad. But keep a lid on it." Then he added cheerfully, "You know I don't believe that religious crap, but if it makes you happy and makes you a better person, I'm all for it."

Like a fool, I took him at his word.

III

A Church to Be Proud Of

You start off with Harry Potter, who comes across as a likeable wizard, but you end up with the Devil. There is no doubt that the signature of the Prince of Darkness is clearly within these books.

— Rev. Gabriele Amorth, chief exorcist of the Vatican

Channeling James Earl Jones

 LINGERED ON THE SIDEWALK like a john at an X-rated theater. I pretended to read the weekly bulletin taped to the window. I glanced nervously over each shoulder, and a voice in my head kept asking: *What's a nice porn writer like you doing at a mean church like this?*

What if someone I knew *saw* me there? Scott's warning was right on the money. It just wouldn't do for a self-respecting homosexual professional to be seen among the faithful. It was too throwback, too neocon, too much like saying I believed in magic. Or had a guilty conscience. Which I did.

There was nothing wrong with church attendance per se. For a straight person. Within reason. On Sundays and holidays, for example. Once-a-week religion on a straight career was like a pocket square: it looked nice, but everyone understood you didn't take it too seriously. Real piety, on the other hand, killed conversations. It was a form of spiritual flatulence on a down-bound elevator.

I was about to turn away and welsh on my covenant with God when a homeless woman halfway down the block shouted, "Got any change?"

Dammit! I yanked open the door and ducked inside. *Change? No, I'm sticking to the deal we made. Swear to You, hope to die.*

Bulletproof glass more appropriate to a pawnshop than a church shielded the information booth in the lobby. A woman of indeterminate age with a skull as narrow as a pencil manned the booth. I smoothed my clothes and tried to project deep spirituality. And maybe heterosexuality.

"Lector training?" I asked.

The woman looked me up and down, as if she were cataloging my sins. This thought visibly passed through her mind: *Priests might need to hear you whine in a box to know, but I had you pegged from the moment you walked in the door, homo.*

She jerked a thumb toward the basement.

Certain people go to foreign lands, seek out strange gods and different cultures, indulge in smoking the local intoxicant, participate in local customs like the consumption of raw aardvark testicles at the birth of the third son, easily absorb languages consisting entirely of clicks and snaps, become inured to the local habit of paying one's respects via presentation of a virgin gecko, and otherwise delight in the company of radically weird strangers as far from home as possible.

Said people are not Boston Irish Catholics. A journey farther west than the local coffee shop gives us hives. When we are looking for a culinary adventure, we switch from Bud to Bud Light. We have trouble pronouncing surnames that don't begin with "O" or "Mc." Shaking hands with strangers smacks of communism. In short, we seek out and cling to our kind, and we have to be dragged screaming to make the acquaintance of others not like us.

The basement frightened me. A dirty velvet curtain flanked a stage with an American flag and a podium. Thirty collapsible tables with folding chairs were arranged between an unused statue of the Virgin and an industrial-strength kitchen. The air stank of cigarette breath, stale coffee, and stainless steel polish. Someone had set out a plastic platter of day-old pastries and enough Equal to choke a horse.

The virtuous had arrived early. A polished, unapproachable Cape Verdean woman was cataloging her gold jewelry; a frumpy Chinese woman sat by herself and looked eager on cue; two soft-shouldered Irishmen with pale blue eyes wore nylon jackets celebrating Teamsters Local 259. It looked like an assembly of actual holy people who tithed, said grace, and never once countercheated against Gram in a high-stakes cribbage match. They no doubt led tidy lives, spent their vacations building homes for the Appalachian poor and making pilgrimages to Lourdes, and were in bed by 9:00 P.M. People, in other words, who had nothing in common with me.

Lo! There's the homosexual! I expected the Cape Verdean to cry out. *Let's burn him!*

I decided to pretend that I had wandered off course while looking for Filene's Basement. I was here not for spiritual substance but for knockoff Prada shoes. Francis the Franciscan Friar whisked me to a seat and buried me in registration forms.

"All are welcome," he reminded me.

If only you knew, Father. . . .

Father Francis divided us into two groups. Eucharistic ministers remained with him. Lectors fell to the purview of a take-charge, no-nonsense priest whose brown robes whisked around him while he walked and whose rope sash cracked like a whip. He had an angular face, an Abe Lincoln beard, and limbs like ax handles. We'll call him Father Abraham.

Using a whiteboard and lots of nervous energy, Father Abraham gave a short history of lay ministry. He explained that lay ministry actually pre-dated the clergy. No distinction existed between clergy and worshippers in the early Church. All ministers were necessarily lay ministers, and no special status attended their ministry. The earliest Christian missionaries were laymen. Many of the religious orders began as lay movements that the Church later clericalized. Saint Francis, the founder of Franciscans and friend to all animals, was a layman.

The origins of the early Church notwithstanding, later Church leaders discovered that God had never actually intended for uppity laypeople to carry out works in His name. Laypeople were to attend liturgy, not to participate in it. For several centuries, the Church limited the consumption, let alone the distribution, of Holy Communion to the clergy. Because the altar was holy, no layperson could enter it.

Vatican II reinvented laypeople. No longer would they sit passively and be the "catchers" of religious activity. Now, the laity would serve as religious "pitchers" as well. (I'll spare you a Handy Gay Vocabulary Alert on this one.) After Vatican II, anyone could read the word of God.

"Anyone?" I asked.

"Anyone," he said. "Of course, you *are* the public face of the Church. So an added burden rests on your shoulders. You need to look and act the part, so that you don't detract from the message you are delivering."

Looking and acting the part wasn't the problem. Truth was, only one thing really worried me about this whole lector business. It wasn't that I suck cock. Or that I write dirty stories. Or that I covet throat lozenges, own a Protestant pew, or look like a serial killer.

No, it was a much more serious matter: no one has ever mistaken me for James Earl Jones. In His infinite wisdom, God gave me a gay voice. It's not precisely lilting or fey, but it has a light, weightless quality — a feathery tone like an insouciant diva offering her jewelry for a kiss in lieu of a handshake. And it doesn't help that I can't enunciate my S's and F's clearly enough for others to distinguish them. My junk mail regularly comes addressed to Mr. Pomsret.

My outgoing voice-mail message plagues me. A hundred times, I've recorded over the old greeting, listened to the new one, rerecorded it, and listened some more. I never quite get the stern, majestic tone that might convey the august power of the law enforcement branch of the United States government to which I belong.

I try the greeting with "U.S.," but it comes out "U.F." I try just "S.E.C.," but that comes out "F.E.C." Stringing the whole thing together sans acronyms and using a diaphragm-stretching deepness of voice that I could barely sustain, I say, "Scott Pomfret, United States Securities and Exchange Commission." I call Scott, play the greeting, and ask him what he thinks.

"You sound like a nancy queen," he says every time.

My two consolations are, first, that I am actually gay. After all, I could have been straight and had a gay voice. Imagine the tragedy, the comic irony, the proof that God has a sense of humor. Second, I take consolation that I'm in reasonably good company. Numerous evangelicals and many of the horse-wranglers from the hate state of Texas, including President Bush II, share this affliction — a squeaky high-pitched whine like a loose telephone wire caught in a brisk wind. Listening to President Bush always gives me that acute sense of mortification you feel when hearing your own alien voice caught on digital audio.

Father Abraham fixed his gaze on me and said in a loud baritone, "As I used to teach young seminarians preparing to say their first Mass, the trick is to make *me* believe that *you* believe. This should be true not just on the altar, but everywhere you go, eucharistic ministers and priests alike. You have personal responsibility with respect to the way you live your life. You must be a witness."

Easy for you to say, I thought bitterly. *You could be James Earl Jones's white brother.*

Before I could chicken out, Father Abraham marched us to the second floor chapel for the dreaded practicum, in which we broadcast the voices God gave us — gay, straight, and anywhere in between. Father Abraham stood in the back row. We trainees huddled like shocked dogs under the glorious stained glass above the altar. The Cape Verdean queen went first. Her Highness rushed through the reading like she was in a race for the finish line.

"Do you have some other place you need to be?" Abraham asked with mock politeness.

"What?"

"*Slow down!*" he boomed. Abraham had no need for amplification.

Her Highness started the reading a second time. Abraham again interrupted. He noted how important em-PHAS-is was. "E-NUN-ci-ate," he chided. "You must enunciate."

Abraham had once been a drama teacher — and I don't mean that phrase as a euphemism for "gay." He was a professor of homiletics — the art of giving homilies, which is what Catholics call sermons — and he couldn't resist the opportunity to show off. With exaggerated diction, he spouted great chucks of scripture, with each character therein given a different voice.

"Do *that*!" Abraham commanded when he had exhausted himself. He might as well have asked Her Highness to turn water into wine.

"Um, OK," she said, close to tears. He mercifully let her get through her text and then slink off to the pews to be alone with her shame and gold jewelry.

One of the nylon windbreakers went next. In a cramped Irish voice that he swallowed whole, he said, "A readin' from the first book —"

"The first thing you need to keep in mind," Abraham said, cutting the Irishman short, "is that the microphone is unkind. It amplifies everything: snuffles, labored breathing, nose wrinkling, gas. Even shyness. God may be forgiving, but the microphone is not."

Once Abraham had reduced the Irishman to a puddle of warm Guinness, I approached the ambo. The microphone radiated evil. Think of the smoking swastikas on the crate holding the Ark of the Covenant in *Raiders of the Lost Ark*. Like the God of the Old Testament, that microphone could perform acts of great cruelty and vengeance. Just when you thought you'd made a covenant with it, the bitch turned on you. It would refuse to amplify a word you said until the moment when you cursed it under your breath; then it broadcast the curse so loud it made your ears bleed. If you laid hands on it, it wilted like an orchid, went slack, and emitted a snap-crackling boom across the entire sanctuary.

"A reading from the First Letter of Paul to . . ."

I couldn't go on. The microphone, in its ever-inventive cruelty, made me sound über-gay. We're talking far-out San Francisco fairyqueen, hand-on-the-hip, triple-snaps-in-a-Z-formation, rainbowribbon-rippling, Maria Callas–worshipping gay. Imagine saying the name "Sosthenes" with a lisp.

"Sorry, Father," I apologized, covering the microphone with one hand.

"Lesson number two," boomed Abraham. "Never apologize! Keep right on going with what you were doing. Don't call attention to your errors. *This is not about you.*"

Three Hale Marys

Between visits to Saint Anthony Shrine and bloody Marys at the gay sports bar, I prosecute people who commit securities fraud. Much like the priesthood, the ranks of the Securities and Exchange Commission are overwhelmed with zealous, righteous, parochial-school-trained Irish guys who believe in big words like Personal Responsibility and Justice and Honor and Fairness and Beer. Like monks in a scriptorium, my colleagues and I spent days, weeks, months, and years poring over documents, reading bank statements, and interviewing witnesses.

Then came a day — a Friday, inevitably — when the work ended. The suspected fraudster's defense lawyer had used every excuse and played every card, confronting me with the decision as to whether to charge the fraudster with a crime. Whether to destroy his life, consign his children to scholarships and his wife to social opprobrium, dim his prospects for early retirement, and perhaps even put him behind bars.

I prayed that I never be tested the way my target was tested. *Thank You, God, for giving me the grace to work for the government so I can't whet my appetite for the good life on an expense account, since I have to pay for every last throat lozenge from my own pocket to avoid coming into conflict with governmental ethics rules.*

God, am I doing the right thing in accusing this poor bastard of fraud? This man whose hand I once shook? This man who is not necessarily rich, perhaps just trying to get ahead, trying to do the best for his family, who nevertheless made a stupid decision, who coaches his kid's Little League team, who is perhaps a lector in his own parish, a religious education teacher, the dude in the next pew, You only know.

Then I remembered that could have been Gram's retirement fund he stole, or it could have been my godchild's college fund. Yet I ached for that confirming voice from the Almighty, saying, *Go ahead, Scott, fry the son of a bitch anyhow. It's OK with me.*

Regrettably, God never once weighed in on these deliberations. He just laughed and said, *That's why you're making the big bucks, Scott. Now, if you put a little higher percentage of that government salary in the collection basket, then maybe we can talk.*

Collection basket! I smacked myself on the forehead. *Shit, I'm late for Mass again!*

My black Oxfords clopped on the marble floor like high heels. The SEC identification cards around my neck flapped wildly on their tether. I bobbed at the tabernacle, cut left into the sacristy, skidded around the corner, and nearly knocked down Francis the Franciscan Friar.

"Slow down," Father Francis murmured. His scolding was soft as a cluster of butterflies. The mixture of lovingkindness and my own breathlessness made me dizzy. I swore Father Francis sent a special plea on my behalf to the Almighty: *Have mercy on this new lector. He knows not what he does.* Because lateness wasn't the worst of it: Fathers Abraham and Francis had enumerated a whole host of lay-ministering sins.

Lay Ministry Rules, Loosely Translated

Francis the Franciscan Friar says:	Scott's Translation:
Arrive fifteen minutes early for Mass.	O.J. Simpson Hertz commercial imitations are frowned upon.
Check in at the sacristy before you sit in the pew.	It's like the locker room before the big game: we put on our lay ministry medallions and our game faces, then wait for Father Francis to deliver the spiritual pre-scrimmage pep talk.
Don't rush the reading.	Most parishioners are thinking about the pretty girl in the third row, whether they put enough change in the parking meter, and whether the Sox will trade in the off-season for some pitching. Give their minds time to catch up.

Prepare the reading ahead of time, and be familiar with its message.	Last thing you want to do is read "Judas" where it says "Jesus." Avoid lightning strikes.
Wear respectful clothing.	Leave the leather chaps at home.
Refer to the pronunciation guide.	God doesn't like it when you make the prophet Habbakuk sound like an invitation to fellatio.
When leading the procession down the center aisle, don't hop, skip, or jump.	Walk with the spiritual equivalent of a pair of cement galoshes.
Don't cause a traffic jam.	Take turns at the tabernacle, and give communicants plenty of room for their pietistic calisthenics.

Mea culpa, Father Francis," I said, dropping my man-purse and swapping my SEC identification badge for a metal cross printed with the word *lector*. I vaulted into place in the pew reserved for lay ministers.

Give or take a few broken hips, some mental disease, and a handful of people who go spiritually adrift, Saint Anthony Shrine has a roster of approximately one hundred fifty lay ministers at any one time. Three are typically assigned to each mass — two to distribute the hosts, one to read, and maybe a spare to change the lightbulb over the tabernacle. Recognizing my rookie status, Father Francis had kindly assigned me to a group of experienced ministers, every one named Mary.

Mary Flanagan's hair was white, but her face was young; tall and thin, she looked much younger than her eighty-seven years. The passage of time had given her a question-mark silhouette. Each week, she dressed in crisp blouses and sensible shoes, and she liberally administered hugs to anyone with a pulse.

Mary Fleming was more reserved. She was shorter, rounder, and thirty years younger. Her eyes sparkled with shy playfulness in the sacristy, but on the altar she always wore her game face.

Mary Flaherty hailed from the Pleistocene age. She had whiskers and walked with a cramped, bent, wide-legged stance, as if she were perennially headed into a stiff wind. In the fall, she wore a Red Sox jacket and tennis shoes. At first it seemed like a victory just to avoid her condemnation, let alone win a word of kindness. Then she'd smile, and the dour puss she wore from a combination of habit and pessimism disappeared. The world surprised Mary Flaherty from time to time.

Ding! The brass bell sounded, and the three Hale Marys stood as one. Francis the Franciscan Friar stepped out onto the altar. He was wearing a simple white cassock pulled over his brown robes, a green surplice, and a stole on his shoulders depicting the five wounds of Christ. (That's hands, feet, and the centurion's spear in the side, for those of you who are counting.)

"In the name of the Father, Son, and Holy Spirit," said Father Francis, launching into the introductory rite. My mind instantly shot to the moon. While Father Francis droned, "blah . . . blah . . . God . . . blah . . . Jesus . . . blah," my inner litany sounded more like this: *Geez! What's with the statue of the Virgin? Somebody ought to rethink the gaudy paint. It makes her look like a harlot. . . . Did Scott rent a car so we could go fetch that pew from Albany? . . . Maybe the fraudster didn't do it. Maybe he really was visiting his elderly mother in the hospital at the time? Maybe the five eyewitnesses were lying.*

I realized Father Francis was staring me down. Uh-oh! The nearest Mary nudged me into the aisle. I dashed up to the ambo, remembering the evil microphone would transform the slightest breathlessness into the sounds of a dirty phone prankster. Fifty parishioners looked up expectantly. Three or four of the loony ones swayed and rocked. The guilty in the back row examined their feet, which in turn made me feel as guilty as any fraudster that had walked through my office door.

In contemplating lectorhood, I hadn't given a moment's consideration to the possibility that regularly uttering the word *God* with a straight face would prove a challenge. It was one thing to mentally run His Name through my head in a moment of extremis (*God, please don't let Whole Foods be out of arugula*), to punctuate someone's sneeze ("God bless!"), or to express the Hibernian morbidity Mary Flaherty loved ("See you tomorrow, God willing").

All that was fine. On occasion, certain members of the Holy Family were useful for moments of surprise and shock: "Mother of God!" "Jesus H. Christ," or "Jesus, Mary, and Joseph!" My mother, a far better person than I, had a novel fix for this sin. She simply converted blasphemy to geography. Instead of "Jesus Christ!" she spouted "Je-RU-salem!" Or, for truly dire occasions, "Fu-DAY-ga." I still don't know where this latter city is, but her tone told me it was nowhere I wanted to be.

In contrast to these easy invocations of God's name, uttering holy words without irony while in the act of worship — *that* made me feel icky. It was like reading porn aloud or accidentally hearing your sister's love-sounds through a bedroom wall.

Needless to say, every eighth word of the Bible contained the name of the Almighty. It might be Yahweh, it might be Elohim, it might be the Most High, but God under any of these names had the same effect. I took to inoculating myself ahead of time against the giddy urge to put ironic quote marks around such words wherever they appeared. "God-God-God-God," I intoned in the privacy of my SEC office as sternly as my gay voice allowed. "Lord-Lord-Lord-Lord-Lord. Jesus-Jesus-Jesus." This exercise only made me feel like one of those saccharine southerners with poofed-up hair and fake boobs who insert "God" into every third sentence and made my teeth itch.

For courage, I looked to the three Hale Marys. Mary Flanagan winked, like she was in with me on this great big cosmic joke. I could almost see the crucifix at her neck dance and her bony shoulders shake with laughter.

Instantly, all doubt vanished. My lips formed the first word of the reading, and I vanished. My mouth opened, and light streamed out. Peace reigned. White flowers cascaded over pots. The smell of cedar incense seemed particularly acute. I swore I detected the scent daubed behind Mary Flanagan's ear, and this suddenly seemed like the personification of faith: that somebody eighty-seven years old would still make the effort to make herself beautiful for Church.

I did just fine.

Thanks Be to the Pedophiles

In January 2002, a decades-long game of Clue came to a horrible, inevitable finale. We Catholics took a peek at the cards in the middle of the board, and the perp was revealed: it was Father So-and-So, in the rectory, with a handful of girlie magazines and a six-pack of beer. Although no friar was implicated in the scandal, the news hit Saint Anthony Shrine like a bomb. What had been a bustling and cheerful sanctuary took on the atmosphere of a morgue.

It wasn't the sexual acts themselves that raised everyone's ire. Show me a Catholic, and I'll show you someone who can name a priest from childhood that everyone knew you should never be alone with. Typically no one complained, most kids steered clear, and we nonvictims carried on with our lives. In a way, Catholics had collectively determined to accept a certain number of diddling priests as the cost of doing God's work.

What really galled us about the scandal was that the Archdiocese of Boston didn't merely shelter pedophiles from prosecution — it actually provided the abusers with fresh meat by assigning the sick priests to new parishes and new victims without disclosing their past sins. Some monster in the grand residence of then-cardinal Law had clearly weighed the personal damage to young boys against reputational damage to the Church and concluded that the boys were expendable.

> **School for Scandal**
>
> In many dioceses around the world, the term *scandal* has won a capital S and has become shorthand for diddling priests and the bishops who enabled them. But *scandal* is also a term of art in the Catholic Church — "To 'give scandal' is to intentionally tempt a brother to sin or to give him occasion to commit it."

When I first read about the scandal, I experienced the standard Catholic response: guilt. It's in my genes. I feel personally responsible for everyone's tears, others' happiness, spilled milk, underfunded schools, untidy bedrooms, unmade beds, and unfolded laundry. It's important to me to make sure that carbon emissions are reduced or eliminated, coaches and teachers made proud, and all sexual activity ends in orgasm.

As for the scandal, I *knew* my participation in the Mass, my support of Saint Anthony Shrine, and my willful blindness in childhood had somehow contributed to and perpetuated the mess. Doctrinal bombs might explode outside the Shrine, but I focused on my God-given task: reading from the Bible. If the microphone squawked, I took a deep breath and ignored it. If the pope squawked, I ignored him. Solitary prayer consisted of covering my ears and singing "*LA-LA-LA-LA-LA*" to drown out unwanted noise.

I thought I could get away with it. I thought I could divide the world into two discrete spheres: one that was gay, messy, and morally cloudy, and one that was antiseptic, Catholic, and enduring. Two fundamentally different worlds populated by fundamentally different people. In retrospect, considering the Church's reaction to the scandal, my religious experience at St. Anthony's had about as much substance and connection to reality as a jolly, tonsured Franciscan on the label of a bottle of Frangelico.

The molesting priests must have told themselves similar stories. Each probably eked out a separate "good priest" world with which he could console himself. In the good priest world, he performed corporal works of mercy and revered God, balancing out in his mind what he did behind the scenes to the altar boys. Unfortunately, each "bad priest" act rippled down through time and affected total strangers at a twenty-year remove with the immediacy of a two-by-four.

Ignoring the scandal was not an option. (Except for Pope John Paul II, whose postscandal 2002 trip to North America notoriously excluded the United States.) The front page was relentless, and everyone and his sister wanted a swing at the target. In my liberal circle, there weren't enough practicing Catholics to go around, so I bore the brunt of people's rage. They demanded:

"How can you support a church that did this?!"

"Why don't you hold them accountable?!"

"Where is your pope now?!" (Not in America, that's for sure.)

I hemmed and hawed, made halfhearted excuses, and shamelessly pulled the Mother Teresa card. But my defense of the Church, however poor, never resulted in substantive argument. Instead, my interlocutors jumped straight for what they viewed as the polemical jugular: "But you're *gay*, dude. You write *porn*."

They had, of course, hit the nail on the head. Although not necessarily for the right reasons. Sure, it was easy to believe that, because the Hale Marys and I tut-tutted together about the scandal and shook our heads and pitied the friars and felt sorry for ourselves and muttered "Je-RU-salem," they and I were in the same boat.

But we were on different oceans. For a gay Catholic, the scandal had a whole extra dimension about which straight Catholics never worried. Within weeks of the scandal's breaking, it became clear that the Church's primary defense was going to be a good offense — against gays.

The Vatican and high-ranking cardinals issued statements linking the scandal to the "problem" of homosexuals in the priesthood. Word quickly leaked that the Vatican was preparing to bar men identifying as gay from the seminary entirely (which it ultimately did in 2005). That arrogant cardinals were turning an administrative nightmare of their own making into the isolated handiwork of a group of horny, marginalized homosexuals in clerical collars left me speechless.

There's nothing gay about shuffling guilty priests from parish to parish so they can diddle more kids. That sin — I came to agree with my inquisitors — was quintessentially Catholic, not gay.

At home, of course, the scandal flung gasoline on the fire of Scott Whittier's belligerent atheism. Everything he had always believed was now proved true. And it was all on the front page of the *Boston Globe*. You couldn't buy publicity like that for the atheist cause.

A lesser man might have afforded himself at least a grin of satisfaction. Not Scott. "It's what I expected," he said, shrugging. "No surprises here."

The lack of triumph in his tone had a single source. Scott Whittier has one opinion about pedophiles: he thinks they should die. Slowly. In great agony. Preferably twisting from a rope tied to their genitals. He couldn't take satisfaction in the Church's downfall, because in his view that downfall wasn't worth the expense to the victims.

After the revelations continued unabated for months, Scott finally sat me down on the pew. His eyes were bloodshot, his expression murderous. The word *Catholic* came from his lips like he was choking on an olive pit. I'd like to say the pit struck my cheek, fell to the good soil at my feet, and germinated into a large, peaceful olive tree that provided us shade and comfort for years.

No such luck.

He complained about the money I dropped in the collection basket at St. Anthony's. He contrasted my political and legal activity in support of gay marriage with my participation in a church that was that issue's primary opponent in Massachusetts. In the weeks that followed, he e-mailed dozens of old news stories, such as the Vatican's condemnation of the 2000 World Pride parade in Rome that ended with the city withdrawing its official sponsorship of the event.

Diddling children, yes. Parades, no. A hell of a slogan for a decaying church to carry into the New Millennium. Je-RU-salem!

Scott asked point-blank, "Why do you keep going to a church that hates you?"

Ouch.

Vatican to the Rescue

I looked to the leadership of the Vatican for guidance. And the Vatican didn't disappoint. On the issue of Harry Potter, for example, Rome took a strong and unequivocal stand. In 2002, the Vatican's chief exorcist, Father Gabriele Amorth, spoke on Vatican Radio and labeled J. K. Rowling's series satanic.

I didn't even know the Vatican had a chief exorcist. Who else was on the payroll? Did Amorth have a staff of junior exorcists toiling away in windowless Vatican cubicles? Was there a grand inquisitor in the office down the hall? A hooded executioner in a small office by the water cooler?

More important, what exactly did the Department of Exorcism do besides taking positions on Harry Potter? Had they, for example, attempted to exorcise the devil in Cardinal Law that made him put the welfare of the institutional Church above the welfare of children? Did they run a school for exorcists, where they started with minor demons, worked their way up to mid-size devils, and then set to work on Satan himself?

I doubted the veracity of the report, but it turned out that Father Amorth was perfectly real. And perfectly serious. And — I am not making this up — his favorite movie is *The Exorcist*. According to news reports, Father Amorth has performed over 30,000 exorcisms. That's a lot of split-pea soup.

In his Vatican Radio interview on the Potter matter, Fr. Amorth said, "Behind Harry Potter hides the signature of the king of the darkness, the devil." Keep in mind, this was five years before J. K. Rowling outed Albus Dumbledore, headmaster of Hogwarts, as a gay man.

Amorth put Harry in good company. Father Amorth said in the same interview that Stalin and Hitler "almost certainly" were also possessed by the devil. Interesting. Adolf Hitler. Joseph Stalin. Harry Potter. Makes perfect sense. According to Father Amorth, Pope Pius XII once tried to perform a long-distance exorcism on Hitler — without success, obviously. Amorth explained, "It's very rare that praying and attempting to carry out an exorcism from a distance works. One of the key requirements for an exorcism is to be present in front of the possessed person, and that person also has to be consenting and willing."

Amorth's concession gave me a very personal sense of relief. Even if he had detected my unsuitability for lector service at Saint Anthony Shrine, he would not have been able to compel the devils within me to get hence without traveling all the way to Boston. But that relief evaporated when further research showed that Father Amorth was not just a crazy old man straying from the reservation. Pope Benedict XVI, then Cardinal Ratzinger (hereinafter "B16" or "the Rat"), was also preoccupied with the bespectacled adolescent wizard. The Rat wrote that Harry Potter contains "subtle seductions, which act unnoticed and by this deeply distort Christianity in the soul, before it can grow properly" in children. Nice to know the Vatican was holding high-level consultations about protecting children from fictional characters while subjecting the same children to predatory priests.

To be fair, Saint Anthony Shrine has its own brand of lopsided, endearing kookiness. Father Justin, for example, is our jazz friar. He constantly riffs on the standard liturgy in ways that catch the flatfooted congregation off guard, somewhere between an amen and a thanks be to God, and not sure whether to sit, stand, kneel, or just shoot the good father and be done with it.

The Shrine attracts more than its fair share of mystics, crazy people, and the devout-against-all-odds — and not just misguided homosexuals like me. A typical Friday mass included:

• The Hero, whose multiple sclerosis had twisted his limbs and stolen his voice. Every Friday, without fail, he propelled his wheelchair up the center aisle by stomping the marble floor with one twisted foot like an angry bull. He bellowed and grunted the prayers and responses out of time in speech as garbled as Chewbacca's. This wheelchair-bound wookie had a reason to hold a grudge against God, and yet he came week after week and made his own pre-Mass ministry, handing church bulletins to all who came through the door.

- The Haunted Man, who communicated regularly with demanding dead people in purgatory. For the sake of their immortal souls, he attended no fewer than six masses a day.

- The Witchy Widow, who wore secondhand shoes and a Victorian black lace shawl fastened over her stark white hair. Before Mass, she flung herself before the tabernacle and prayed madly, lips moving but making no sound. During Mass, she stayed out of step with the coordinated responses and prayers of the other parishioners, like a sour note in a marching band. After communion, she kissed the feet of the brass Jesus and never once acknowledged another living soul.

Who is the Holiest of Them All?

The Haunted Man and Witchy Widow are contestants in a penitential variety show, the goal of which is to outdo one's neighbors in acts of piety and abasement. Other contestants include Deep Bowers, Exaggerated Genuflectors, Floor Flingers, Prayer Bellowers, Demonstrative Bead Counters, Forehead-on-Pew Slumpers, Large-Cross Wearers, Early Arrivers, Late Stayers, and, I imagine, a few with thorns in their underwear and a dungeon at home where they whip themselves at night.

Participants in Ye Olde Piety Show never accept communion from a eucharistic minister, however extraordinary he or she might be. Apparently, someone told them that communion only works if you take it directly from an ordained priest. They change lines, cross-check their compatriots, duck, and backtrack to the other side of the sanctuary solely to avoid receiving communion from the unordained. To them, lay ministry is as newfangled as power door locks, cell phones, or the Internet. Where's the magic in the sacraments if any post–Vatican II homosexual can administer them?

When participants in Ye Olde Piety Show do approach the priest, the religious fireworks really begin. They leave plenty of room between themselves and the communicant in front of them, so when the path is clear, they get a two- to three-step running start to fling themselves at the priest's feet with tongue outstretched.

Even the artwork at Saint Anthony Shrine was a little off-kilter. A row of panels in the second-floor chapel pictures twelve apostles — but not the right ones. A Simon is missing, replaced by Saint Paul, who was not an apostle. In a rendering of the Last Supper, Judas makes no appearance, and no women whatsoever have shown up, although the Gospels put both at the scene.

All this kookiness reminded me of the Native American craftsmen who deliberately engineer errors into pottery. The flaw is the point where the spirit enters the work and gives it life. So, too, for Saint Anthony's: the Shrine was a veritable Swiss cheese through which the Spirit flowed at a steady clip.

Of course, kookiness is all fine and good until someone burns at the stake. Local Saint Anthony's kookiness was endearing, but high-level Vatican kookiness was too much to bear. Like the Hale Marys and Ye Olde Piety Show, like Fathers Abraham, Justin, and Francis, like so many Catholics, I just wanted a church of which I could be proud. This yearning was another form of learned helplessness: I was passively looking for a savior to restore my pride, as if the Savior we had wasn't enough.

IV

Love, J2P2

Join us in a diplomatically intricate, ethically ambiguous, and sometimes publicly humiliating tightrope walk toward Jesus.

— Jim Naughton, Anglican Diocese of Washington, D.C., referring to the controversy over the ordination of gay bishop Gene Robinson

Happy Birthday

HRISTOPHER HITCHENS BE DAMNED. If you want proof of the existence of God, you have a couple alternatives. First — and I think this evidence is irrefutable — Dick Cheney and Alan Keyes each have a lesbian daughter, and Lynn Cheney in turn has a child. These facts bear witness: Not only is there a God, but He's a funny son of a bitch.

If you need additional proof, you can pray to the Lord and see if He answers. I, for example, had prayed for a new savior to restore my pride in the Church. On my thirty-fifth birthday, God delivered. The pope appointed Seán Patrick O'Malley to be the new archbishop of Boston.[†]

Given the timing, I concluded that O'Malley was a gift-wrapped, sealed-with-a-kiss love offering from the Almighty Himself.

[†] The accent known as the fada changes the meaning of the word. "Sean" without the accent means "old."

The friars at the Shrine shared my optimism, in part because Archbishop Seán, as he preferred to be known, was one of them — a brown robe! He was a Capuchin, a kissing-cousin branch of the Franciscans from whom cappuccino takes its name. One friar announced, "We are called to be peacemakers, to heal wounds, unite what has fallen apart, and bring home those who have lost their way. . . . That's what the [Vatican] had in mind when they appointed [O'Malley]."

Personally, I couldn't help but ascribe tremendous virtue to a man who was said to speak six languages, and who, like me, loathes cats and had been caught red-handed in the decidedly un-Franciscan act of shooting them with a squirt gun. At first glance, O'Malley came across as a likable wizard.

Not everyone in the archdiocese shared my enthusiasm. Archbishop Seán's habit of wearing his habit inflamed the sartorial jealousy of diocesan priests, who suffered in basic black and a dog collar. Never permitted to wear a sash and dress, they cattily referred to O'Malley as the Brown Bag.

At the Shrine, he also had his skeptics. A few weeks after the Brown Bag became archbishop, a stranger waited after Friday mass. She had a broad Irish face, a fire-hydrant body, and an aluminum walker. I had never seen her before. Flooded with guilt, I racked my brains for the sin with which she was preparing to confront me.

I dodged around the holy water font, feinted for the shrine of the Holy Virgin, and made a beeline for the side door. But she had good foot speed for a lady with a walker and cut me off at the statue of Saint Anthony.

"I want to let you know," she said sweetly, "you read beautifully. I really enjoy coming to this Mass."

"Th-thank you," I stuttered.

I discreetly knocked on the wooden platform supporting Saint Anthony. If there's anything a Catholic boy likes less than being confronted with his sins, it's being confronted with praise. Praise makes you proud, and pride goeth before a fall, and no doubt this woman's good wishes would boomerang back and knock down my immortal soul.

To reduce the karmic backlash, I put on my best aw-shucks

voice. "It's not me. I just read what's in the Book. God's word and all that."

"*Well*," she said, raising her voice. This was not a woman who tolerated contradiction. "*I* appreciate it. It takes my mind off of *all this*."

"All this" was the phrase parishioners at Saint Anthony Shrine used to denote the pedophile priest scandal, and it gave me the opportunity to change the topic from the pitfalls of pride and praise.

"But O'Malley's coming," I reminded her.

"So's the Lord," she snapped, "but I'm not holding my breath *all this* is going to change soon."

But it did change — or seemed to change. O'Malley's first acts gave reason for hope. He insisted on being called by his first name. He hired my former law firm with the goal of reaching settlements with the victims. He rejected the luxurious trappings of Bernard Law, his pandering predecessor. Gone was the mansion, gone the orgiastic installation ceremony. Seán took up residence in the rectory of the Cathedral of the Holy Cross, auspiciously located in my gayborhood, the South End, and used proceeds from the sale of the mansion to compensate victims.

O'Malley's first homily as archbishop of Boston described how lepers converted the heart of Saint Francis. All his life, the sight of lepers had disgusted Francis, until one day, by the grace of God, Francis embraced a leper and kissed him instead of fleeing and holding his nose. This homily made my heart leap.

Brother Seán, I thought, *aren't gay men America's lepers?*

Seeking a big wet smooch of reconciliation, I sent Archbishop Seán a welcome letter. I wrote that I looked forward to his coming and restoring pride. Basically, I pinned my hopes on Bishop O'Malley's arrival as if it marked the return of Christ himself.

I never got any sort of reply. The Brown Bag was too busy, no doubt, fixing all that was wrong with the Church.

Calculating the Odds

Shortly after the installation of Seán O'Malley as archbishop, Scott Whittier and I launched Romentics, the first-ever line of romance novels featuring gay men. We modeled them explicitly after the Harlequin line.

The venture was Scott's idea. For years, he had watched Gram and his mother devour truckloads of cheap Harlequin novels. After reading, they coded the novels with their own shorthand ratings scale on the first page: "good story," "nice," and, very occasionally, "sexy." This latter rating was no compliment. For Scott's mother and Gram, sex got in the way of the story.

Scott and I had a different perspective. We wanted *every* reader to write "sexy" on the flyleaf of our Romentics novels. Sex was integral to our characters' relationships and necessary to driving plot. Ours were romances, yes, but romances with testosterone. Blushes and saving your maidenhead for marriage simply wouldn't do.

Our first romances appeared on November 1, 2003. They had intentionally sassy titles: *Razor Burn* and *Hot Sauce*. Warner Books agreed to publish the latter, and this stamp of approval attracted media, beginning in Canada — natch — with a profile in the *Globe & Mail*.

But it wasn't until the *Boston Globe* profiled us that news of my venture got back to the Shrine. The Friday after the *Globe* came out, I showed up in the sacristy a few minutes before Mass. The three Hale Marys had already arrived. We went about our usual business, which consisted mostly of watching the sacristan pour out a bag of unconsecrated hosts — *Oops! Dropped one! Five-second rule!* — and set out the chalice and ciboria.

It didn't surprise me that no one mentioned the *Globe*. My conversations with Mary Flanagan in particular were always lopsided. She never asked a single question about my personal life, not even where I lived. It was "Don't ask, don't tell." That is how old ladies get along in a changing world: they converse at a level of generality that allows everyone to pretend nothing has changed. Then they die. At eighty-seven, Mary seemed no different.

An elevator led from the friars' quarters directly to the sacristy, much like the pole in a firehouse. When the alarm rings, the friars dash to the lift, go down it, and go to work. About ninety seconds before Mass was scheduled to began, the elevator doors opened, and Father Myron McCormick stepped into the sacristy, blinking a moment in brilliant benevolence. He was ancient, completely bald, and had long, wizardlike fingers that accentuated his medieval brown robe.

"Hello, Scottie," he said. Father Myron is the only person besides my mother and my godson who calls me Scottie. "Hello, Mary. And Mary. And Mary."

I have always been a spiritual size queen,[†] and Father Myron was a man of enormous spiritual endowment. His eyes exuded kindness. He never failed to greet me enthusiastically, taking my hand in both of his. His manner was what you might expect from someone named Myron: he wore big, nerdy glasses and had an endearing spastic awkwardness. To be in his presence was like taking Valium; immediately the restless spirit calmed and anger diminished. I couldn't imagine him harming a housefly. Archbishop Seán himself had stopped by the Shrine for the express purpose of making his confession to Father Myron.

Recovering from his stunned benevolence, Myron drifted around the room, laying hands on each and every person in the room. He opened the wardrobe that contained a rainbow of vestments for the various masses of the liturgical year and hooked his cane over the top of one of the doors. Myron was addicted to this cane that he never actually used, carrying it everywhere and forever hanging it on altars, chair rails, counters, doorknobs, and forearms.

Myron slipped vestments over his robe. The Hale Marys paraded out to the first pew. I took a last look at the day's reading. Mass was supposed to begin, but Myron paged through the lectionary (known as "the Book") as if he had all the time in the world. All of a sudden, as if the Book reminded him of books in general, he turned and asked, "How's your book coming, Scottie?"

"*My* book?" I thought he was referring to the lectionary.

"I read about it in the *Globe*," he said.

My eyes widened, my knees weakened. I wanted to explain that I was not Scottie at all. Rather I was a National Security Administration operative living under a false identity while engaged in a top-secret

---

† Gay Vocabulary Alert: A size queen is a gay man with an "open door policy," for whom the phrase "the bigger the better" was coined.

undercover operation, which regrettably required me to leap immediately through the nearest stained glass window and make my escape.

"Um, my book's good, Father Myron. Which, uh, reading do you want me to do? The feast-day reading? Or the regular one?" *Or the one with the shower scene that involves whipped cream?*

"Where can I get a copy?" Father Myron asked brightly.

An image — a very unwelcome image — flashed through my head: Myron reading my smut:

> The first kiss tickled the spot behind his ear. The hard cock was a firebrand against his backside. Slicked with soap, Troy's hands moved one circle on Brad's chest, one on his right hip. Gradually the circles grew closer and closer to Brad's crotch. He tried to turn, but Troy would not let him. Like a man arrested, Brad placed both his palms on the glass, spread his legs, and lowered his butt slightly. First there was a finger, then two . . .

It wasn't that I was ashamed of the poetry of this passage. Sexuality is a gift from God, and can be sacramental in the right circumstances. And the sexual congress in our novels always took place in the grossly conventional context of sacred and enduring unions between men who were destined to live happily and monogamously ever after.

No, what made me uncomfortable was the fact that Myron was a priest and a saint. He belonged up on that altar (read: pedestal). I wanted him to be glassed in and safe, like the dolls in the lobby of the Shrine: NOT FOR SALE. Putting aside Myron's saintliness, the last thing I wanted was for this to get back to Archbishop Seán. I didn't want him to get a bad first impression or become distracted from restoring pride in the Church.

A store carried my books a hundred yards from the Shrine, but I suggested, "Why don't I try to get you a copy sometime, Father?" I had absolutely no intention of doing so.

Myron grasped my hand in both of his. "Would you?" he said. He wrung my hands warmly. "Thank you, Scottie. Thank you."

It wasn't that I wouldn't, I told myself. Rather, I would delay it. For years.

The Cardinal Spellman School

"The last thing I need," Mary Flanagan declared one day in the sacristy, "is yet another edict from Rome about how I'm supposed to approach the tabernacle or where I'm supposed to put the used ciboria after Mass."

A Eucharistic Place Setting

The altar is the table at our cloth-napkin restaurant. We don't wrap the utensils into a paper napkin twist and put out crayons for the place mats. Here's what you'll find on a properly set eucharistic table:

- Ciborium: Soup bowl used to carry wafers for consecration and distribution.
- Paten: Dinner plate that carries the presider's portion. Since bread is all there is for dinner, there's no separate bread plate.
- Chalice: Wine (and water) glass. There's typically just one, so the presider never has to worry about poaching from his dining partner.
- Cruets: Just like those used for salad dressing, but these hold water and wine, respectively.
- Purificator: A napkin used to wipe holy schmutz off the edge of the chalice between recipients.

In stark contrast to the tenacity with which Rome clung to tradition, edicts concerning the eucharistic ministry changed weekly. According to the latest instruction, the leftover consecrated hosts were not to be returned to the tabernacle after communion was distributed.

They were to be left instead on the windowsill in the ambulatory between the altar and the sacristy, so that the sacristan could judge whether sufficient host remained for the next mass.

"It feels like I'm leaving crumbs for birds," Mary Fleming complained.

Mary Flanagan announced she was going to ignore the edict. "Sooner or later," she said defiantly, "they'll go changing the rules on us again."

For most Catholics, particularly lapsed Catholics, Catholicism is a religion of screwy, random rules paired with fantastically grave consequences. We think of the Thou Shalt Nots, the Ten Commandments, nuns with wooden rulers, confession before communion, holy days of obligation, altar boy rubrics, when to sit, stand, and kneel, how long to fast before Mass, don't touch the host with your hands, orgasm-free sex tips, and, of course, don't take the Lord's name in vain, goddammit. Throw in a few Thou Shalts, for good measure, and don't ever get caught alone in the rectory with Father Feel-Me-Up. The Church created the specter of a moral minefield of a world and then pointed the way to safety: strict obedience.

While Vatican II loosened things up a little, Pope John Paul II (known affectionately as J2P2 because his aging, hunched physique increasingly resembled the wheeled droid from *Star Wars*) inspired a rules-based backlash. He hired bishops and priests who made a fetish of obedience and congratulated themselves on their denial. They made a golden calf of rubrics and rules and encouraged a diminishing number of followers to gird their loins and lash their own backs, and they thought less of those who did not lash in time.

Mary Flanagan and many of the eucharistic ministers had a looser approach to Catholicism. They put the "cat" in Catholic. Getting them to follow a common set of prescribed rules was like the proverbial herding of felines — without the benefit of the Brown Bag's squirt gun.

"Is anyone not getting their communion because of me?" Mary asked belligerently. When she heard nothing but God's own silence in response, she said with great satisfaction, "I didn't think so!"

Father Bear-Daddy was Mary Flanagan's nemesis. Bitchy,

impatient, passionate, and demanding, he suffered no fools. Father Bear-Daddy — unlike Father Abraham — was, at heart, a "drama teacher." The clues were legion:

- Father Bear-Daddy owned a miniature greyhound, eight inches high at the shoulder and all of twelve pounds.
- He subscribed to *Bay Windows*, the local gay paper.
- He also received other harder-core mailings — "Stuff I don't touch!" according to one parish employee.
- He had a finely developed sense of gay vanity. When I referred to the friars at Saint Anthony's as "old," he became indignant.
- At the party celebrating the thirtieth anniversary of his ordination, a pastoral associate joked that she meant to buy him pearls to wear, but thought it would look too Mardi Gras.
- Father Bear-Daddy was the Shrine's decorator-in-chief — his taste inspired by a Victorian bordello. Imagine extravagant purple and scarlet swashes of silk streaming down from the rafters under which one had to duck to reach the ambo, collections of lilies that spread out from the altar like a rash, and lighting so low that anyone on the altar could pass for twenty years younger.
- Father Bear-Daddy had read *Hot Sauce*.

But he was no mincing nancy. A burly, handsome satyr of a man, he sported a better-to-eat-you-with smile, a full head of close-clipped hair, and a goatee. Had he made an appearance in civilian clothes in Provincetown on Bear Weekend, he would not have been out of place.

Handy Gay Vocabulary Alert!

Q. What's a bear?
A. A bear is a fat, furry homosexual. Bears do not get as much TV time as the wispy queen, but they are nevertheless a very

important piece of the homosexual menagerie. Bear Weekend is their annual gathering in the gay beach resort of Provincetown, Massachusetts. Subspecies include cubs, and, at the thinner end of the scale, otters and wolves. Bear faghags are known as Goldilocks.

Rules mattered to Father Bear-Daddy, and pity the eucharistic minister who crossed him. Bitch-slapping wasn't out of the question. Take, for example, the rules about consumption of communion on the altar. (Did you even know such rules existed? It makes you think of how closely you flirt with perdition every day, doesn't it?) Typically, as the presiding friar consecrates the bread and wine, the eucharistic ministers line up next to the altar. The friar distributes the consecrated host to each minister. Then both friar and ministers consume the host simultaneously.

Once when Father Bear-Daddy was presiding, a wayward eucharistic minister filling in for Mary Fleming accepted the Eucharist and immediately lifted the host to his mouth. Father Bear-Daddy whirled, his vestments lifting up around his hips like the skirt of a flamenco dancer. He slapped the offending hand. The host flew. The entire congregation gasped. Hand on hip like a steaming kettle, Father Bear-Daddy pointed sternly to where the host fell until the hangdog minister retrieved it. For a moment, I thought Father Bear-Daddy was going to take the host back and expel the offender from the sanctuary.

As a result of this transgression, Father Bear-Daddy convened all lay ministers for a refresher course. He charged around madly, emphasizing the need for rules and spelling them out for us with great emphasis.

"No *tongues*," he said. "When you're up on the altar, you will take communion in hand — put one hand in the other and form a cup to receive the Lord. *Capisci?*"

We all nodded dumbly to indicate, yes, we understood what he was saying.

A skeptical look passed over Father Bear-Daddy's face. Then he exploded: "You should be smooth, simple, and dignified when you take communion. Those who make *quandamas* — that's Italian, it means

'a big show' — those who make *quandamas*, they don't understand.[†]
There shouldn't be a bow or genuflection or fireworks. It's communion, for goodness' sake. It's not time for you to show everyone else how
pious you are, with sackcloth and ashes."

For the briefest moment, I thought he was joking. I glanced at
Mary Flanagan. Surely, this spelled the end of Ye Olde Piety Show.

Father Bear-Daddy hopped off the chancel — the raised platform
at the front of the church — and wandered halfway down the pews
like a talk show host among his studio audience. "These people who
take communion on the tongue, they think they're being *traditional*!
They think they're being more *pious*! It's *ignorance*, that's what it is!
What's traditional is the *hand*, creating a vessel for the Lord."

Father Bear-Daddy loudly slapped one hand down on the other.
The sound rang out like a shot in the deathly still sanctuary.

Father Abraham, who had been lurking in the wings, stepped forward. "What Father Bear-Daddy is saying is that you shouldn't go out
of your way to express any stray feelings of holiness you may experience just because you are on the altar. In many ways good ritual is
good drama. The spotlight should be on what's important. Therefore,
there's no need to genuflect or otherwise reverence the tabernacle on
your way up to the ambo or when otherwise involved in the liturgy.
Your involvement alone expresses the proper reverence for God."

Mayhem ensued. Hands flew up. Voices rang out. Everyone and
his sister had a different opinion about how the liturgy should be carried out. Half of the eucharistic ministers wanted to be assured they
were doing no wrong. The other half, who could conceive no possibility of their own imperfection, were determined to help Father Bear-
Daddy explain the rules. A nun who could barely speak English
bitterly complained about the quality of lecturing she had experienced.
A pinched woman with multiple lapel pins prescribed particular
points of proper genuflection. They revisited rubrics long since rejected, offered suggestions for further improvement, and did everything short of adding a mariachi band to the music mass.

---

† *Quandamas* isn't actually Italian. Father Bear-Daddy later confessed to me that he
had invented the word on the spot.

Mary Flanagan rolled her eyes. Father Bear-Daddy became visibly agitated. "Mary Flanagan, you're not dead yet, are you?"

Mary wisely took a moment before she answered to be sure she had the correct response. "No, not yet."

"Good. Then you can still learn how to do things a little differently."

White-knuckled, eyes blazing, Father Bear-Daddy was not by nature a populist or a democrat. "You *all* can," he said, pacing back and forth on the chancel and then up and down the center aisle. Taking a deep breath, he summoned benevolence and patience from what was clearly a depleted store. "The Church is not a people gathered to congratulate itself on its own righteousness. It is a communion gathered for mission."

He returned to the safety of his cherished theme. He began railing about those who took communion on the tongue: "They bite, they snap, they scratch, they lick, they fling themselves to the floor. . . ."

Lips curled in disgust, he acted out each of these forms of faux veneration. Then he glared into the pews as if we ministers were personally responsible for his close encounters with saliva. I, for one, felt not a little proud that I had been taking communion manually from the beginning. Father Bear-Daddy made it feel like a safe, morally unambiguous practice.

Mary Flanagan stood up in her pew, slipped into the aisle, and threw her arms around him. She laughed herself to tears and patted him on the back, thereby undermining all his precious dignity.

"I've been taking communion for eight decades, give or take a couple of years," she said. "I guess I've never seen someone put so much thought into it as you do."

The Rules

All this talk of rules and all these people presuming there was some contradiction between my gay life and my Catholic life got me thinking. What exactly were the Church's rules regarding "persons with a homosexual tendency" (their lingo)? Most people believe that the Church isn't a gay man's best friend. But like a typical lawyer, I wanted the nuts and bolts, the unglossed, official line with all the nuances and loopholes. Sometimes we think we know something, but when we return to the original source, our knowledge can prove mistaken.

After all, when it comes to its most prominent leaders, the Church itself doesn't throw away the spiritual baby with the homosexual bathwater. Francis Cardinal Spellman, bishop of Boston and later head of the Archdiocese of New York, for example, was notoriously gay. His particular fondness for Broadway musicals and their chorus boys earned him the nickname "Fanny Spellbound," yet the Church named numerous high schools after him and offered him up as a model of virtue.

How bad could being a "drama teacher" be?

I consulted my trusty copy of the 1878 Baltimore Catechism.

The Baltimore Catechism

A widespread torture device used to destroy the knuckles of three whole generations of American Catholic schoolkids while simultaneously eradicating all independent thought, the Baltimore Catechism is a primer. Its question-and-answer format gives standardized responses to questions of doctrine, morals, and all things Catholic. American students had to memorize the responses and regurgitate them word-for-word on demand, beginning in kindergarten.

If you failed to recite the correct answer in the proper words?

"You got the ruler," my father recalled ruefully sixty-five years after the fact, "which happened with an alarming degree of frequency in my case."

Page 124 set forth the following teaching:

> *Q. Which are the Four Sins that cry out to Heaven for vengeance?*
> A. 1. Willful murder; 2. Sodomy; 3. Oppression of the poor or of widows and orphans; 4. Defrauding laborers of their wages.

Q. *Why are they said to cry out to Heaven for vengeance?*

A. Because on account of their horrible wickedness they seem to cry out to Heaven for punishment.

Morally equating the insertion of bodily tab A into bodily slot B with "willful murder" struck me as a tad extreme. Most people — gay or otherwise — believe in a hierarchy of sin. It is worse to kill, for example, than to have consensual premarital sex with someone you love. Rape and child molestation aside, I imagined that the worst sins were not sexual acts.

Surely the Church had modernized since 1878. Notwithstanding its claim to "constant" teaching, the Church does introduce new ideas from time to time — like papal infallibility in 1870. Here's the current catechism:

- Homosexual acts are intrinsically disordered, contrary to the natural law, and close the sexual act to the gift of life.
- They do not proceed from a genuine affective and sexual complementarity.
- Under no circumstances can they be approved.
- Homosexual persons are called to chastity.

Riffing further, under the leadership of B16, the Congregation for the Doctrine of the Faith (successor entity to the Inquisition) has stated that "The particular inclination of the homosexual person is not a sin, [but] it is a more or less strong tendency ordered toward an intrinsic moral evil; and thus the inclination itself must be seen as an objective disorder. . . . It is only in the marital relationship that the use of the sexual faculty can be morally good. A person engaging in homosexual behavior therefore acts immorally." Why is this behavior immoral? Because, according to said inquisitors, "To choose someone of the same sex for one's sexual activity is to annul the rich symbolism and meaning, not to mention the goals, of the Creator's sexual design."

The United States Conference of Catholic Bishops (USCCB) echoed this view: "Homosexual acts do not reflect the complementarity of man and woman that is an integral part of God's design . . . and are not in keeping with our being created in God's image and so degrade and undermine our authentic dignity as human beings." Je-RU-salem! Bottom line? In the Church's view, I'm a defective straight guy.

Even when making allowances for our human dignity, the Church can be cramped and ungenerous. For example, in 1992, the Congregation for the Doctrine of the Faith under B16's leadership said, "What is at all costs to be avoided is the unfounded and demeaning assumption that the sexual behavior of homosexual persons is always and totally compulsive."

Well, imagine my relief.

Searching for good news to hang my homo hat on, I found only these teachings:

- Homosexual persons must be accepted with respect, compassion and sensitivity. Every sign of unjust discrimination in their regard should be avoided.
- Full and active participation by persons with a homosexual tendency in the Church is encouraged, but the Church has a right to deny roles of service to those whose behavior violates her teaching.

The USCCB discouraged coming out to the general public. A coming-out party limited to "family members, a spiritual director, a confessor or members of a church support group" was permissible. The *Boston Globe* didn't qualify as a church support group.

Seeking redemption, I turned to Rome's teachings on porn, hoping it might rank low in the hierarchy of sin. No such luck. According to the Church, "pornography . . . perverts the conjugal act [and] does grave injury to the dignity of its participants . . . since each [participant] becomes an object of base pleasure and illicit profit for others. . . . It is a grave offense."

Crap. I was worse off than I thought. Even my dignity was at risk. Do not pass go. Do not collect $200. Go straight to jail. By the Church's rules, the best I could hope was that God looked down on me and nevertheless concluded: *Well, at least he's not a willful ax murderer.*

Make Me Believe That You Believe

After President Bush invaded Iraq, Father Bear-Daddy asked the other friars to insert a prayer for peace in the liturgy. One day, after the new prayer, an unshaven Irishman wearing glasses and a filthy cable-knit sweater ranted, "If you want peace, you need to get George Bush and his stinkin' wife out of the White House. Then you'll have peace."

Acutely discomfited by the sound of his gutter voice in the Shrine, the rest of us prayed louder. It wasn't so much his skepticism about the prayer that bothered us, but that he had disturbed our insular sense of peace.

The Shrine attracted a distinctly God-and-me-alone crowd. Even the offer of peace — when parishioners turn to one another and say "Peace be with you" and, in most churches, shake each others' hands — was more solitary at Saint Anthony's. Typically, my fellow communicants made do with a nod or a grunt. Occasionally, in a bout of enthusiastic bonhomie, someone might wave a limp hand.

When I was new to the Shrine and actually reached out my hand, the woman to whom I was offering peace blanched. She permitted only the slightest fingertip touch. The communicants sought a relationship with God, but not with each other. Who knew what sins lurked beneath the placid faces of praying men? Some people you like better if you don't know too much about them.

Case in point: Archbishop Seán. His first chance to rant occurred exactly three weeks after Scott and I launched our gay romance line. On November 17, 2003, the Supreme Judicial Court of Massachusetts ordered the Commonwealth to open civil marriage to gay couples.

The court's decision actually made me cry. I had been taking testimony from fraudsters in a windowless room all day long. Afterward, I trudged back to my desk and popped open my Internet browser. As I read the headline on CNN.com, my backbone slipped out of me. Tears streamed down my face. I ran from office to office trumpeting the victory like a herald angel. I threw open my office window: a crowd of triumphant gays was gathering at City Hall Plaza. It never occurred to me that anyone could possibly deny our joy.

But before the ink was dry on the court's order, Archbishop Seán denounced it: "It is alarming that the Supreme Judicial Court in this ruling has cast aside what has been . . . the very definition of marriage held by peoples for thousands of years. My hope is that legislators will have the courage and common sense to redress this situation for the good of society." I'm not sure why I expected anything different. Seán was a Vatican man. *What about the lepers, Seán? Remember them?*

The Friday that followed the court's decision, I made sure I wasn't late to Mass. Rumors had been flying that Archbishop Seán had asked priests to read a statement condemning gay marriage as a "national tragedy" at every Mass in every church in the archdiocese. Since I wasn't yet out to the friars — except perhaps Myron and Bear-Daddy — I expected the worst. Filled with foreboding, perched on the edge of my pew, I swore to myself that I would storm out if they read Archbishop Seán's statement.

Francis the Franciscan Friar presided. The pews were full, the Marys were cheerful. The day's Gospel reading was from Matthew: the second greatest commandment is to love your neighbor as you love yourself. Father Francis never read the archbishop's statement. Instead, his homily focused on that word, *love*.

"So often," Francis said, "we regard love as a feeling. We say, 'I'm in love.' But gospel love is a verb, an action word. One loves through acts. This is what Jesus meant, when he said 'love one another.' How you actually feel about a person is largely irrelevant, as long as you act toward him with love."

I hardly heard any more of Father Francis's homily, because a different, louder voice spoke up inside me. In Francis's sense, I realized, I had to learn to love the Church. How I felt about it was secondary. And since love involves action, I could not sit around and wait for Archbishop Seán to surprise me with a change of heart. I had to love him, actively.

Francis concluded, "One of the most neglected acts of love is to pray for a person, and in particular to pray for wisdom."

It was an instruction: I had to pray for Seán. I had to pray for his wisdom. I had to pray that he would see the error of his ways.

Errors, I thought, *are where the spirit enters.*

Make me believe that you believe.

My course of action suddenly became obvious: what the archdiocese needed was not a ministry to the gay and lesbian community, but a ministry to the Church *by* the gay and lesbian community. Archbishop Seán, his fellow bishops, and the Vatican itself obviously didn't understand. Archbishop Seán had not met me and Scott. He knew nothing of gay love. Like Myron, he had not yet read *Hot Sauce*.

If I explained it the right way, Seán would see the light. He was a linguist. I just had to speak to him in the right language, to say the right words. If I reasoned with him, he'd surely come around to my point of view. I wasn't asking for a miracle, after all. I didn't plan to ask Archbishop Seán to serve as grand marshal in the gay pride parade. I just wanted him to witness the dignity and power of love between men and to acknowledge that a gay man could be as good a Catholic as any other. God and I had worked out an arrangement concerning the Sabbath, right? We could work something out on this score, too.

V

Lives of the Saints

It is necessary that all the Pastors and the other faithful have a new awareness, not only of the lawfulness but also of the richness for the Church of a diversity of charisms, traditions of spirituality and apostolate, which also constitutes the beauty of unity in variety: of that blended "harmony" which the earthly Church raises up to Heaven under the impulse of the Holy Spirit.[†]

— Pope John Paul II, "Ecclesia Dei"

Beheadings, Burnings, and Other Children's Literature

 COME FROM A LONG LINE of drama queens. My father used to throw temper tantrums over the loss of the shavings catcher on a forty-nine-cent pencil sharpener. My paternal grandmother bullied us grandchildren into unwilling Rockettes for a home rendition of "Jingle Bell Rock."

Even the family dog was a drama queen. My sister, God bless her, used to dispose of her used female sanitary products in the bathroom wastebasket. Occasionally the dog would hunt these products down and pull them out for inspection. On one of these occasions, I tried to remove the Snausage substitute from his jaws. Rather than give up the bloody goods, the dog fled. I chased him down the hall, skidded the

---

† "Charisms" are "those gifts and graces of the Spirit that have benefit, direct or indirect, for the community."

corner, and dived for his little dog ankles. When captured, he growled, snapped, whined, and promptly went into a week-long sulk. (Needless to say, wresting my sister's tampon from Fido's jaws marks the exact moment in which I lost any residual chance of being a straight man.)

The first indication of my own drama queenliness was my obsession with Butler's *Lives of the Saints*. I turned to martyrs the way other kids discovered the Hardy Boys or Judy Blume. The *Lives* contained nonstop hangings, burnings, stonings, spearings, beheadings, drownings, slashings, quarterings, scourgings, immersions in boiling oil, stretchings on racks, defacings (nose, ears, eyelids, and underlip cut off), beatings to a pulp, and being forced to watch your daughters die and to drink their blood. And that was just October!

Butler's *Lives of the Saints*

Butler's *Lives of the Saints* is a month-by-month, multivolume compendium that gives biographical information for virtually every saint ever canonized in graphic, uncompromising, and horrifically bloody terms. It was a must-read for Catholic kids before Harry Potter.

My consumption of the *Lives* mirrored my sinfulness. Murdering a pet gerbil called for a half-dozen martyrs and three saints. Thoughts of naked boys cost me ten virgin saints, preferably female. Failure to pass the collection basket at home Mass meant a whole month's worth of saints' feast days. Had I made it two and a half times around that Irish chapel, I would have to have read all four volumes from cover to cover.

I committed dozens of the lives to memory as faithfully as my father memorized the Baltimore Catechism. Even today I can tell you that, after being beheaded, Saint Justus picked up his severed head and went out to meet his brother. Saints Crispin and Crispinian — nearly as gack-inducing as Scott & Scott, don't you think? — defied their tormentor's attempts to boil and drown them, which so infuriated the tormentor that their persecutor jumped into the fire he had prepared to roast them alive. Step aside, X Games. Martyrdom was the extreme sport of the early Christian period.

The influence of the *Lives* in my life became obvious. A messianic craving for martyrdom expressed itself in quixotic and self-destructive ways:

• I chose Thomas à Becket as my patron saint. I ached for someone who had been fed to the lions or tortured to death by having his skin peeled off and eyes plucked out, but my pastor assured me that a sword through the skull was sufficient suffering for sacramental purposes.

• Under the influence in New Orleans, I imagined myself to be the Great White Hope who was going to unite the black and white races. I marched down Canal Street with my arms spread wide, embracing black strangers. A guardian angel whisked me back to Bourbon Street before anyone embraced me in return with a baseball bat to the head.

• I conceived of a program modeled on the Peace Corps called Homosexuals for the Heartland, in which armies of gay men would go to Iowa to impart faith, friendship, and fashion sense.

Law school largely purged any messianic impulse. The only time the *Lives of the Saints* seriously crossed my mind thereafter was when a thousand-dollar-an-hour lawyer explained how his fraudster client was the incarnation of Mother Teresa.

Martyr from the Mothballs

Archbishop O'Malley brought the martyr in me out of retirement. I vowed to be this holy homo, a progressive porn god, who would lead the faithful by the nose (or some other extremity) to a new openness to gays in their midst.

To prepare myself, I cracked open the *Lives*. In honor of the Shrine, I flipped straight to Saint Anthony.

Bingo! Saint Anthony had been a lector, just like me! At the feast of the Pentecost in 1221, Anthony preached before a great assembly of fellow Franciscans. He had no prior speaking experience, and he stumbled at first — no doubt on Sosthenes and Habbakuk. But then his voice filled with the Holy Spirit, and he wowed the assembled audience with his oral skills.

As an itinerant preacher, Anthony attracted upward of 30,000 people at every sermon. He needed a bodyguard to protect him from fans armed with scissors who wanted to snip off a piece of his habit as a relic. He called on the rich and powerful and accused them of greed, tyranny, and luxurious living. When no one listened, he preached instead to the fish in the sea. (Ecclesiastical history doesn't record whether the flounders repented.)

Anthony was no martyr; he died of natural causes. When exhumed as part of the canonization process, his body had decomposed, except for his tongue, which remained healthy and whole. Anthony is the patron saint of lost and stolen items, sailors, travelers, and fishermen. (Do fish have ears?)

Lost dignity, stolen lives, a traveler in an alien world — it was a perfect fit. A man whose sermons caused people to patch quarrels and brought mortal enemies together! It even turned out "Anthony" was the thirteenth-century equivalent of a screen name; his real name was Fernando. (Can you hear the drums?) Saint Anthony became patron of my own cause, and my fishing expedition started with Archbishop O'Malley.

The Stalker's To-Do List

1. Buy dark glasses.
2. Find someone who knows Cardinal Seán's most embarrassing secret from middle school.
3. Google.
4. Listen to Guy Noir episodes on *Prairie Home Companion.*
5. Consult Massachusetts antistalking statute.

6. Blurk a conservative Catholic blog to figure out what makes the enemy tick.[†]
7. Google more.
8. Take Fernando as a screen name.
9. Induce Father Myron to drop a dime on Cardinal Seán and give up the fruits of the confessional — the masturbation and the temper tantrums, the moments of doubt, the regret over beating up on the gays, the clandestine sticking of pins in a B16 doll he borrowed from the case in the lobby at the Shrine.
10. Find Archbishop Seán's calendar of public appearances.
11. Learn Archbishop Seán's screen name.
12. Have a friar make a religious doll of Archbishop Seán with religiously correct undergarments into which I could stick pins.
13. Give Archbishop Seán a big wet leper's kiss.

Stalking the Archbishop

"Quiz me!" I demanded. "Ask me anything."
Scott looked at me like I was crazy. "I don't want to."
    "Quiz me!"
    "I'm not going to quiz you about your archbishop," he said. "I don't want to encourage your craziness."
    "QUIZ ME!"
    "Can't we just commit the sin that cries out to heaven?"
    "No."
    Scott sighed. "OK," he said. "What's his favorite color?"
    "Brown, of course! He's a Franciscan. Ask me something else."
    "Favorite movie?"
    "*Diabolique*. He's not all about angels."
    "When was he born?"
    "June 29, 1944. Too easy. Ask me something hard."

---

† *Blurk* (v) tr. To read a blog without commenting on or contributing to it. From *blog* + *lurk*.

"How many altar boys has he diddled?"

"Very funny. Zero — as far as I know."

"Does he have any idea that you exist?"

I was stumped. "I'm not sure," I said. "Does it matter? This is going to be like *Roger and Me*. I just want to get in his face and give him a kiss."

"Michael Moore wanted to kiss Roger Smith?"

"Stay with me, Scott."

"Lemme get this straight —"

"So to speak."

"You want to kiss the cardinal?"

"Metaphorically speaking."

"Why?"

"Why not? We all could use a little love."

"I thought you wanted to confront the bastard."

"I do — with love."

"I see. Well, wear a condom, wouldja?"

"A condom?"

"Metaphorically speaking. I don't want you bringing any metaphorical infections home."

What I Learned about Archbishop Seán on My Summer Vacation

These are the highlights of my Brown Bag dossier:

The Good

- No recorded views on Harry Potter's satanic nature. In fact, Seán admitted to having read *The Da Vinci Code* and joked publicly about Mary Magdalene being portrayed as Mrs. Jesus Christ.
- Emphasis on the lost art of homiletics. Seán instructed his priests that they should stress creativity, humor, and — thank God — brevity.

- Passed police background check prior to his appointment. (Call me old-fashioned, but ideally my bishop has no criminal record.)
- Lifework heretofore focused on missions to immigrants and the poor. Seán opened an AIDS hospice in the Virgin Islands and had known Mother Teresa personally.
- Had a screen name. Upon his ordination in 1965, the Brown Bag changed his moniker from Patrick to Seán.
- Demonstrated ability to change his mind. In 2000, he refused to condone Irish Catholics' eating corned beef with their cabbage on St. Patrick's Day because the feast fell on a Friday during Lent. After protests and national media coverage, he revised the decree.

The Bad

- On May 18, 1999, O'Malley testified in a legislative hearing in Massachusetts that gay parents could "open the door to polygamy and incest."
- According to a priest who met with O'Malley: "He doesn't talk. It's the big dilemma for most priests. He's like a sphinx. . . . He just sits there."
- According to another priest, "He's a 'company man.' He's cautious and likes to limit conversations to noncontroversial issues."
- Archbishop Seán likened prochoice candidates for political office to "the KKK without the sheets."
- The motto on his coat of arms is *Quodcumque dixerit facite* (Do whatever he tells you) — not the slogan of a man likely to buck the Vatican.
- He was born near Cleveland.

The Ugly

- According to a priest and mental health professional: "O'Malley has an illness, a mental illness. If he's in a room of people, he just stands there with his arms crossed. Doesn't say a word. If you ask him how he's doing, he says fine. If you say you're bleeding arterially, he just nods. The guy is in over his head."

- In 2000, then-bishop Seán invited the chief judge of the Massachusetts Superior Court to speak at a dinner. A few days before the event, O'Malley rescinded the invitation. He told her that he would not feel comfortable sitting at the same table, because she had spoken out in favor of gay civil rights. He offered to reinstate the invitation if she publicly distanced herself from her remarks. Rather than admit to O'Malley's disinvitation, the event's organizers disingenuously announced that "circumstances beyond her control" had kept the judge from speaking.

Love Letters to the Archbishop

To confront the archbishop, I hit him where it counted. I mustered all my courage and wrote him a nasty note. I imagined all the auxiliary bishops cowering behind their desks at the chancery as they absorbed my withering prose. *Careful*, they'd whisper to one another, *or he'll write another one*!

Here's my letter:

Dear Archbishop Seán:

I write to you with the idea of reconciliation. I am one of your flock. I am a lector and a practicing Catholic. I am also a gay man in a long-term monogamous and committed sexual relationship with the man I love. Your behavior toward gay members of your flock — in word and in deed — does not reflect the love that I take from the Gospel.

Let me assure you that I hoped for the best from you. The announcement of your appointment came on my birthday. My richest experiences have been with Franciscans, so your Capuchin background was itself a reassurance. Your knowledge of languages suggested an ability to speak across boundaries that seemed absolutely necessary for a fractured Boston. Your history among less privileged flocks was an inspiration — it suggested you would spend far more time on the sins of the world then on the sins of the flesh.

Sadly, you have disappointed. You have chosen to exercise not merely moral authority, but *political* authority: I cannot understand how you justify involving yourself with necessarily ephemeral and transitory political movements. It demeans your spiritual authority. You should get out of the business of appearing with political figures like Mitt Romney and encouraging that political petitions be presented and signed at and after Mass. You demean the office and the sanctuary.

Can you truly believe a child is worse off with a lesbian mother than none at all? Can you possibly believe that a civil marriage demeans a Catholic religious marriage any more than, say, Britney Spears's "marriage" did?

The best solution would be for us to witness together. My hope is that by witnessing together, it will become evident that we share far more than those things that divide us. Therefore, I'd like to ask your permission to serve as lector at one of your Sunday Masses at the Cathedral. Please let me know if you will permit this and let me know what dates may suit you.

Several days later, a thick envelope with red lettering appeared in my mailbox. The return address was the chancery. A Reverend Kickham had signed it. *Kick-him*, I thought. *The cardinal's playing a big joke on me*.

Bracing myself for brimstone, I perused Reverend Kick-Me's response. It was . . . sickeningly inoffensive. At first blush, the good reverend provided me with nothing to rage against. I felt like I had been talked down from a ledge, and now the nice men in white coats were going to take me to a clean, padded room.

Reverend Kick-Me soundly rejected my request to serve as a lector during a Mass over which O'Malley presided. According to him, Archbishop Seán rarely said Mass at the cathedral in our gayborhood, except for special events for which the hosting organization chose its own lectors.

As for my complaint about the archbishop's condemnation of gay marriage, Reverend Kick-Me wrote, "The Archbishop acknowledges that some of the Church's teachings are a source of concern to some people. Please know that the Archbishop does not seek to cause any person upset or distress."

I wrote back that it wasn't necessarily the Church's teachings that caused immediate concern; the vigorous attempt to have those teachings inscribed in the civil law, on the other hand, did trouble me. While I appreciated his politeness, to say the archbishop didn't seek to cause upset or distress was disingenuous. This guy testified that gay parenthood might lead to polygamy and incest. This guy wrote that the institution of same-sex marriage merely reflected "an exaggerated emphasis on the preferences and conveniences of individuals" and that the Supreme Court decision mandating marriage equality was a "national tragedy." This guy endorsed the statement that "no same-sex union can realize the unique and full potential which the marital relationship expresses," and said that recognizing same-sex civil marriage "risks diminishing our humanity."

"Forgive me for being overly sensitive, Reverend," I wrote. "I guess my feelings are easily hurt. But the Archbishop's proclamations demean our worth and cheapen our love, so by their nature they cause upset and distress. To perform an act while knowing its natural consequence means the actor (Seán) must have also intended the consequence. I don't mean to advise you on public relations, but wouldn't it be better (and more honest) just to admit to seeking the consequence of our upset and distress, but claim instead that Seán believed that in the long run the bitter medicine would be good for us?"

Reverend Kick-Me wrote back that Seán would be glad to greet me personally at Christmas Mass if I wished.

The South End Catechism

Q. Why seek a kiss from the Brown Bag?
A. Catholics are genetically programmed to seek blessings. Blessings justify what we're doing anyway and give our projects a boost. It stems from a fundamental lack of self-confidence.

Q. *Have you spoken to God?*

A. God has never given me the time of day. But then again, I wouldn't have presumed that, if I heard a voice, it was God's. I like to imagine God is busier than that, concerning himself with war and famine and grace and matters more important than me. I fool around with men, I don't rob banks.

Q. *Don't you want to know what He has to say?*

A. Of course. But Pat Robertson makes a living speaking to God, as if he were a celestial psychotherapist giving God fifty-minute hours on the heavenly divan. Pat isn't shy about letting us know what the Almighty has to say.

Q. *Doesn't scripture condemn homosexual activity as an abomination?*

A. Yes. And Leviticus also condemns the consumption of shellfish. Last week, Archbishop Seán launched a campaign to eradicate lobster rolls.

Q. *Any other Old Testament surprises?*

A. Well, if you get picky and take the Old Testament literally, even Jesus gets condemned: Deuteronomy says, "Cursed be everyone who hangs on a tree."

Q. *What else is the Bible good for?*

A. ʼIt makes a nice doorstop.

Q. *Answer the question, Counselor.*

A. Here's a better answer: southerners invoked scripture to justify slavery, pointing out that neither Paul nor Moses had ever objected. Jefferson Davis wrote, "[Slavery] was established by decree of Almighty God. . . . It is sanctioned in the Bible, in both Testaments, from Genesis to Revelation." Indeed, if you read closely, the Bible not only sanctions slavery but also provides that, so long as you only incapacitate your slaves for a couple of days but don't kill them, you can beat them mercilessly (Exodus 21:20–21). By contrast, abolitionists had only a couple of flimsy passages in Galatians and Philemon on their side.

Q. Generally speaking, aren't priests good people?

A. The word *cleric* derives from the Greek word *kleros*, which means a casting of lots or a roll of the dice.

Q. Are there other groups the Church used to hate but now loves?

A. Oh, yes. Gentiles, for example. The Jews regarded them as unclean and their practices as evil. Yet outreach to Gentiles is a central theme of the New Testament. Don't even get me started on how the Church treated the "perfidious Jews," only to change its mind after the Holocaust.

Q. What's the next book you and Scott are writing together?

A. *The Harry Potter Code.* The Vatican will have it banned and us exorcised. We say, bring it on, Father Amorth. We'll only incapacitate you for a couple of days.

Advanced Thinking

As a public school Catholic, I endured a decade of Continuing Catholic Development, which was also known as "Sunday school," though in my town it took place on Wednesday afternoons. (Mine wasn't the first deal with God, apparently.) Parochial school students were, of course, exempt from CCD, as much from their natural virtue as from the expectation that their continuing Catholicism was being adequately developed.

Our CCD teachers were mainly laypeople, with the occasional substitute nun to keep us on our toes. In fifth grade, a teacher posed this moral conundrum to my class: given a collapsed building in which some victims are gravely hurt and likely to die but easily reached, while others are not gravely injured but difficult to reach and will die from lack of oxygen if not soon rescued, how would you go about rescuing people?

My answer was to blind yourself and go methodically from one person to the next, saving whomever fell first in your path.

The teacher called my answer "advanced thinking."

"No thinking about it, really," I said. "Just common sense. You can't save everyone that falls down in front of you. You have to move on, stop thinking about it, put it out of your mind, don't dwell."

The teacher knew better. It was advanced thinking or nothing, and her mealy public approval in front of the rest of the class made me want, even as a little kid, to put a bullet in my brain.

But advanced thinking seemed like a pretty good model for getting to Archbishop Seán. I could confront dozens of people before I finally confronted him. I imagined it would go like this: Scott and I would hit all the gay marriage rallies, hold hands, and sing "You're a Grand Old Flag" until we went blue in the face. Pastor Bob and Mr. Sodomy would instantly see the error of their ways. Mr. Sodomy would drop his "No Butt-Fucking" sign and turn back for Appalachia, remarking, "That bald-headed gentleman with the chip on his shoulder about his archbishop was remarkably persuasive. Homosexuals should definitely be entitled to equal rights under the law."

Pastor Bob would say, "Yeah. Too bad about the gay voice."

"Yes," Mr. Sodomy would say, "he reminds me a little of our beloved president, but with a three-digit IQ."

Then Pastor Bob would suggest they both drop to their knees. "Let's pray for the bald gentleman to get a nice manly voice. Maybe then he can find the husband God Himself has selected as his mate."

How to Come Out to Hardcore, Bead-Counting Catholics

1. Talk butch. Advocate the virtues of a two-deep zone and a four-man front in a second-and-long situation. (Sounds hot, doesn't it?)
2. Resist attempts to be set up with a nice Catholic girl.
3. Spend half a year referring to your boyfriend sans name or gendered pronouns.
4. Float Mr. Rogers–like observations comparing the rainbow to the diversity of God's children.
5. Wear lavender frequently. Pay no heed to comments that you must be very secure in your heterosexuality to wear such a color.
6. Remark on the joys of all-male communities who share

particular friendships, vacation together, and think highly of a muscular man in a loincloth affixed to a torture device. Clarify that you are referring to priests, of course.

7. Stop trying to speak like a Hollywood harlot who's chain-smoked too many Lucky Strikes. Embrace the gay voice God gave you.

8. Offer to loosen the kinks from the hot new friar's muscular back.

9. Get outed in the *New York Times*.

10. Break out the sex toys.

The reality of my confrontations proved considerably more mundane. Take the Hale Marys, for example. Each had a thoroughly Irish name and sufficient stubbornness to outwait the Second Coming of the Lord, so I planned my coming-out carefully. Most days before Mass, I did a once-over in the bathroom mirror at work to rid myself of any direct or indirect indications of homosexuality: a little concealer on the hickeys, sleeves pulled over the entrance stamp from the gay club, shed the rainbow flag, lose the copy of the local gay paper, etc.

Only my perennial lateness undid my plans. One cold November Friday, I had no time for precautions. Fraudsters on the mind, I raced into the sacristy late. Mary Flanagan greeted me with a great big hug. Her face glowed.

"Oh," she asked, "what does your pin say?"

I looked down in horror at the political pin on my lapel. *Oy vey.*

She peered closer. I resisted the urge to cover her eyes as you might a child gawking at a car wreck.

"Hi!" she read aloud, sounding the words out like a child learning to read. "I'm . . . loved . . . by . . . a . . . second-class . . . gay . . . citizen."

Seconds ticked by. Light years. Eons.

Then Mary threw back her head and laughed. She hugged me again and kissed me on the cheek. "I love you."

It turned out Mary had a confession of her own. No, she didn't munch rug. She came out as a thoroughbred professional faghag since before I had been born.

"Every Sunday," she said, "I go to Aunt Sadie's — do you know Aunt Sadie's?"

I did. It was a gayborhood boutique that sold fabulous, overpriced, one-of-a-kind versions of various housewares so wealthy gay men could exhaust their disposable income in an orderly fashion.

"Do you know Mr. Ho and Mr. Mo?" she asked, naming the gay men who ran the store. (Straight people tend to assume that all gay men know one another; it's true we have all probably slept with one another at one time or another, but we rarely use our real names.)

"Well, Mr. Ho and Mr. Mo have a piano in the store, and every Sunday . . ." Mary regularly patronized Aunt Sadie's to drink mulled hard cider and crowd around a grand piano with a dozen gay men singing show tunes.

Hallelujah!

A few weeks later, one of the regulars at Friday mass cornered me in the Shrine's lobby. "You're the famous author!" she squealed. "I saw you read at Borders! What's your book again? *Salsa*, or something?"

"*Hot Sauce*," I mumbled.

"What's it about?"

A light dew formed on my bald head. "It's a novel," I said.

"I've *got* to get it."

I suggested she try the *Q Guide for Wine and Cocktails* that Scott and I had written. "You're Irish," I explained. "You must fancy a wee drop now and again."

"No," she insisted, "I want the novel." She continued to pester me for my novel's title. Every time someone new came into the Shrine, she introduced me as the "famous writer." A dozen people vowed to converge on Borders the next day.

I debated managing expectations, but in the end I just sent them off. Call it another inadvertent coming-out party. It was time to stop apologizing for my gayness, as if a wayward child had inadvertently broken the ceramic candy dish of decorous conversation.

God Hates Fats

The last person standing between me and Archbishop Seán was a coworker we'll call Tony Cinnabonini in homage to his diet and ethnicity. Cinnabonini had signed a petition in favor of an amendment to the Massachusetts constitution banning gay marriage.

Before incapacitating him for a couple of days, I prepared for the workplace showdown. I consulted my lesbian boss, the SEC Equal Employment Opportunity Office, the SEC Office of Ethics, the union-management relations person, the Collective Bargaining Agreement, Father Bear-Daddy, Cinnabonini's supervisor, my mother — in short, just about everyone but Gram and the good Lord Himself. Only the EEO lawyer supported me, waxing nostalgic for the old days when — I am not making this up — she came under gunfire while confronting the mining industry on behalf of female coal miners.

Everyone else said, "You must be *nuts*! Don't engage him."

"His baby is two years old," I explained. "I just can't wait for God to bless him with a gay son or for his daughter to grow up to be a porn star. I have got to incapacitate him for a couple of days right now — before he has a chance to vote to restrict gay rights."

One Friday mass soon after, the Gospel reading told how Jesus stuck his fingers in the ears of a deaf-mute. "Be opened!" Christ commanded, and the deaf-mute instantly could hear.

I took it as a sign. I snuck up behind Cinnabonini and gave him a wet willy in the right ear. "Be opened!" I cried.

OK, I didn't actually do this. The EEO representative specifically told me not to. But I did corner Cinnabonini in his office, brandishing my four main talking points: the financial security of same-sex marriage; questions of health-care rights; the message-sending power of same-sex marriage (since others internalize the inequality as a license to do us violence); and questions of equality with the elderly who can get married and the heteros who marry but don't want or can't have kids.

Cinnabonini nodded throughout my discourse. But when I first mentioned a "Catholic perspective," he interrupted me to describe the circumstances around his signing the petition.

"There was no hate," he insisted. "They just pitched it as defending the sacrament of marriage, making sure those vows have a special place. To be honest, I didn't think that much of it. Everyone was signing the petition as they went out the door, so I signed it, and my wife signed it. I don't know that I would sign it if we had to do it again."

That surprised me. "Why not?"

"My wife's getting liberal in her old age," he said. "She's been watching Rosie O'Donnell. She sees how Rosie cares for those kids. She thinks now that gays can be as good parents as anyone."

"Maybe better," I murmured. "Thank God for Rosie." We take our bigotry-reducing lessons anywhere we can find them.

"Anyhow, I hear what you're saying," Cinnabonini said. "If I can split sacramental marriage from civil marriage, I would do it. I would vote against the amendment."

"But they're already pre-split for you, like an English muffin."

"Huh?"

"If you get married in the Church but don't get your marriage license from City Hall," I explained, "you're not legally married. End of story. Similarly, if you go to City Hall but aren't blessed by a priest, you're not sacramentally married. Two totally separate concepts. Only the timing and the Church's willingness to be an agent of the state links them."

Cinnabonini continued to nod, but clearly didn't get my point. In desperation, I invited him to join me at Mass. I told him about the friars' belief that the Vatican's stance is a cruelty. Playing this card made me feel like I was betraying Father Francis.

"I see what you're saying," he said. "I try to do what the Church wants, but I think about it. My Protestant friends always laugh at me. They say I do whatever the pope tells me to do. Not true. I think about it. My parents were divorced," he explained.

"You're losing me," I said.

"That's why marriage matters so much to me. I try to do the right thing. I bring my whole family to church on Sundays, I volunteer at the church, I go to the International House of Pancakes afterward with everyone who is involved."

"But gays aren't asking for sacramental marriage or the Church's blessing to go to IHOP," I countered. "Most of them don't want it. They want to make a civilly recognized vow to each other, just like straight people do. The Church can withhold its blessing, but the state should not."

"Did anyone else in the office sign?"

"Not that I know of."

Cinnabonini then ratted out another one of our colleagues. "You should talk to her," he said.

"Maybe I will," I said. "But what about you?"

He scratched his head. "It's still against the Church. Nothing you say changes that."

"So's gluttony," I fumed, "but that doesn't keep you and your wife from stuffing your faces at IHOP until you're both big as houses."

Actually, I didn't say this. Not to him. But I said it afterward to Scott — over and over and over.

Obviously, I had some homework to do in the charity department. The Hale Marys were all fine for comfort (and, apparently, show tunes), but I needed gay spiritual warriors and martyrs more advanced than me to assist my quixotic quest to convert Archbishop Seán. I couldn't greet him on Christmas Eve alone.

VI

Land(s) of the Misfit Toys

Charlie: I am the official sentry of the Isle of Misfit Toys. My name is —
Rudolph: Don't tell me: Jack.
Charlie: No, Charlie. That's why I'm a misfit toy. My name is all wrong. No child
wants to play with a Charlie-in-the-Box, so I had to come here.

— from *Rudolph the Red-Nosed Reindeer*

Cruising for Catholics

Y NEW GET-RICH-QUICK SCHEME? — personal ads for spiritual lonely hearts. Craigslist, ManHunt, and Match.com be damned.[†] I want a site where you'd see the following:

- Purebred Buddhist with light karmic burden seeks similarly highly evolved being with nice yoni for frequent tantric sex and occasional satori.
- Heterodox Hindu to share passion for mosquito swatting and Philly cheese steaks.
- Ye Olde Piety Show participant looking for fellow liturgical dramatists skilled in the fine art of prostration.
- Catholic strip-club patron looking for blushing, gorgeous,

---

† ManHunt.net is a matchmaking Web site for gay men seeking romantic encounters of limited duration.

virgin parochial schoolgirl raised by nuns to be mother of my children. Must be OK that I sleep around.

- Lutheran humorist seeks mate with good posture and collection of Old Testament knock-knock jokes.
- Ecumenical Unitarian Universalist group seeks anyone with a pulse.

My ad would look like this:

> Gay Catholic erotica writer seeks spiritually advanced, robust, homo-friendly, charity-filled warriors for Archbishop-smooching, light lectoring, and religious furniture shopping. Nongay voices preferred. Likable wizards welcome.

Getting venture capital for this enterprise proved challenging, so I had to stick to hunting down gay Catholic warriors the old-fashioned way: by cruising.

The GLBT Spirituality Group at Saint Anthony Shrine was my first stop. Having just finished the poet Trebor Healey's book on the mystical aspects of the raunchy, half-goat gods he imagined us homosexuals to be, I expected a roomful of cheerful satyrs — robust, hairy men who regularly ventured into the wild to beat drums and pat mud on their genitals. I'd whip them into a frenzy, and together we would fart, scratch our balls, and storm the chancery.

Here's the roster of people who actually attended my first meeting:

- Two closet cases visibly racked by the guilt of gay desire
- A tightly wound gay seminarian, whose every word was like a marble flung at my eye
- A pale, rail-thin wraith who had swallowed a Baltimore Catechism whole
- A pot-bellied Episcopalian retiree
- A tight-lipped, out Diocesan priest named Picasso, who had the world-weary manner of a debauched whore
- Mama Bear, a six-foot-two, queeny, bald, slump-shouldered man who radiated unctuous concern

Their pale, terrified faces gaped at me. My sudden appearance in the doorway symbolized to them the arrival of Opus Dei come to haul them off to hell's eternal fires.

"Don't worry," I said. "I'm just one of the gang." I joked that we should invite Archbishop O'Malley to join the group. They blanched.

"We can't do that!" one of the closet cases shrieked, not raising his eyes. He was thickset, perhaps forty, but with a young face and jowls that trembled. He had the soul of an accountant, so let's call him Abacus.

"Why not?"

"They'll come down on us," Abacus whined. "They'll shut us down."

Mama Bear and Picasso co-led the meeting. Obviously a veteran of group work, Mama Bear focused on process. Every time someone expressed an idea, Mama Bear repeated it back in the modern-day call-and-response of the feel-good, padded-room group psychotherapy approach. We spent a quarter of an hour just debating whether we would check in with the group's members to see where they were at and to assess their expectations.

Self-revelations and confessions followed. Apropos of nothing, the seminarian brought up the burden of his celibacy. Picasso mentioned that he painted. Abacus reported that his confessor had told him he was going to burn in hell. Mama Bear explained that he was trying to come to terms with the possibility of monogamy in his gay marriage after twenty years of mutual infidelity. The other closet case brought up how humiliated he felt when his priest preached against gays and gay marriage.

To counteract this heavy pall of shame, I tried to project resolute positivity, determined cheer, and a brash bonhomie completely contrary to my nature. I offered one of those banal, hopelessly chipper Hallmark-card confections that could have formed a lynch mob from a group of Poor Sisters of Saint Clare, let alone a bunch of desperate homos: "You should see these humiliations as graces and grow from them," I suggested brightly.

Silence descended over the room. Mama Bear pouted. Picasso sighed. Abacus clicked some beads.

"Are you saying we deserve to be humiliated?" the seminarian asked. It was like being quizzed by Travis Bickle.

Then the pale wraith — let's call him Job — lifted his head from the table and spoke for the first time.

"Let me tell you about humiliation," Job said. "I shat myself in a cafeteria today. It's my gastrointestinal. Everyone saw me, but pretended not to. I think it was the chocolates I ate. I just had three. They were Mardi Gras chocolates. That's humiliation."

Dumbstruck, the group nodded in agreement.

"Last time I shat myself, I was alone," Job added. "The time before that was in a shelter, but someone cleaned up the mess while I was off looking for paper towels."

For all his humiliation, Job was looking on the bright side. The grace of the shelter worker's efficiency clearly impressed him.

After that first meeting, I prayed: *Beheadings and burnings are one thing, God, but you can't possibly ask me to endure another tale of intestinally misbehaving Mardi Gras chocolates.*

Getting no response from the Almighty but significant affirmation from a flock of pigeons crapping on the crucifix above the Shrine's front door, I took my quest for gay warriors on the road.

Dignity

Boston gave me a choice among gay Catholic groups: one was called Dignity and the other was called Courage. While the groups' differences, theological and otherwise, are legion, they may be fairly summed up as follows: Dignity members get to engage in the sin that cries out to heaven for vengeance; Courage members opt for celibacy.

I struggled with this difficult choice for three long milliseconds, then I opted for Dignity. The basement of the Episcopal Church where Dignity met had laminated flooring, half-flaccid balloons pinned to lockers, antismoking posters, a drop ceiling, random playground balls, and an altar that looked like a wooden sawhorse. We took name tags at the door and sat in folding chairs arranged like an encounter group. A keyboard rested on a card table. A pixie lesbian with a brass bell of a voice led the five-person choir and shook her maraca (not a euphemism for booty). Someone had scrawled the hymn numbers on huge sheets of yellow-lined paper taped to the wall.

A retired Marist priest led the liturgy. His homily focused on his formation as a priest. He said he had spent fifteen minutes every morning contemplating the sinfulness of some aspect of his life. Every evening, he examined his conscience rigorously to see where he had failed.

"It was all about identifying yourself as a bad and worthless person," he said.

But his message to Dignity came straight from Mr. Rogers's neighborhood: "You are all good people," he assured them, "ninety-nine percent of the time."

No one but me seemed to disagree. The Dignitarians were obviously far more spiritually evolved. My goodness percentage topped out in the low teens — at best. Hell, even during the Marist's homily I was deconstructing my fashion-challenged fellow worshippers, who had adopted wholesale the suburban-dyke-with-kids look — orthopedic sneakers, elastic waistbands, oversize sweatshirt with drool stains, and Red Sox caps.

Dignity's liturgical procedures mandated such strict gender equality. They hailed the Holy Spirit with all three pronouns, alternating among he, she, and it. Wherever possible, the liturgy used the word *God* instead of masculine pronouns and nouns, but the gender-neutral construction often caused blips in the rhythm of the prayers: "Our Father and Our Mother, who art in Heaven. . . ."

An old dyke took the first reading, and a young gay man did the second. Taking alternate verses, the two collaborated on the Psalms. I half expected them to use an eco-friendly game of Rock, Paper, Scissors to determine who would get the Prayers of the Faithful.

Prayers of the Faithful

This call-and-response segment of the Holy Sacrifice of the Mass occurs shortly after the homily, when the congregation fervently gives thanks that Father Longwind's homily has finally ended. We also pray for clothing of the naked, comforting of the sick, world peace, and similar types of happy nonsense.

But the Dignitarians' capacity for egalitarianism had outstripped my imagination. The entire assembly participated fully in the Prayers of the Faithful. They shared their "celebrations and concerns," so we prayed for a few birthdays, some elderly parents, a dying partner, a cancerous mother, peace in Scotland, oppressed minorities everywhere, the immortal soul of Gloria Gaynor, and reasonably good weather during the annual conference of DignityUSA in Austin, Texas. They appealed to the predilections and causes of so many splinter groups that it completely undermined the communal nature of the experience.

After the celebrations and concerns, we remembered our dead aloud. Names of the dearly departed boomed from every throat in a macabre cacophony of remembrance that threatened to wake many of those named from their eternal sleep.

At the exchange of peace, I extended my hand to my immediate neighbor. Dagger glances shot from every corner of the room.

Is my fly down? Did I not wash my hands? Do they know I'm not 99 percent good?

Someone muscled my offending hand aside, and a series of strangers quickly moved in for full-body contact. The dyke sitting next to me gave me a kiss on the mouth. Everyone in the room had to be hugged — some of them twice. An average friar at the Shrine could have crammed two Masses into the span of time it took the Dignitarians to exchange peace.

Aside from the lesbian lip-lock, you might have expected that all the bodily contact wouldn't have bothered me. After all, in my pre-Scott dating years, I enthusiastically engaged in far more intimate acts with complete strangers without batting an eyelash — or at least I wanted to. But Dignity's service was *so* over-the-top inclusive that it estranged me.

Three laypeople joined the former Marist at the eucharistic sawhorse. The priest and a gay man handled the host: pita pockets torn into triangles. (Did Christ serve hummus at the Last Supper?) Two women took charge of wine. Before approaching the sacred sawhorse for our consecrated pitas, the Marist reminded us that there was a gluten-free "host alternative" as well as consecrated grape juice for those with "special needs," apparently a euphemism for alcoholism. By the end of the Mass, Saint Anthony's old, cold anonymity and male-urinal-style worship — standing as far apart as possible from the next guy — had never seemed so good. The Dignitarians might be just the right people to hug Cardinal Seán to death, but otherwise I would have to find my gay warriors somewhere else.

Taking Heart

During my undergraduate years in upstate New York, near the Canadian border, tales of Jesuit missionaries to the Mohawk drew me in. The Jesuits had a stellar reputation for courage. Priests captured by the Mohawk reportedly prayed unceasingly while the braves scraped off the priests' skin with sharpened seashells and snacked on severed fingers. Even after the Mohawk cut out their tongues, the priests continued to say rosaries. So much did the Mohawk warriors admire the priests' bravery that they cut out the Jesuits' hearts and ate them so as to inherit the Jesuits' courage.

With these hearty missionaries in mind, I set out to find equally brave clerics to serve as my fellow foot soldiers. Here's what I found:

- Number of diocesan priests under O'Malley: 525.
- Number of religious-order priests in the archdiocese: Approximately 500.
- Estimate of the rate of homosexuality among priests: 30 to 50 percent.
- Number of priests in the Boston area who came out publicly to their parishes and the world at large: 0.

- Number of priests who signed the petition "Roman Catholics for Equal Marriage Rights": 1.
- Number of priests who testified that the social justice teachings of the Church precluded support for constitutional amendments banning gay marriage: 4.

Butler's saints and martyrs had no competition in Boston.

The Rainbow Church

A church that celebrates as its central rite a eucharistic ritual "in which an all-male clergy sacrifices male flesh before images of God as an almost naked man" and in which unmarried men regularly share a residence has got to be the gayest church in the whole wide world. Take, for example, liturgical vestments: they come in more shades than a pride flag and have more meanings than any arrangement of colored hankies you might wear in your back pocket.

- Violet, purple, or blue for Advent and Lent
- White from Christmas to Christ's baptism, from Easter to Pentecost, and for feasts for the Virgin Mary
- Red for Good Friday, Pentecost, and feasts of martyrs
- Green for non-feast days
- Black and white for funerals

So, if you are a liturgical top, and it's June, you wear . . . Oh, never mind.

In private, many priests told me they disagreed with the Vatican's teaching on civil recognition of committed gay relationships. Some of them ignored the archbishop's direction to preach against civil marriage and to collect signatures from the parish for a petition to ban same-sex civil marriage. But not one — not a single one — actually preached in favor of recognizing civil same-sex marriage.

"If there is this whole network of priests who believe that justice requires being more welcoming of gay Catholics and recognizing gay civil marriage, why are they not speaking out?" I asked.

The answer from one priest: "I like my day job."

"But you're not doing your day job," I argued. "Your day job is justice."

"I can do more from within than without."

"So what do you do?"

"I put all that anti-gay-marriage literature from O'Malley on the table way in the back of the church. That's like relegating it to the netherworld," he said, proud of being such a rebel.

One of the priests I spoke to, a generous and generously proportioned prelate named Father Butterballino, proposed, "Maybe if I lived in a society where coming out as gay was like mentioning that you are left-handed, then I'd come out."

"But you won't live in such a society *until* people like you come out."

"True," Father Butterballino acknowledged. "But I'm not going to be the first."

Over and over, it was the same refrain: fear of job loss, fear of opprobrium, fear of being tainted by perverts and pedophiles, fear of loss of ministry. But where were those priests who decided social justice, personal integrity, and the possibility of saving a youth considering suicide was worth the risk? Where were my Berrigans, liberation priests, and prelates who stood up to Nicaraguan death squads? Where were my Jesuits?

Clerical Comings-Out

In the early 1970s, Tom Brokaw interviewed Father John J. McNeill, a Jesuit, on NBC. "Are you gay?" Brokaw asked. McNeill acknowledged that he was. This admission kick-started a tradition of clerical coming-out:

- 1987: Robert L. Arpin announced from the pulpit that he was gay and had AIDS. He died in 1995.

- 1997: Martin Kurylowicz came out to his parish in a newsletter and at Holy Thursday services. His boss, the bishop of the Grand Rapids diocese, supported him.
- 2002: William Hart McNichols of Taos, New Mexico, came out in a *Time* magazine article about closeted priests.
- 2004: Fred Daley, a priest in the Diocese of Syracuse, announced publicly that he was gay after becoming fed up with the Vatican's attempt to scapegoat gay priests for the scandal. His parish gave him a standing ovation.
- 2005: Rich Danyluk came out to his parish. He later explained, "There's a passage in Scripture that God said to Jesus, 'You're my beloved son in whom I'm well pleased.' I believe God says that to every male, and he says, 'You're my beloved daughter,' to every woman. Finally, that sunk into me, that I don't need a priest or a bishop or a pope to tell me who I am."
- 2005: A Jesuit retreat director from Bloomfield Hills, Michigan, Thomas J. O'Brien, came out in the *Detroit Free Press* in response to the ban on gay priests in the seminary, writing, "I am coming out as a gay, chaste Jesuit priest because it hurts too much not to."
- 2006: Jim Morrison came out to his Louisiana parish and bishop as a celibate gay man. He said he was not looking for approval, but only trying to be more true to himself, his parish, and his God.

For many, coming out costs them dearly. In 1974, McNeill (a cofounder of the New York chapter of Dignity) argued in his book *The Church and the Homosexual* that the Bible doesn't condemn homosexuality. After studying its contents for three years, the Vatican initially approved the book's publication. Two years later, however, Rome rescinded its permission, and the Rat ordered McNeill not to speak to or write in the media. When O'Neill refused to discontinue his ministry to gays, the Rat caused McNeill's expulsion from the Jesuits.

When I expressed dismay to a diocesan priest that only about 8 of America's 45,000 priests had come out of the closet, he said, "I think that more have than you know. It just hasn't been public. I know priests who have come out to people who they think are trustworthy." Quoting Matthew Shepard's mother, he said that people ought to come out wisely, safely, and not to people who might hurt you. He sighed, then added, "I think if we get the word 'sex' out of homosexual, it might be a lot easier."

Shortly after, I had lunch with Father McSlutty, a sexually active gay priest. While we perused the menu, Father McSlutty waxed rhapsodic about the pleasures of coming out to himself and becoming comfortable with his own body. A byproduct of this new comfort, he said, was the ability to urinate without stage fright for the first time in his life.

But Father McSlutty also had a confession to make. Not only had he failed to come out or speak out in support of gay people, he had preached Archbishop O'Malley's party line, delivering a homily that lumped homosexuality in with adultery, masturbation, and fornication. He seemed genuinely surprised that two gay men in the parish had confronted him afterward. When Father McSlutty saw the couple again the following week, the men rightly snubbed him, and their cold shoulder hurt.

"There is a language we have to speak," Father McSlutty pleaded, "a language of gay, tentative at first —"

"That's the language of the closet," I pointed out.

"You've got to understand that a priest can't wear a sign that says, 'I'm gay-friendly.' If a priest says he is gay-friendly, it means 'I accept the homosexual lifestyle of cruising and acting out and supporting others who do these things.'"[†]

"Assuming you accept the idea that there is a 'homosexual lifestyle,' and that your description aptly characterizes it," I said.

"You need to find ways to gently reveal your gayness, so that your

---

† "Acting out" is the priestly euphemism for cruising for anonymous sex, as Father McSlutty knew from personal experience.

pastor can pursue the subject if he wishes. The priest may be trying to say something to you that he can't say in public. You have to listen."

"Gays don't want to play games anymore."

"I understand that. They spent a lot of effort to come out of the closet. I know. But they should play the games for the sake of the rest of us, out of charity if nothing else, so that the priest can become part of their lives. Priests can't afford to get stuck on positions and stands." Father McSlutty shrugged. "I'd love to have gay couples in my parish. But gays have to compromise. They can't be flamboyant. Hugging is OK. But being demonstrative . . . no." Then Father McSlutty looked up at the cute waiter in the tight black pants and made eyes at him.

Womenpriests: Invasion of the Compound Nouns

One group of priests with hearts that no self-respecting Mohawk would turn down were the Roman Catholic Womenpriests, an international organization of ordained women whose members traced an unbroken apostolic succession through a European (male) bishop ordained by Rome, who had ordained one of their number in a secret ceremony.

My local womanpriest, Jean Marchant, told me that gay men played a key role in her decision to become ordained. For years, Jean had directed spiritual care at a hospice for patients suffering from complications of HIV/AIDS. The birth families of many patients had disowned them for being gay.

"It was very powerful work," Jean said. "I saw the sacredness of these relationships up against the lack of family support, the lack of societal support, sometimes even in the face of lack of support from the gay community, which at that time was not very accepting of those who wanted to live in relationships. The level of commitment and care was extraordinary. They were doing the dirty work. They were showing up every day."

Fast forward to 2004. By then, Jean had taken a job with the Archdiocese of Boston, coordinating the work of chaplains and others who visit the sick at the archdiocese's seventy hospitals.

Two incidents drove Jean to break with the Church. First was how the archdiocese set about closing parishes for fiscal reasons. Jean warned that parishioners needed a grieving process to ease the transition. O'Malley's then–vicar general — archdiocesan chief operating officer — Richard Lennon, assured her that no such process was necessary. As Jean predicted, the closings turned into a major fiasco. Renegades continue to occupy some of the closed parishes to this day.

Second was the archdiocese's campaign against gay couples. The Massachusetts Catholic Conference, a lobbying organization funded by the archdiocese and chaired by Archbishop O'Malley, made available a video designed to be shown during Mass in place of the homily.

According to Jean, the video "was a piece of propaganda. What shocked me, what I most remember, was a scene that showed an elderly woman in a hospital bed with oxygen tubes and everything. This was shown next to a picture of a gay couple. And the movie said, 'If gay marriage is approved, it will take resources from those who need it most.'

"I am still speechless. It showed no respect for the dying woman and no respect for the reality of same-sex couples. If you have to revert to fear tactics . . ." She trailed off, clearly upset. "It had the opposite effect on my marriage. I was working with people [at the HIV hospice] who had had spiritual commitment ceremonies. The impact was: Wow! If these people can make it work without the support we straight people have! Whenever I see a gay couple in love, it makes me look at my own marriage and say, I know I could do better."

Jean had wrestled with a call to priesthood all her life. The afternoon that she watched the video, she e-mailed a womanbishop, "I'm on board." In March 2005, Jean was ordained to the deaconate. In July 2005, on a boat on the Saint Lawrence Seaway, she was ordained to the priesthood. Jean worked for the archdiocese for another year, at which point she disclosed her ordination and resigned.

Orthodox Catholic bloggers viciously attacked her in print, calling her a liberal Protestant mole, a kangaroo, a tool of Satan, and a worn-out 1960s-reject poncho lady. Nearly all the womenpriests were forbidden to accept communion. Certain bishops targeted fellow womenpriests for special condemnation in the bulletins of their home parish. By way of contrast, no church bulletin I found accorded space to single out a pedophile priest or his pandering bishop in the same way.

Despite the bad press, when I spoke to them a year later, the womenpriests, more enthusiastic than ever, were training a new group of female candidates for priesthood.

"We are not all gay or lesbian, but we are in solidarity," one womanpriest told me. "We know the value of people, the value of diversity, the injustice. Whatever we do, we will be part of the solution and not part of the problem."

Forget the GLBT Spirituality Group, I thought. *Forget Dignity. Forget the fainthearted clergy. Give me womenpriests!*

Unfortunately, the womenpriests were already booked. They had their own cause: getting the Church to recognize vocations among women. Still, it was good to know that although my spiritual Craigslist ad went unfulfilled, I wasn't the only heretic in the archdiocese.

VII

God Bless Ireland

The language of faith is prayer. Prayer is a language that allows us to communicate with our heavenly Father.... Some people have forgotten that language. Without prayer we become spiritually disoriented, our relationships suffer, we begin to be isolated, alone, confused, and often overwhelmed.

— Archbishop Seán O'Malley, July 30, 2003

Wookie Prayers

ANY PRIESTS, including Jean Marchant, report an early childhood obsession with playing priest. While the rest of us were outside playing Kick the Can, they built home altars, murmured blessings, and pressed younger siblings into roles as altar servers.

My early prayer life consisted mainly of beseeching. I prayed for new Legos, more snow days, and the return of my "gabum" — my filthy security blanket, which some well-meaning stewardess on an Aer Lingus flight mistook for a potential cholera menace. (Don't think I've forgiven you, wench.) I prayed that no one make fun of my penis in the locker room at the YMCA, that I pass the Hail Mary–Our Father test, and that my brother inflict only temporary damage on my limbs during the vicious dodgeball games at Catholic summer camp.

By my teen years, my prayers consisted almost entirely of a single plea: *God, please don't let me be gay. Let it all just be brotherly affection, an artist's eye for the male form, a passing curiosity as to what it might be like to wear my sister's tutu. Find for me, God, the perfect chick, who will really understand my needs.* ("A chick with a dick, in other words," Scott said years later.)

As the years passed, even without benefit of a proper parochial education, theological sophistication took over. I regularly tried to game the prayer system. If the Almighty cottoned on to the fact that I liked something and gave thanks for it, He — in His Old Testament wisdom — would snatch it away. With this in mind, I gave thanks for increasing premature baldness. My prayers were pro-chromedome, in favor of dead follicles. Grateful for every strand on my pillowcase, I assured the Almighty baldness was the best thing that had ever happened to me:

> *Are you there, God? It's me, Scott. Thank you for this yarmulke-sized tonsure. Thank you for all its wonderful advantages: not having to wash my hair, not worrying about high wind, and not having to be concerned about having to date girls anymore. Speaking of which, please don't make me gay, either.*

God did not take the theological bait. It proved maddeningly difficult to pull one over on the All-Knowing, so prayer slipped by the wayside for a decade. When I arrived at Saint Anthony Shrine, I met people like Sherwin, a gay former member of Opus Dei, who regularly dropped Sorrowful Mysteries and Glory-Bes and Liturgies of the Hours into conversation. Sherwin had a rosewood rosary with carved roses for beads that stank of rosewood oil. (Overkill much?) He also had a finger rosary for driving. Filled with energy and not the least self-consciousness, he rattled on about morning prayers, evening prayers, prayers in the car, prayers with song, and blahblahblah.

"What are you talking about, dude?" I asked. "You pray in the morning *and* the evening *and* in the car *and* . . . ?"

"Yeah," he said brightly. "How about you? How's your prayer life?"

He might as well have asked me what my boccie life was like. "Well, I do try to squeak a short one in after I brush my teeth," I said.

The smile on Sherwin's face froze.

"Also after communion," I said, "if I'm not planning an afternoon of trying to put people in jail for securities fraud."

The light in his eyes went out.

"Belly-button-lint gazing," I begged. "Does that count? That I do all the time."

Poverty comes in many forms. The look on Sherwin's face told me I had found mine. If the government ever got into the business of doling out spiritual welfare, I'd be first in line.

A few years at the Shrine and a steady campaign of saintly intercession by people like Sherwin produced minor improvement: good old-fashioned beseeching came back to me. I prayed that the networks cancel Ye Olde Piety Show on account of its low ratings. I prayed for the conversion of Bay State politicians on the same-sex marriage issue. My most fervent requests went skyward for the gay conversions of Brad Pitt and Jerry Falwell — each for a different reason, of course.

Dealmaking also re-entered my repertoire: If God permitted me to survive this lightning-stricken hike in the Rockies, I'd devote myself to a porn-free life of charity and chastity. I offered to swap three-quarters of my everlasting soul in return for President Bush getting caught soliciting police officers disguised as underage boys in the public restrooms on the Capitol Mall.

Over time, dealmaking and beseeching gave way to occasional thanksgiving and, of course, prayers for others. My parents had always been big on bedtime prayers. They began with the ghoulish standby:

> *Now I lay me down to sleep,*
> *I pray the Lord my soul to keep.*
> *If I should die before I wake,*
> *I pray the Lord my soul to take.*

followed by *God Bless Mommy and Daddy* and litanies of siblings, aunts, uncles, cousins, godparents, babysitters, schoolteachers, garbage collectors, old ladies who lived alone, and starving children in Africa. I had approximately 3,700 Irish cousins, so it took an hour each night just to get through the list. In the interest of efficiency, I developed a clever shorthand; I just prayed for Ireland as a whole — and Africa. *God bless Ireland. God bless Africa.* That way, no one missed out, and I skipped to the all-important beseeching portion of my prayer program.

At Saint Anthony Shrine, my greatest concern was keeping my prayers for others fresh. I constantly sought people I hadn't yet prayed for or hadn't prayed for lately. I wanted to keep it interesting for God, and be a sassy, unpredictable petitioner, pulling in a soul from left field that He hadn't heard about in a long time.

Soon, I was resurrecting people from my distant past, those whose acquaintance was so short I didn't catch a name, those who had always annoyed me, fraudsters bound for the Big House, those who were going to hell no matter what I did, and the little children who lived next to my grandparents in Ireland and woke me at dawn like a firing squad, shooting relentless questions at me in hopes that I would say something — anything at all — in a Boston Hahvahd Yahd accent I did not actually possess. *God bless Ireland.*

A heavy workload and my perennial tardiness gave rise to the following prayer:

> *Now I arrive in church so late,*
> *I pray the Lord not strike my pate.*
> *If I forget the words to read,*
> *I hope that He will intercede.*

God bless, uh, um . . .

By virtue of proximity rather than by virtue of virtue, the Hale Marys received thousands of requests for blessings. The friars received fewer, because they had a head start in the salvation game, and it was time to give someone else a fighting chance. My skinflint prayer for O'Malley went something like this: *Lord, may You not cause Seán to catch typhoid pneumonia.*

Chewbacca always proved easy to pray for. His arm had atrophied. One leg drew up into his hips. He held his oversize head at an angle so that he appeared to be an aquatic creature surfacing from the deep. An insulated canvas lunch box hung over the back of his wheelchair. He usually parked near my pew, leaving just enough room for me to exit to do my readings. During the introductory rite, his bellows and grunts were like the ill-timed, incoherent snorts of a beached whale — a vast, proud, dying animal — and they regularly threw me off my rhythm, which made me realize how much I depended on others to recite my prayers in the same measured tones as me.

But God had left Chewbacca the ability to laugh, provided Francis the Franciscan Friar had decent homiletic material. *God bless Chewbacca. God bless every snort and bellow. God bless all of us who race to shake his crimped hand at the sign of peace, hoping that his holiness might rub off.*

Tabernacle Sports

Racing to touch the hem of Chewbacca's wheelchair wasn't the only competitive sport at the Shrine. Welcome to the Saint Anthony Regional Ultimate Tabernacle Fighting Championships.

Our contestants, two fellow lay ministers, were replacing one of the Hale Marys who was playing hooky. In one corner was a black man with a Bill Cosby face, a pear-shaped body, and a sport jacket matched with basketball sneakers. In the other: the Cape Verdean queen whom Father Abraham had reduced to tears. Her Highness had a gorgeous accent, sensible heels, and a magnificent booty.

Before the presider had finished his homily, Cosby and Her Highness jumped the gun. They leapt from the pews, dodged Chewbacca, and sprinted toward the tabernacle faster than the disciples to the tomb of the risen Lord. In front of the tabernacle, Cosby and Her Highness jostled for advantage like a couple of basketball players beneath the rim. Her Highness went for the bread. Cosby boxed her out. She feinted left for the cruets, but Cosby's bulk prevailed. Loading up on bread, chalice, water, *and* wine, Cosby downshifted his smug expression into servility and barreled toward the altar, conveying the ciborium of consecrated hosts as if it were the platter bearing John the Baptist's head.

Muttering to herself, Her Highness returned to her pew. Had she a Cosby doll in hand, she would have riddled it with hairpins. She prayed fiercely for Cosby to screw up — chalices to fly, the body of Christ to hit the floor, communion wine to stain the altar linens.

At the sign of peace moments later, she turned to me and said, "Peace be with you."

"And you, Your Highness," I said, and I damn well meant it. Her Highness may not have the same moral underpinnings, but she had the heart of a womanpriest — and infinitely more booty.

The sanctuary filled with distractions: the clamor of delivery trucks in the rear of the church; an impatient taxi driver blaring his horn; the mutterings of Her Highness; the siren of an ambulance come to pick up the body of a homeless man; the pre–Vatican II rosary whisperings of participants in Ye Olde Piety Show; and Chewbacca's grunts. Secular musings overwhelmed my prayer experience: *How many copies of* Hot Sauce *did we sell at the Castro reading? . . . Is Her Highness a closet lesbo? Could she be recruited if I found her the right girl? . . . How could Scott and I put new life in the naughty-altar-boy game?*

The communion line arrested my vagrant attention. Parishioners moved toward the altar like boxcars in a railroad yard. Their steady, mechanical, inevitable motion reassured me, as did Father Francis's murmuring "Body of Christ," the communicants' responding, "Amen," the squeak of shoes on marble, the flutter of hands at the sign of the cross, the bob of genuflection, and the beatific expressions.

And the asses — *Mea culpa*. Here's where the vagrant mind causes trouble. Her Highness wasn't the only person blessed from behind. God had been generous:

> *God bless the intense student with blue eyes, a strong nose, tight buns, and a heavy backpack who gave twice as much as I did to the collection basket. God bless the salt-and-pepper investment banker, a dead ringer for Anderson Cooper, who plopped his plowable posterior in a pew near the right-hand aisle. God bless the Latino with blue-collar biceps, a bubble butt, and thighs like an Olympic speed skater.*

I was head-over-heels in love — with the student, Anderson Cooper, the Latino — every one of them. And not a mere crush, not a catch-his-eye-he's-kind-of-cute-I'd-do-him-on-a-slow-night passing fancy. I'm talking Love with a capital *L*: immediate, 150-proof, throw-your-Armani-coat-on-the-ground-so-he-can-walk-over-puddles-and-not-get-his-feet-wet, please-walk-across-my-chest-in-your-stiletto-heels-and-make-me-carry-your-suitcases, this-alone-would-content-me kind of love; love that makes you put aside breathing and nutrition in favor of showering the object of your tumid affections with fistfuls of expensive rocks and bright shiny bling of every description; love that made me realize what I had previously called love was mere turds in a toilet, a tissue of indiscriminate lies, a maggotry empty of substance or meaning.

Was it sinful to check out the other communicants? Would it have been more godly to block them out, to pretend that I was eating alone, to keep my eyes closed and my hands clasped and my face tilted toward the floor? No, gazing at them became a form of wordless prayer, a raid on the inarticulate as pure as Chewbacca's grunting, an expression of gratitude for the richness of the world He had created.

God bless the Shrine, Amen.

Baltimore Catechism Apocrypha

Q. Does God hate fags?

A. No, that's an unfortunate misspelling. God hates fats. And flags, too. Mindless patriotism that results in hopeless wars on foreign people does not please Him. Anyway, God couldn't hate fags as much as I do when a pair of dime-a-dozen, bleached-blond, impossibly gorgeous, smooth-chested, plucked, pouting pretty boys with pipe-cleaner arms sipping Cosmos and texting madly about Paris and Lindsay put themselves between me and my martini, goddamnit. *That's* hate.

Q. What caused the drop in religious vocations among straight men?

A. Gays. Bishop Wilton Gregory, former president of the U.S. Conference of Catholic Bishops, has blamed a frightening "homosexual atmosphere or dynamic that makes heterosexual young men think twice" about entering the seminary.

Q. What are the rules of the eucharistic ministry?

A. Start with a centering prayer. Then wash your hands. (God only knows where they've been!) Set out the bread, water, and wine in their respective containers. Get the key to the tabernacle. Reverence it. Make sure spare hosts are available in case there's a rush. Sit in the first pew. Make eye contact with the communicants. Deny communion to the gay ones. Say "Body of Christ." Place wafer in whatever body part is offered. Bring unused hosts back to tabernacle. Kneel. Lock them up. Put the key in the sacristy. Return to pew. And if you screw up, we'll turn you over to Father Bear-Daddy.

Q. *What's with all the holy dishwashing the priest does with the goblet and little brass cookie plate? Can't the Church exploit illegal immigrants to do that like the rest of us?*
A. You're going to hell just for asking that.

Q. *What does a cry out to heaven sound like?*
A. Lots of kissy noises, snuffles, grunts, and aaahhhs. Not unlike straight sex, actually. But without a woman's voice asking, "Are you done yet?"

Q. *Why does eyebrow plucking invariably cause a gay man to sneeze?*
A. This is one of God's enduring mysteries.

Captain of the Team

A few weeks after the showdown between Her Highness and Mr. Cosby, Father Bear-Daddy summoned me and the other members of the Lay Ministry Committee to a cramped fifth-floor room at the Shrine. The first order of business: the bait-and-switchers, a new breed of wayward communicant, who were rumored to approach an unsuspecting eucharistic minister with tongue lolling, only to stick out cupped hands at the last minute. Or they came with hands out, but opened wide with no time to spare. The Lay Ministry Committee discussed the phenomenon at length, but all I could think about was a filthy parochial-school joke about pedophile priests that an old girlfriend recently told me. You know the one — it ends with the immortal punch line, "In the mouth or on the tongue?"

"This brings me to a more general point," Father Bear-Daddy announced. "We need to bump up the liturgy a notch. I want the *best* lectors for the high holy days. I want to increase our membership. I want to make the music really zing."

It was unclear whether Father Bear-Daddy was envisioning putting on a mass or marketing a Broadway musical.

"It's important," he continued, "that the faithful get a seamless worship experience."

The other committee members and I exchanged looks.

One of them, whom I had always suspected of being an Opus Dei infiltrator, said, "We might want to start by making sure the lectors are actually Catholic. I noticed the sign-up form requests you to list your occupation, but not your religion."

The suggestion had the whiff of a purge, which I instinctively resisted. "Have we really had a problem with people passing themselves off as Catholics solely to get access to the pulpit?"

"Well," she said, "I think it's important. It's not like it was in the old days."

Father Bear-Daddy growled and let loose with one of his trademark pastoral f-bombs. He was impatient with the "old" Saint Anthony Shrine, which the faithful invoked regularly to oppose his grand plans for a total ecclesiastical makeover.

	The Old Saint Anthony	The New Saint Anthony
Parishioners	Night owls, cab drivers, bar patrons, *Boston Herald* reporters, riffraff	Milquetoast homosexual government attorneys
Friars	Brown-robed, thrice-knotted, and sandaled	Brown-robed, thrice-knotted, and sandaled with Internet access

Mass/confession schedule	Thirty-five Masses on holy days, going well beyond midnight	Banker's hours, closed on federal holidays
Fund-raising techniques	Collection basket	Paid development officer
Sins	Anything you didn't dare confess to your parish priest	Anything you didn't dare confess to your parish priest, including watching YouTube clips of Britney
Votives	Wax candles, wicks, and live flames	Electric bulbs that provide three minutes of light for a dollar

At Saint Anthony Shrine, the old and new coexisted in uneasy tension. Minor theological adjustments like blessing gay unions and womenpriests certainly seemed in order. But some innovations went too far. For example, Father Bear-Daddy took inordinate pride in the newly installed Franciscan Giving Center — an ATM-like donation station in the lobby on which some friar had posted the sign "Credit/Debit for Jesus." At the time, the Shrine was the only Catholic church in the country to have one. Several major newspapers printed a photo of Father Bear-Daddy with his arm around it.

It was mortifying. The Orgasmatron in Woody Allen's *Sleeper* came to mind.

The Reconciliatron™

The Giving Center presaged an entire line of automated faith machines. Once the old friars retired and the shortage of priests became acute, the Franciscan provincial would install another automated station in the confessional called the Reconciliatron.™ Simply type in your sins, and the Reconciliatron™ gives you computerized absolution. Just be sure to get a receipt. You'll want to have your records in order when Saint Peter undertakes an audit of your life at the Pearly Gates.

I explained to Father Bear-Daddy that, I, too, harbored a nostalgia for the harder, older times that had existed long before my first appearance at the Shrine. Bitterness, backwardness, and repression seemed more honest.

"You've confused all that old-fashioned baloney for honesty," Father Bear-Daddy replied. Only he didn't use the word *baloney*, or anything else you could print in a family newspaper.

Lector Boot Camp

If you hang around long enough, someone will inevitably put you in charge of something. This was how Father Abraham's lector-training legacy passed to me — including his hardcore philosophy. When you're going to the proverbial mattresses, you don't want Magic Fingers and a waterbed. You want a thin, inflatable camping pad that deflates beneath you in the night. You want your pith helmet for a pillow. You want a moth-eaten wool blanket. Life in the trenches should not be feel-good consolation.

Ten of the faithful showed up to the first session. They sat in folding chairs around a wooden table in the dingy second-floor classroom where the GLBT Spirituality Group met. Highlights included a bearded, disabled man with two amazingly dexterous foreshortened arms like a *Tyrannosaurus rex*, yet another Mary, and two college-age women whose perfect skin suggested they hadn't committed a sin in their lives.

We kicked off with an hour-long lecture on the practical theology of lectoring: "Read the selected text. Understand the selected text. Know the selected text. Proclaim the selected text." Then we drilled a copy of the current lay ministry rules, which had bulked up since the days of my training to four single-spaced typed pages. After a turkey club sandwich break, the lector candidates marched over to the sanctuary. For half an hour, they drilled the opening processional until they could walk the liturgical pace in their sleep.

For combat training, they took to the pulpit with the lectionary in hand and that nasty microphone at their lips. They sucked.

"Um, great liturgical pace approaching the pulpit, Mary," I said, emphasizing the positive. Experience taught that lector candidates generally reacted poorly to being told they made Chewbacca sound as if he had been taking elocution lessons. "I loved the way you held yourself stiff as a pencil and were not able to let loose anything more articulate than the yip of a lapdog. Now, let's work on everything *else* about your performance."

I strode to the far reaches of the church, cupping my hand to my ear, playing the "I-can't-HEAR-you" game. "Slow down," I shouted. "EM-pha-SIS." The subtle attractions of words like "Heil" and "Achtung" and "totalitarian state" were becoming clear to me.

"For God's sake, man," I called out. "You're not informing us there's a spill in aisle five. You're proclaiming the *Word!* Let your voice ring out. I want Seán O'Malley himself to hear you, all the way up there in the chancery.

"Look up!" I shouted. "Look up at the end of the sentence. Hold my gaze. You a criminal? Are you *lying* to me when you read His word? Why can't you look up for more than a split second and hold my gaze?"

The candidates' voices strengthened. Their diction sharpened. Their eye contact tightened like a vise. One of the sinless college girls stopped swaying in the pulpit like a gospel singer in a purple muumuu, and the other removed from each phrase the question mark and rising inflection that made the commands of Scripture sound like dubious propositions. By the time the commissioning Mass rolled around, a veritable army of lectors had formed, a crack verbal fighting force, lector ninjas. After Mass, we exchanged bear hugs and high fives.

"My lector trainees," I crowed, burgeoning with pride like a father whose son has just hit a Little League home run or burst the prom queen's cherry. "Broadway showstoppers, each and every one. Amen."

VIII

A Habit Worse Than Porn

Being Irish, he had an abiding sense of tragedy that sustained him through temporary periods of joy.

— William Butler Yeats

Give Us This Day Our Daily YouTube

Y WILY NEMESIS, Archbishop Seán, went hog-wild in cyberspace. He didn't open a ManHunt account — I imagined him posting a profile of himself raising the hem of his brown dress to show off his shapely gams, and promptly wished I had not — but he did join the blogosphere. He launched *The Brown Bag Blog* (not its real name), to which I occasionally posted helpful theological commentary, such as "Get a life" and "Go back to Cleveland!"

The Boston archdiocese didn't land me in digital hot water. For that, blame Justin Cardinal Rigali of Philadelphia. Cardinal Justin — a known womanpriest hater — started posting weekly commentary on scripture and other issues to YouTube. I had been a YouTube virgin, but after spending a few moments with Cardinal Rigali's clips, my cherry officially popped. YouTube orgies followed.

I typed "alligator attacks" and watched four grisly videos involving severed limbs.

"Birth defects" — "celebrity sex" — "third-degree burns" — "gynecological plastic surgery" — "plane crash."

The most shocking footage featured William Shatner singing Elton John's "Rocket Man."

The addiction started innocently with just a cardinal, some scorch marks, and a few severed limbs. Nothing that threatened health or welfare, only on weekends and after work hours.

But put aside your crystal meth, your cigarettes, and your chronic masturbation. Nothing hooks a gay man like YouTube. Soon loved ones also fell into the sordid habit. Scott and I came to spend more time on YouTube than we did engaging in the sin that cries out to heaven. Our romance-writing enterprise ground to a halt. My anemic prayer life hit the skids. Stalking the archbishop fell by the wayside.

I lay on my back on the Protestant pew and stared at the ceiling. Scott sat at the laptop.

"Try 'starving African children,'" I said.

Clickety-clickety-click.

Pause.

"What'd you get?"

Click.

"AWWWWW!" Scott cried out. (To me, not to heaven.)

The monitor showed a miasma of bloated bellies, stretched skin, and flies in eyes.

"Enough," I said, feeling queasy and responsible for world hunger. "Try 'Britney on the beach,'" I said.

Clickety-clickety-click.

"Nude," I added.

Clickety-clickety-click.

Scott surveyed Britney with the dispassion of a clinician. "D cups," he said. Guessing boob size was Scott's favorite party trick. He had a 99 percent accuracy rate.

"Type in, 'Hot twinks.'"†

---

† A twink is a young, tall, thin, smooth-chested gay man with insubstantial intellectual gifts but a prodigious desire to please. My kind of guy, in other words.

"No way," Scott said, keeping me honest. "How about 'Married men on the down-low' instead?" ("Straight" men appear often in Scott's porn stories.)

"No chance."

Instead, we viewed Saddam Hussein's hanging, Mitt Romney getting into a bitchfest with PETA after Mitt strapped his dog to the roof of his car, and Idaho senator Larry Craig's "wide stance." Even the Womenpriests were on YouTube!

Picasso Paints Provincetown

Starlets with pill problems check into the Betty Ford Clinic. YouTube addicts take off to Internet-free lodgings in Provincetown, Massachusetts, a gay beach resort and artist haven that also happens to be a vacation mecca for gay priests, celibate and otherwise.

An art gallery there was showing a series of strikingly bold paintings of the male figure: strong, masculine, and subtly erotic. The series was called *Man Emerging*. The artist? None other than my friend Picasso from the GLBT Spirituality Group at Saint Anthony Shrine.

Books I Took with Me on My Big Fat Gay Summer Vacation

- The Catholic poet Anne Porter's *Collected Works*
- The poet Don McKay's meditations on rock, *Strike/Slip*
- Wayne Hoffman's novel *Hard*, about a year in the life of a group of gay men
- Cardinal Bernadin's *Gift of Peace*
- *Faith Beyond Resentment*, by gay Catholic theologian James Alison
- Dan Savage's *The Kid: What Happened after My Boyfriend and I Decided to Go Get Pregnant*
- Andrew Sullivan's *Virtually Normal*
- Kathleen Norris's *The Cloister Walk*

Note the absence of porn. Who says I can't be redeemed?

"Wow, Picasso! Has the archdiocese had anything to say about your exhibition?"

"Why should they? There's not a penis in the whole *Man Emerging* series," he snapped indignantly.

It was still unnerving to hear the word *penis* coming from priestly lips. "No reaction at all?" I pressed.

He admitted that there had been some unpleasantness when he first linked his artistic Web site to his parish's site. Conservative Catholic bloggers circulated the link. Picasso said he received over 200,000 hits in that one month. He also received a personal invitation to the chancery.

"I was ready for them," Picasso said. "Look at Michelangelo! I had my art history lined up."

That was a frightening proposition: a gay man armed with art history.

"So what happened?" I asked. "Did they fire you? Send you to a retreat for your exhaustion? Assign you a new parish like they did with the pedophiles?"

"The bishop asked me to delink my site from the church's."

"No art history?"

"None."

"No new parish?"

"Same old place."

We chatted for a while, and I asked how Picasso had first come to the GLBT Spirituality Group.

"I was flirting with Mama Bear on the subway," Picasso admitted. "He was wearing a baseball cap with a rainbow bear."

"You still go?"

"No, but you should go back. They're still around."

I promised I would. My sense of superiority had gradually faded. Porn writing tends to keep you honest and humble. It also keeps you from ever holding elective office, but that's another matter entirely.

GLBT Spirituality Redux: The Bishop's Blessing

The Group had dropped the B and T. It was now just lettuce and bread: the group's official name became G-L Spirituality Group.

"No one is unwelcome," said Mama Bear, but he suggested that B and T spiritual issues were different.

Desperation no longer filled the windowless classroom. Travis Bickle, God help his soul and those of his future parishioners, had gone off to finish seminary work. The closet cases had diminished by half. A pink tablecloth covered the back table, now stacked with pint bottles of water and a few juice boxes. Multigrain snack bars formed tidy blue, red, and green pyramids.

And women had joined! Martina, a boyish lesbian, endlessly fingered a long purple necklace that looked like rock candy. Clearly she had had older brothers; she tried to — but would never fully — make up for all the things she hadn't been able to say when she was a girl. She spoke in unrestrained bursts about gay spiritual books she had read, a welcoming church she attended, and the need for gender-inclusive language.

A token straight couple, Ward and June, sat next to Martina. They looked like they had been through hell. The gay son they claimed to have must have been a demon: I pictured a nasty Chelsea S&M barebacking pagan sex worker meth queen antichrist democrat with a voracious taste for my porn.[†]

Ward and June nodded vigorously when Mama Bear suggested that their main goal ought to be to find a way both to affirm their love for their child and to remain loyal to Church teaching (and the Republican Party). Looking a little ashamed, Ward acknowledged that he knew it was a Catholic group, but he recommended *The Good Book* by Peter Gomes, the Protestant chaplain of Harvard University. "It's

---

† A *democrat* is . . . oh, forget it. There are so many gay vocabulary words in that sentence that I could spend a whole chapter on it. Google them yourself.

worth reading," he said shyly, as if the book was on the Vatican's prohibited list.[†]

To make Ward feel better, I copped to the truth: "I have a Protestant pew and a Protestant boyfriend. I know just what you mean."

Emboldened, Ward said, "One of the problems is that people don't go to confession anymore."

"I've got nothing to confess," Martina snapped.

Mama Bear swooped in to remind the group that this was a meeting about gay spirituality, not a bitch session. He suggested we take two minutes to hold hands to show our unity. We sang a verse of "We Are One."

"No," Ward explained, "what I mean is, not going to confession makes our pastors less effective. In the sixties and seventies, when everybody went to confession, priests learned about humanity and it softened their hearts. It helped them see how life is really lived."

Boy, I thought, *I could educate some of those pastors about humanity right quick. Burn their ears. Crash confessionals all over the state, all in the name of softening hearts.*

Like a stenographer, Alphaba scribbled down virtually every word spoken, as if she were going to report it back to the archbishop. She had a weathered face and a blunt voice that was like getting slapped in the face with a sapling. She reminded me of a wounded dog under a blanket — vicious, angry, thrashing, drawing out its own intestines as if it could remove its agony and choke it down. At fifty-five, she acknowledged that she was newly "exploring these feelings" and new to "all this." Neither the word *gay* nor the word *lesbian* crossed her lips during the entire hour.

Next to Alphaba sat Magoo, a red-faced drinker and self-described sissy-boy run to fat and glasses. His legs trailed away from his upper body like a nasturtium spilling over an iron railing. He came to the meeting because a priest had told him that gays were just defective

---

† The Index Librorum Prohibitorum was a list of books banned by the Catholic Church. First published in 1557, the Vatican updated it until 1966, when it was finally abolished.

straight people. He said that when he came out to his mother, she responded, "I still love you." He had expected a "but" to follow. He had expected her to rattle on reflexively about Church teaching. The "but" never came.

"It was the first time my mother has ever had an original thought," Magoo said, "the first time she wasn't a wind-up automaton, where the Church pulls a string and the words come out of her mouth. She finally allowed that the Church might not have all the right answers."

The last member of the group, the Landscaper, wore a green T-shirt advertising his trade. Much of the time, he sat on his own oil-stained hands with his face down and his shoulders hunched. Explaining that they conjured up gay pride marches and men in leather, he proposed excising the words *gay* and *lesbian* from the group's name. (Did Mama Bear flinch?) I didn't have the heart to tell the Landscaper that the average Boston Gay Pride parade consists of big-name advertisers, employee affinity groups sponsored by major corporations like Fidelity and Bank of America, and religious groups like the Jesuit Urban Center, Religious Coalition for the Freedom to Marry, Integrity (gay Episcopalians), A Common Bond (gay Jehovah's Witnesses), Affirmation (gay Mormons), Q-Light (gay Quakers), and OrthoGays (gay Orthodox Jews).

And Brazilians, dressed in feathers, boas, very short shorts — and very little else. (As one priestly acquaintance observed, "They're very talented.")

The landscaper's suggestion about the group's name led to discussion of the group's legitimacy.

"The bishop blessed the idea of the G-L Group here at Saint Anthony's," Mama Bear said.

"What bishop?" demanded the Landscaper.

"He gave his blessing," Mama Bear repeated firmly, dodging the question.

At that moment, Job wandered in carrying a flyer that he had found in the lobby. "I'm trying to figure out what it says."

Mama Bear snatched the flyer from his hands. "Where did you get this?" he demanded. Job looked as if he were going to have another unfortunate Mardi Gras chocolate moment.

Mama Bear first tore the flyer in half and then asked mildly, "Do you mind if I tear it up?"

"What is it?" Job asked tremulously.

"I don't want to talk about it," Mama Bear sniffed, dropping the halves in the trash. Job gazed longingly at the basket. Oblivious, Mama Bear launched into a long-winded diatribe about some crazy nut-job who had been terrorizing the Shrine. That morning, the nutjob had ascended the pulpit during the seven o'clock mass and started raving. Father Bear-Daddy had the lunatic physically removed from the Shrine.

"I've been telling Father Bear-Daddy to get a restraining order," Mama Bear fumed.

Everyone looked both giddy and spooked. Our strangeness to one another suddenly became manifest; each of us was a potential danger.

As the meeting broke up, the Landscaper approached me at the elevator.

"You want to go to dinner?" He flashed me a lascivious look.

"I think you're looking for Ward and June's son," I suggested gently, wanting to explain to him that I was a domesticated satyr, with a three-piece suit, a pocket square, a tumbler of calvados, and vanilla sins.

"Whaddaya say?"

"Um, no thanks. I'm meeting my boyfriend for dinner tonight. Next time."

The Landscaper turned from the elevator.

"Not coming down?" I asked.

He shook his head and returned to what was left of the group to see if he could scare up a date. I should have directed him to the doughnut social at the Jesuit Urban Center.

Captain Handsome Is My Copilot

Scott and I were booked to do an erotic reading in Manhattan. Our flight was delayed, and fellow passengers hovered about the jetway like mosquitoes around standing water. My prayer life got an instant boost.

Please don't let us get stranded here, God, I beseeched. *And please do not let this family with seven toddlers sit in the same zip code as us.*

As if in answer to my prayers, a deep baritone voice spoke from behind. "Excuse me."

The voice emanated not from God or James Earl Jones, but from the pilot — six-foot-two, blindingly white teeth, Mitt Romney hair, a titanium jaw, manly handshake, and piercing blue eyes.

The toddlers gazed at him in awe.

I gazed at him in awe.

"Hello, son!" boomed the pilot. He knelt next to one of the toddlers and ruffled his hair. Then he glanced at the parents with an expression that said, *You better be raising this child right, or Captain Handsome is going to come and clean house.*

Waving my government ID frantically, I parted the toddlers. "Excuse me, kids, pardon me. Step aside, please. I have some urgent business with Captain Handsome up in the cockpit."

Scott yanked me back down into my seat.

I protested: "You're depriving this man who has our lives in his hands of something he desperately needs — namely me?! Suppose his soul is in agony. Suppose he ends it all and takes us and all these children with him."

"Captain Handsome can do just fine without your ministrations," Scott growled.

"He needs help," I said. "His soul is crying out to me. Forgive him, Captain Handsome," I mouthed toward the cockpit. "He knows not what he's doing."

As my luck would have it — and perhaps as divine retribution for the adultery in my heart — the woman sitting in front of us farted steadily from the moment we took off. She proved to be an odiferous imperialist colonizer, counting on people like me to turn the other cheek, as it were.

Don't get me wrong. I admired her gumption. She had picked small and winnable battles. She was not by any means an egoist. She was not, like me, trying to take on an entire archdiocese and a thousand years of tradition with a handful of damaged homos, hugging Dignitarians, and priests with good urinary function but little courage.

On the other hand, it hardly required a parochial education to discern the evil of her ways: even the youngest toddler aboard that flight agreed there was something profoundly immoral about not owning up to your own gas.

I prayed for spiritual guidance: *Should I blind myself to greater indiscretions, God? Should I speak to her because she was the one You placed in my way? What would Captain Handsome do? Mmmmm, Captain Handsome . . .*

Ultimately, I gave her a taste of her own medicine. We farted and counterfarted over most of Rhode Island, eastern Connecticut, and Long Island Sound. It was only when we were about ten feet off the runway in New York that I realized my counterfarting campaign had caused me to forget the necessary Hail Marys.

"HailMaryfullofgracetheLord'switheeblessedartthouamongst —"
BOOM!

The rear wheels touched down, then the front. Rubber screeched. The woman in front of me gasped — or perhaps just farted again. The plane bounced once and lurched left. The flaps went up, and the brakes squealed. We rolled to a stop.

My vengefully flatulent nature and raw spiritual laziness had endangered a whole planeload of people. *Mea culpa, mea culpa, mea maxima culpa.* Not even Captain Handsome could make a plane take off or land safely unless someone aboard was madly reciting pleas to the Virgin on behalf of each and every passenger. Hey, he has his work; I have mine.

IX

The Godfather

Pain is no more reason to avoid friendship than is sacrifice to avoid virtue.

— Saint Augustine

How to Read Just Right

HE BAR IN LOWER MANHATTAN had no name. Purple light bathed the back room. The crowd was bohemian — women were big and dykey, men tattooed, patched, scrawny, and visibly gay. Every shirt was made of hemp. The room overflowed with decaffeinated tea, isms of every variety, and organic dark chocolate from endangered forest areas and socialist collective farms. At the back of the bar, a talented lesbian erotica writer educated us about strap-on devices, distinguishing the "softie" she wore on days she expected no action from the more rigid member she sported when she expected something hot, wet, and delicious.

My friend Tim stuck out like a sore thumb. Tim all but screamed heterosexual. His uncle had famously impregnated Tim's aunt despite having a vasectomy, a condom, and arm restraints. Tim's grandmother boasted relentlessly about such legendary feats of virility. This genetic inheritance suggested Tim's semen contained not merely good swimmers, but spermatic Houdinis.

He showed up in a suit and silk tie, fresh from a meeting of Alabama bankers that involved discussions of Daisy Duke, queer-bashing, muscular foreign policy, personal relationships with Jesus Christ, and whatever men from the South bantered about when they got together.

My text for the evening was a short story, "Sucksluts Anonymous." It went something like this:

> I was born a suckslut. I sucked my thumb in the delivery room when there was nothing else. Teachers and babysitters used to remark on my perseverance. I wore my pacifier to a nubbin. As a child, I could suck the color off a lollipop. Everlasting gobstoppers lasted ten seconds. Popsicles didn't have a chance to melt in my mouth. Chrome off a trailer hitch? You betcha. Every Boy Scout leader this side of the Mississippi wanted me in his den.

Tim signaled for a third martini.

The Ten Commandments of Reading Gay Porn

1. *Thou shalt be a stranger.* Strangers are hot — especially aggressive strangers who make you call them "sir."
2. *Thou shalt not laugh.* Laughter is the anti-porn. Don't crack a smile. It's like giggling when God smites Job.
3. *Thou shalt get to the action in 150 words or less.* Pornography is not the time for endearing sweet talk over bottomless cups of tea.
4. *Thou shalt prepare and practice ahead of time.* Nothing spoils the heat of the moment like stumbling over "butt cheeks" or substituting the word "caught" for "cock."
5. *Thou shalt not use "firebrand" for the male member more than five times in a story.* This one goes without saying.
6. *Thou shalt not sweat reality.* In real life, there are fluids to clean up, and licking honey off your loved one's inner thighs always

proves to be a horrifically bad idea (especially if you live any-where near a nest of fire ants), but these realities should not con-strain the action.

7. *Thou shalt not get too descriptive.* The audience is going to hear what it wants to hear. "Hot" will conjure twink for the chicken-hawk, hairy Harley-rider for the bear, Michelin man for the chub chaser. Less is more. Remember, it's like the Pentecost: everyone's going to hear the message in his own tongue.

8. *Honor thine antecedents.* He-he, his-his, him-him. It all gets very confusing, and anatomical impossibilities frequently result.

9. *Thou shalt not indulge in too much "sexy voice."* You have a gay voice, sister. No amount of guttural come-hither will ever change that.

10. *Thou shalt not act out the action.* Don't masturbate the micro-phone. Reading porn, like reading scripture, is not about you.

After the reading, we hustled a visibly shaken Tim to a restaurant in Chelsea. It was French in affect but Irish in provenance: the chalked menus for foie gras hung on thick wooden beams over the Guinness taps. My then-eight-months pregnant friend Erin sat on my right. Suf-fering from occasional contractions, she spoke about her pregnancy-induced passion for black porn. Across from me sat a fellow SEC attorney, a blond woman with thick calluses on her knuckles and crazy stories about her abusive dojo master.

Tim sat uncharacteristically silent. We assumed he was still in shock from the readings. He only interrupted when he learned that I had volunteered at the free legal clinic that Saint Anthony Shrine had just opened.

"Your perverse loyalty to the Catholic Church amazes me!" he snapped.

"It's only weekends," I said. "Well, Fridays."

Scott interjected, "What about your GLBT Spirituality Group meetings? Those are Wednesdays!"

The whole table fell silent. Unbenownst to me, the dinner was a staged intervention. They had become worried about my Catholicism.

We love you, Scott. We want to help you and support you, but your Catholicism is affecting all of us.

"Maybe a *few* Wednesdays," I acknowledged. "Just to blow off steam. It's not like I missed work or it's affecting my relationships."

Scott scoffed. Tim demanded that I defend my Catholicism on the spot.

"Can't we talk more about black porn and abusive dojo masters?" I pleaded.

"Seriously," Tim said, "why are you Catholic?"

"I believe in magic."

"What?"

"Religion fills a basic hunger. It's one part community, one part thankfulness, and one part awe and wonder. You guys know what I mean?"

They did not. Universally nonreligious, they congratulated themselves on seeing clearly and walking without a spiritual crutch.

"Why specifically *Catholic?*" Tim pressed. "That's what I'm talking about."

I wondered whether I could strategically knock a candle onto the checkered French tablecloth, spackle their eyes shut with Guinness-flavored foie gras, and escape in the confusion. Coming out Catholic to a table of confirmed Manhattan liberals was like being boiled and drowned with Saints Crispin and Crispinian.

"There's no financial connection between my church and the Archdiocese of Boston," I said defensively. "My money is not going to Archbishop O'Malley."

"You know the scripture you read is the same scripture that's used to justify the repression of people just like you, don't you?"

"I never once read aloud the passages so valued by the antigays — Leviticus, Corinthians, that stuff. The Catholic lectionary has suppressed the problematic passages."

"You're a cafeteria Catholic," Tim said.

"How consistent with the Gospels and Pauline letters is the idea that submission to Church authority is the true mark of discipleship? Look at Joan of Arc. They burned her at the stake before they made her a saint."

"Scott, you're no Joan of Arc," Tim said.

With more confidence but less ambition, I cited statistics as if we might win the Most Valuable Religion award:

- The Archdiocese of Boston educates nearly 50,000 students each year in Catholic schools.
- Catholic hospitals in the Boston metropolitan area care for more than 1 million patients annually.
- 200,000 individuals receive social service outreach from the Church.

"Look at all the good Catholics do," I pointed out. "I'm proud to be part of it."

"So why are you writing that crap?" Tim snapped.

"Crap? Don't tell me you didn't learn something tonight."

"If I never hear another word about a 'softie' for the rest of my life," Tim said, "I will die a happy man."

"Porn's not so bad. I mean, ever since Augustine put the shame in sex, characterizing it as a disgusting but necessary act, the Church has put sexual sins at the forefront of its rulemaking — while claiming to follow a Gospel, focused on social justice, featuring a prostitute among Jesus's followers. But there *is* a hierarchy of sins. Most people agree that writing porn is better than murder."

"Not exactly a high bar," Tim remarked.

"Porn writing may actually be beneficial," I countered.

"How so?"

"It blunts Augustine's shame and returns the focus of sin to acts that have actual victims."

"I don't see how you reconcile it with going to church."

"Ah, but that's where you're wrong, Tim. The skills of reading porn are very much like reading the Good Book. Practice, preparation, enunciation, drama. Take it from me," I said. "Tonight's reading actually helped me to be a better lector. I'm no longer afraid of the icky parts."

Improbable Friendship

At the end of a G-L Spirituality Group session, Mama Bear cornered me. "You," he said. "You come here often. Want to join the group's leadership team?"

"Do I have to quit writing porn?"

"No."

"Sign me up."

Meeting regularly, we hashed out what topics the group would address, and whether to invite Archbishop Seán to our meetings, and emergency procedures in the event of a visit from an armed right-wing nutjob, and whether Martina felt her womanhood had been sufficiently validated, and the efficacy of saint medallions, and the relative merits of liturgical dance. (On the latter, Mama Bear was pro. I was con. As a matter of public record, the Vatican has come out against liturgical hula.)

The meetings were an early glimpse of what hell must be like. We coddled feelings and gave them spa treatments. Microscopic minutiae received subatomic attention. Centering prayers preceded all discussion. Correctness reigned. And Mama Bear's process-oriented feel-good remarks topped out at the terminal level:

- "Are people OK with that?"
- "We need to unpack this notion."
- "Can we take that up later? — It's a good question. Really."
- "Where are people with this?"
- "We need to check in with people."

In contrast to Mama Bear's style, snap decisions followed by hard charging down whatever path the decision dictated best characterize my modus operandi. Until such time as the decision proves hopelessly wrong. At which point, I charge hard back to where I started, tail between my legs. Then I make a new snap decision, and go hard-charging down another path. And so on, until I drop from exhaustion.

Then wiser minds prevail and lead me, head down, to the correct decision, which has been painfully obvious to everyone else for three millennia. These opposing styles produced the obvious result: I was continually and inadvertently hurting Mama Bear's feelings.

Fortunately, Mama Bear didn't like to suffer in silence. Not naturally assertive, he had obviously spent time — perhaps years — learning to stick up for himself. He always promptly informed me of my transgressions so I could feel guilty and apologize. And my apologies always entailed my bruising his feelings all over again. Mama Bear and I talked more about our feelings in a single week than Scott and I had over the entire length of our relationship.

From this precarious beginning, friendship grew. There was a slyness to Mama Bear that felt innately sexy. He seemed like he might want to introduce a little more raunch into the group, to make it more real and less ethereal. "It's fine to talk about the virtues," he pointed out, "but how are they to be acted out in the gay-lesbian context? Where is God when you are in the midst of an orgy?" He understood the attractions of Captain Handsome and communion booty.

Mama Bear was also shirt-off-his-back generous. One day, a Franciscan leather vendor (no kidding) was hawking his wares on the sidewalk outside the Shrine. I mentioned that I had been looking for a leather armband for my biceps. (The one Scott bought for me proved embarrassingly too big). Without hesitation, Mama Bear promised to supply me one from his personal stock.

Mama Bear also generously shared his colorful history. Because he was born just after the death of a female cousin, Mama Bear received the male version of the cousin's name. At age four, his grandmother gave him a scarf and women's shoes to play with. His mother, who worked as a housekeeper, allowed Mama Bear first choice of the cast-off clothes the rich people gave her. His basement became drag-queen heaven. Later, he got a job at a convent and "borrowed" the nuns' garments on wash days, traced patterns on them, and made his own elaborate habits.

When he was thirteen, Mama Bear's parents closed down the basement nunnery, because, they told him, it was time for him to start acting like a man — specifically, a priest. At the time, Mama Bear had

an acutely developed religious life. He took communion daily. He held
long conversations with God in which he tried to make sense of the
differences between him and other boys. He recognized God in flora,
fauna, and heat lightning and regularly discussed the merits of the various religious orders he considered joining.

From fourteen, Mama Bear also had an acutely developed sex life.
In his rural town in the mid-1960s, he found the few other sexually active men in a public toilet outside the town hall. At his first breakup
with an older man, he came home to his mother in tears. He explained
that he was gay, and why he was sad. He found himself comforting her
as she wept and berated him. And then she said, "I know who the man
is. I'm going to call the police." Mama Bear swore up and down that he
would deny everything. They didn't speak about the topic for another
fifteen years.

One afternoon thereafter, Mama Bear wandered into confession.
The old ladies in the pews rattled their rosaries with joy at the sight of
a teenager coming to confession unattended. Their excitement turned
to horror when they heard the priest shout from the confessional, "You
did *what*?" As Father Hypertension ranted and raved, Mama Bear
took note of the vocabulary. He said, "I don't know what exactly
'abomination' and 'perversion' mean, Father Hypertension, but I'm
going to look those words up. I *do* know I don't believe you because
you are too angry about it." He never confessed to a priest again, pre-
ferring to keep his sins between him and God. (Gram would be so
proud.)

At eighteen, Mama Bear left home for Boston. Still deeply religious, he made the rounds of the local churches and settled on Saint
Anthony Shrine as his spiritual home. Still deeply sexual, he made his
rounds of the cruising grounds and nightspots. In the 1970s and '80s,
Mama Bear struggled to integrate his religious and sexual experiences,
often frightening away sexual partners by launching into enthusiastic
postcoital thanks to God for the wonderful orgasm. "God was there,"
he explained. "How could I deny Him?"

Mama Bear was religiously promiscuous, too. He found like-
minded souls at Dignity. He attended Mass at the Jesuit Urban Center.
He took spiritual direction from a nun who had never before worked

with a gay man but was willing to try. He joined the lay ministry at Saint Anthony Shrine. In fact, long before I realized I was gay, he had come out to the friars and the Lay Ministry Committee. In many ways, Mama Bear proved to be my ancestral forebear.

Mama Bear's extraordinary talent for ritual, reaching out, celebrating and cementing relationships, and talking freely about them astounded me. As Scott has made clear several times, usually at high volume, my approach consisted of: If I love you, you have to guess it. If I am angry, you must divine it. And never ever mention desire aloud.

Infinitely creative, Mama Bear, too, had the Broadway bug. He proposed, produced, codirected, and starred in a G-L Spirituality Group prayer service called Sisters and Brothers Together. Mama Bear promised that it would draw on a dozen religious traditions and involve seven languages, chant, song, psalm, incense, silence, commentary. And, of course, dance.

Before the service, a half dozen stepladders and a full-body wolf suit folded up on a chair behind the altar came to my attention.

"Didn't Francis the Franciscan Friar tell you?" Mama Bear asked. "We nominated you to be the wolf."

If dance was on the schedule, wolf suits were certainly possible. I fell for it.

Mama Bear led the service, and next thing I knew I was flapping my arms, flowing like water in the pew, and spinning a hula hoop around my hips. We drew twenty-five people, all of whom, like me, seemed a little unsure of how to act during this strange service — when to stand, when to speak, when to dance. Job drifted in and out as the intestinal urge hit him. Ward and June clung to each other nervously. Martina belted out brash a capella hymns in a voice like a trumpet. Alphaba fidgeted like a bag of elbows in the back pew.

"I think that went well," Father Francis said afterward.

"It went OK," I conceded. "But if Mama Bear threatens me with another prayer-dance, I'm through."

The Godfather

I don't know what it is, but something about a religious, hula-hooping gay man makes people do the craziest things. Case in point: when word leaked out about my Catholicism, however suspect, straight people swarmed to me like flies to honey. To understand this phenomenon, take the following multiple-choice quiz:

Why on earth would someone ever entrust me with the spiritual care of his or her offspring?

(A) The Church requires a Catholic to be in good standing in his parish, and there are only so many of us left from whom to choose. (At last count, Massachusetts had approximately five active Catholics.)

(B) The birth parents calculated that I would produce no biological heirs who might compete for my inheritance.

(C) Someone had too many margaritas the night before the baptism.

(D) I could post the baptism on YouTube.

(E) I love children.

If you picked (E), you get an F. Notwithstanding my ability to produce gas on demand, children terrify me. Not simply because of the fragility of their little limbs and noggins and budding psyches — one look at a child, and my mind automatically recites a rosary of the Horrible Mysteries: crib deaths, car accidents, nasally lodged Legos, Saranwrapped breathing passages, abductions, pedophile priests, electrically tortured canines, stroller malfeasance, butter-fingered babysitters, kindergarten bullies, malfunctioning playground swings, lead-painted toys, and stolen gabums.

More than all that, though, children (and dogs) possess an innate ability to recognize the truth of one's inner being. And so they put me in mortal fear of being unmasked — a whole line of children and barking dogs pointing at me with mouths open, like Donald Sutherland in *The Invasion of the Body Snatchers*.

My godparenting was godawful: First Communions missed, ages forgotten. Why couldn't the squalling toddler yank himself up by the diapers and bone up on *Business Week* so we could discourse intelligently on what — other than greed — was causing all these hedge-fund meltdowns that occupied every waking minute of God-Daddy Scott's working day? On my first godchild's first birthday, my co-godparent — out of the country at the time — shipped the child a hand-carved, life-size antique wooden horse last used during the battle of Troy. My stuffed Elmo from Toys "R" Us paled in comparison and highlighted my patent inadequacy for the job.

I wanted to pull my toddler godchild aside and give him a real-world lesson straight from the heart:

> Listen, you little twerp. Lemme explain how it works. I'm not here to shower you with gifts and money. I'm here in case Mommy and Daddy die in a tragic car crash. Stop sniveling. Crying gives you crow's feet, and then no man will ever want you. Now go get God-pa another throat lozenge.

I foreswore further godchildren — until my niece Mikaela was born. A child perfect in every other way, she lacks three fingers on her left hand. My brother Bruce and his wife requested that I be her godparent.

What better excuse for turning down godparenting than one that came from the mouth of Archbishop Seán himself?

> Dear Reverend Kick-Me,
>
> Remember me? — the annoying gay guy wanting to serve as a lector at a Mass presided over by Archbishop Seán?
>   I've got a question: Can a gay man licitly serve as a godparent?
>
> Love and leper kisses,
> Scott

The chancery hadn't responded to many prior inquiries and invitations, but this question elicited a response. Reverend Kick-Me assured me that he knew no position taken by the archdiocese or the Church concerning an openly gay man being a godfather, nor did he expect one to be developed.

With no theological excuse available for turning down the request, I asked my brother plaintively, "Why me? Wasn't Captain Handsome available?"

"Because you understand what it's like to grow up different," Bruce explained.

Ah, yes.

The Theology of Baldness

Between bouts of YouTube and apologies to Mama Bear, Tim's spiritual intervention gnawed at me. I knew I should have had a better explanation for remaining Catholic, but every time I came up with one, the Vatican and/or the archdiocese countered with a fresh condemnation of gay people. It was like a game of spiritual table tennis.

Spiritual Table Tennis Scorecard

Take a minute to fill out the handy scorecard below. Award positive points for compelling reasons to remain Catholic, and negative points for gratuitously mean-spirited or misguided condemnations by the hierarchy.

Scott's Reasons for Remaining Catholic	Points (+/-)
Spiritual S&M. I want a religion that wants more of me than I can deliver.	
The question is not, Why stay, but Why leave? We aid in our own exile by leaving.	
The Church is the original *wiki*. There's shared wisdom in shared worship.	
I don't pack my bags for Polynesia every time I disagree with the Bush administration.	
If you forgo weekly mass and accept religious experience only when it hits you over the head, you'll starve spiritually. Your soul will look like Kate Moss. No one wants a Kate Moss soul.	
I can no more shed my Catholicism than my gayness.	
Faith is a gift, and God didn't include a gift receipt.	

Vatican/Archdiocesan Remarks	Points (+/-)
The Rat: "Allowing children to be adopted by persons living in [gay] unions would actually mean doing violence to these children."	
The Rat: "The Church . . . cannot admit to the seminary or holy orders those who practice homosexuality, present deep-seated homosexual tendencies, or support the so-called gay culture."	
Bishop Allen Vigneron of Oakland, California: "A homosexual is not properly ordered to relationships with persons of either sex."	
Archbishop O'Malley: Same-sex civil marriage is a "national tragedy."	
Archbishop O'Malley: Same-sex marriage is "an attack on the common good."	
The Rat: Same-sex marriage is a threat to world peace.	
TOTAL	

Strangely, the Church's campaign against gay issues made my worship seem more mad and divine. In the twenty-first century, it's no longer spiritually impressive to dance as Pan on a rural hillside, fucking boys and scarfing hallucinogenic mushrooms. It's been done a thousand times since Robert Bly.

But Gothic churches, hard pews, and stained glass presented huge opportunities for ecstatic madness. They represented spiritual gold mines where I and thousands of other self-flagellating gay albino monks named Silas could celebrate the bawdy, unkempt Spirit and an untidy, misunderstood God.

Tim's question turned upside down:

> *If not Catholic, then what? What else can I do with this instinct to bow my head for a blessing, to genuflect at a tabernacle, to bark out a Hail Mary just before the wheels hit the tarmac?*
>
> *With whom shall I share these moments that tend upward? What would I do with this inarticulate yearning to give thanks, to give praise, to look for grace?*
>
> *Other than priests, whose job it is to pluck something worthwhile out of a text, to ask unsettling questions of me? Who else will give me spiritual sticky notes to reorient me to what is good?*

This spiritual frenzy pressed me for a way to explain my holy outrage in terms Seán could understand. I needed a spiritual bridge, a tunnel from my condominium straight to the chancery, a way of speaking to him that he could not fail to hear. After all, not every bishop opposes legislation in favor of gay unions. Sixty-two-year-old Bishop Raul Vera of Saltillo, Mexico, gave his support to a civil-union bill modeled on France's pacts of civil solidarity, saying, "As the Church, we can't assume the position of homophobes. We cannot marginalize gays and lesbians. We cannot leave them unprotected." Similarly, the bishops of New Zealand endorsed a civil union proposal. The Vatican's ambassador to Spain, Monsignor Manuel Montiero de Castro, told a conference of Spanish bishops that "there are other forms of cohabitation [besides marriage between one man and one woman] and it is good that they be [legally] recognized." Even here in Massachusetts, one of Seán's brother bishops testified before the legislature that — while he opposed gay marriage — the question of distributive justice regarding who should get spouselike benefits was a topic ripe for discussion.

My breakthrough came while watching a clip of Archbishop Seán on Catholic TV. Between the two of us, I realized, Seán and I had almost as much hair as a naked mole rat. *Baldness* would be my bridge!

Out came the writing tablet:

Dear Archbishop Seán:

Imagine a different Church, one that proclaims that baldness is intrinsically disordered yet proscribes all attempts to cover bald heads as morally inferior to hairdos of all kinds — even those from the Seventies.

You and I would both be in trouble in such a Church. Wearing your bishop's miter would be an act of grave sin. Yet, isn't that how God made us — bald? Isn't it our nature? Isn't it arbitrary to forbid someone to act on baldness's imperative — to cover your head against the winter wind?

This is how I experience the Church's condemnation of homosexuality and homosexual activity. It denies that God made me and that grace might inhere in loving another man.

Moreover, even if I accepted your idea that God's intended use of sexual organs was solely for procreation and that same-sex desire was therefore defective, why do we not treat other physical defects the same way? Is my goddaughter Mikaela to circumscribe her activity on account of her handicapped hand? Do you preach that blindness is somehow a question of moral culpability? Has the Church issued a fatwa prohibiting the use of Braille?

Good Lord, Seán! That kind of thinking is a throwback to when we blamed people for their infirmities and suggested they were a punishment from the Lord. To be sure, this outlook is vintage Old Testament, so it's clear how a well-meaning person might make a mistake.

But now we have science to explain outbreaks of disease and deformity. We no longer need to ascribe them to an angry deity. Well, unless your name happens to be Jerry Falwell, who assigned moral freight to AIDS, Katrina, and Tinky Winky, and who saw God's retribution in 9/11.

Love and blessings,
Scott

It seemed so reasonable, I could puke. After all, Christ Himself had made my argument two thousand years earlier. Just substitute "bald" for "blind" in the text of John 9:2–3, "His disciples asked him, 'Rabbi, who sinned, this man or his parents, that he was born [bald]?' Jesus answered, 'Neither he nor his parents sinned; it is so that the works of God might be made visible through him.'"

My missive to Cardinal Seán ended with a long P.S. that stated five simple ideas:

1. The Church does not accept that the "plain meaning" of the Bible should in each and every instance be credited as God's law. My Baltimore Catechism includes the following teaching:

    Q. Are all the passages of the Bible to be understood according to our modern manner of expression?

    A. No. Some of the passages of the Bible are not to be understood according to our modern manner of expression, since they contain certain figures of speech, parables, and literary forms used by the people of ancient times but not employed in the present.

No one has adequately explained why some passages (advocating slavery or headscarves for women in church) should be ignored, while others, allegedly antigay, should carry weight.

2. Procreation does not adequately or essentially distinguish heterosexual from homosexual love.

    Heterosexual couples, including the elderly, can marry, and their sexual union is blessed even though they cannot procreate. Sex expressly intended to be nonprocreative is permitted; we call it the rhythm method. It's hard to credit a reason as rational if it's applied selectively.

    Besides, for God anything is possible: conception in a gay couple is at least as probable as a virgin birth. Lord knows that Scott and I are going to keep on trying in hopes the Holy Spirit blesses us with a child.

3. The Church's teaching has been anything but "constant."

    The idea of teaching that cannot change is itself a heresy known as

scotosis — the deliberate and willful darkening of the mind that results from refusal to acknowledge God's presence and power at work.
It suggests that the Holy Spirit no longer moves in the hearts of men,
and that the Spirit is now merely resting on Its heavenly laurels.

The notion that the Church has never changed teachings is a
patent absurdity. Early in his papacy, for example, B16 abolished
limbo, the place where unbaptized babies had been consigned thereto-
fore. The Immaculate Conception and the Assumption of Mary became articles of faith in the nineteenth century. Marriage only became
a sacrament in the twelfth century. Saint Augustine invented original
sin in the fourth century. The Eucharist only became a central part of
the liturgy in the second century, justified post hoc by the Last Supper.

As a letter to the editor in the *San Francisco Chronicle* put it:

> Remember that the Church has, at one time or another, con-
> demned heretics to death, supported the practice of human
> slavery, denied the possibility of salvation to non-Catholics,
> denounced the American Bill of Rights, and, of course, con-
> demned Galileo for claiming that the Earth moved around
> the sun. With that in mind, I would suggest . . . remem-
> ber[ing] the immortal words of Oliver Cromwell, "I be-
> seech you, in the bowels of Christ, think it possible you may
> be mistaken."

Luckily, Archbishop Seán, you don't suffer from too much love for
constancy in the bowels of Christ: witness your change of heart concerning the Saint Patrick's Day Corned Beef Debacle.

4. The sin of Sodom isn't what you think it is.

The Old Testament passages don't condemn loving same-sex relationships; they condemn the failure to be hospitable to one's guests.
Even the Web site of the U.S. Conference of Catholic Bishops acknowledges this point:

> Israelite tradition was unanimous in ascribing the destruc-
> tion of Sodom and Gomorrah to the wickedness of these

cities, but tradition varied in regard to the nature of this wickedness. According to the present account of the Yahwist, the sin of Sodom was homosexuality (Genesis 19:4–5), which is therefore also known as sodomy; but according to Isaiah (Isaiah 1:9–10; 3:9), it was a lack of social justice; Ezekiel (Ezekiel 16:46–51) described it as a disregard for the poor, whereas Jeremiah (Jeremiah 23:14) saw it as general immorality.

Thus, as Nancy L. Wilson, a Metropolitan Community Church bishop, said, "It is the Church, not queer folk, which has been most obviously guilty of the sin of Sodom, refusing hospitality to queer people and offering rejection and violence."

5. There's a hierarchy of scriptural imperatives.

According to Vatican II pronouncements, "In Catholic doctrine there exists an order or hierarchy of truths, since they vary in their relation to the foundation of Christian faith." This makes sense: Christ Himself identified two commandments above all others: "Love the Lord your God with all your heart, with all your soul, and all your mind. This is the greatest and most important commandment. The second most important is like it: Love your neighbor as you love yourself."

With this in mind, we can reread those scriptural passages purportedly outlawing homosexual activity not simply in a different light (i.e., the light of modern experience), but also through a lens that recognizes other passages of higher import and greater generality that take precedence over more particular, culturally conditioned passages. Slavery provides a clear example. The Bible condones the "peculiar institution" in many particular passages, but in light of contemporary experience, such passages appear inconsistent with the highest command to love your neighbor as yourself.

I sealed the envelope with a kiss, stamped it, posted it outside the Shrine, and waited impatiently for Archbishop Seán to see the error of his ways.

This Is Not about You

On the afternoon of Mikaela's baptism, the everyday human menagerie surrounding the Shrine put Boston's corporately sponsored gay pride parade to shame for all its variety and wonder. Behold:

- bovine midwestern tourists shying away from dark-skinned youths and the elaborate mating rituals of H&M-bound queens
- buskers and con artists
- homeless people
- religious lunatics
- tour guides in colonial-era dress
- a protest march of the union of Hispanic workers who clean 99.9 percent of Boston's office towers
- college kids asking whether I had a moment for the environment
- political supporters of perennial fringe candidate Lyndon LaRouche
- heavyset lesbians intent on getting Fidelity Corporation to divest from Darfur

Inside the Shrine, calmness reigned. The slow drip of countless Masses from my youth, the years of witness and worship, ran in my veins. A candle burned. My face flushed. The microphone squawked. Chewbacca laughed. I prepared to slip out of myself and into the text, to obliterate myself for a moment.

A glorious melody from my mouth silenced the street outside. Beautiful phrases flew out, escaping like sparrows. The world stopped turning. The events I narrated came to life around me. Cedar billowed around the altar. An old woman in the second row skipped a whole decade of her rosary, raised her face to the altar, and revealed that she had once been very beautiful.

Each word of the Responsorial Psalms rose and burst, a shower of dandelion seeds scattered by a hard breath. Each verse became an aria capable of shattering glass. Each phrase came out like a silken stream, a mesh of golden threads, numerous as the stars in the sky.

My brother bore Mikaela to the baptismal font. He stared down at her with an all-consuming love, making desperate bargains with the little one — *Don't you get sick, baby Mikaela. Don't you leave us. Don't disappoint* — and simultaneous bargains with the Big Guy — *Watch over the little one, protect her from harm, and, if you fuck with me on this, God, I will chase you down to the ends of the universe and wantonly destroy your creations.*

Thanksgiving, unworthiness, urgency, and awe all filled me at once. Swaddled in clean white linen, daubed with water and chrism, Mikaela wailed and shook her little imperfect fist, inarticulate and full of life.

"Power to the people, little sister Mikaela," I whispered. No doubt the Spirit would enter here — in that small fist, that big Womanpriest heart, those power lungs.

I whispered to her, "You're going to need that ferocity, angel. From here on out, it's a lifetime of forgotten birthdays and hastily wrapped gifts and only the occasional 'God bless' before bedtime."

She bopped me firmly on the chin.

This is why I'm Catholic.

X

Excommunications ʼRʼ Us

Priest: Your Eminence, what are we going to do about all these young people living together before they get married?
Cardinal Law: If they put down the same address, presume it's a duplex, and ask no questions.

— as related by Walter Cuenin

The Vatican Paperwork-Reduction Program

 EAN MARCHANT'S SISTERS, the first Roman Catholic Womenpriests, were ordained on the Danube in 2002. The following year, on the feast of Mary Magdalene, the Vatican formally excommunicated them in a document signed by the Rat. Additional ordinations followed, culminating in a highly publicized ceremony in Pittsburgh in 2006 in which seventeen North American women became womenpriests and womendeacons. At least two American bishops, Timothy Dolan of Milwaukee and Justin "YouTube" Rigali of Philadelphia, announced that they would forward the names of their local womenpriests to the Vatican for disciplinary proceedings. (No one likes a tattletale, and no one likes a copycat, either: the two bishops' statements read nearly word for word.)

Most American dioceses, including Boston, set out a slightly different message: there was no need to excommunicate the women formally. They were automatically excommunicated (called a *latae sententiae*) by virtue of their actions.

The womanpriest movement continues to grow. Five ordination ceremonies, each involving multiple women, took place in North America alone in 2007. If the Vatican insisted on formally excommunicating each of the renegades, it would have to shanghai poor Reverend Amorth from his busy exorcism schedule and put him to work processing excommunication decrees. And then who would keep an eye on Harry Potter?

A Short History of Excommunication

The first major heretic in the Church, Arius, taught that Jesus, though divine, was not the equal of God the Father. In 325, at the Council of Nicea, over 300 Church leaders condemned Arius's teachings, declared him a heretic, and excommunicated him.

The practice proved more addictive than YouTube. For the next thousand years, priests dispensed excommunications like breath mints. Apostates, heretics, and schismatics could all apply, of course. But excommunication also resulted from reading forbidden books, belonging to forbidden societies, killing popes and bishops, stealing from the Church — or because you happened to own a property that the local potentate fancied. The potentate paid the local bishop to excommunicate you. You were seized and burned, your family was dispersed, and the local potentate henceforth enjoyed spectacular views from your bedroom window.

In fact, medieval abuse of excommunication helped bring about the Reformation. When the Church addressed certain Protestant critiques at the Council of Trent, voices of reason gently suggested that Church authorities lighten up and save excommunication for truly grave offenses.

Pope Pius X led another bout of excommunications, famously declaring that there ought to be "no questions, no subtleties, no opposing of personal rights to [the pope's] rights, only obedience." Pope Paul VI ratcheted the temperature down a few notches: he didn't even censure a single theologian for radical views. In the mid-twentieth century, Pope John XXIII announced, "Today the spouse of Christ [i.e., the Roman Catholic Church] prefers to use the medicine of mercy rather than severity. She considers that she meets the needs of the present age by showing the validity of her teaching rather than by condemnations."

Pope John XXIII's flirtation with mercy didn't last long. No sooner had his corpse and that of his short-lived successor JP1 gone cold than J2P2 and B16 retrofitted excommunication with renewed chic. Clip and save the FAQ below in the event of your own excommunication.

------------------------ cut here ------------------------ ✂

Excommunication FAQ

Everything you always wanted to know about excommunication but were afraid to ask.

Q. What exactly is excommunication, and what does it mean for me?
A. It means you are placed "outside the Church." No more receiving or administering sacraments or having church-based prayers said for you. (Private prayers are kosher.) And, of course, your long-suffering mother won't love you anymore.

    The real punishment, however, stems from this item of Catholic dogma: "There is no salvation outside the church." Excommunication means you are going to hell for sure — unless you repent.

Q. Do they do that anymore?
A. Excommunicate? Oh, yes. You can't call yourself a bishop anymore unless you've demonstrated your conservative cred by excommunicating a few members of your flock.

Q. Do they still tear your bowels out and burn them in front of you?
A. Not so much. Excommunication gets a little press, a lot of fist-waving, low-grade threats against your associates, some nasty blogging, and nonsense about wanting you back as soon as you recant. It's not unlike a low-level Mafia spat on the Jersey shore.

Then, Brangelina does something remarkable like copulating, and the media forget the whole incident.

But if you're a priest or nun, you're screwed. The Church takes your job, paycheck, and housing, and boots you into the street.

Q. *But who's actually been excommunicated (or at least threatened with excommunication)?*

A. Henry VIII, Martin Luther, Juan Perón (spouse of gay saint Evita), Galileo, Miguel de Cervantes, Joan of Arc, Joe DiMaggio, all divorcés who remarry, and, of course, the mayor of Benidorm, Spain, in the 1940s for authorizing bikini wearing.

Q. *Yesterday's news. Who's been excommunicated lately?*

A. The better question is, Who hasn't been threatened with excommunication lately? In 1999, Father James Callan was excommunicated for performing marriage ceremonies for gays and allowing women too prominent a role on the altar, and Sinead O'Connor caught the Vatican's attention when a splinter Catholic group ordained her as a priest and she insisted on being known as Mother Bernadette. Since 2000, the Church has also excommunicated a married bishop in Africa, improperly appointed bishops in China, bishops that do not accept the reforms of Vatican II, and a priest who held a funeral service for his dog. 2006 was a banner year for actual or threatened excommunication: offenders included Madonna, for performing a song three miles from Vatican City while strung up on a crucifix; Father Ned Reidy, for refusing to follow Church teaching on homosexuality and — do you sense a theme? — the ordination of women; and Father Rouville Fisher, for joining Rent-A-Priest, an organization of married priests that performs priestly services for a fee.

Q. *Don't some bad guys get excommunicated, too?*

A. Hitler remained a Catholic in good standing until the end.

Q. *Is excommunication necessary?*

A. No. Many impatient bishops skip straight to dessert. They don't bother with excommunication; instead, they withhold sacraments ad hoc. Witness, for example, Bishop David Ricken of Wyoming, who in 2007 ordered that a married lesbian couple who had been vocal in support of same-sex marriage be denied communion after they appeared in their local paper on Ash Wednesday with ashes on their foreheads.

Q. *What's the difference between threatening excommunication and actually carrying it out?*

A. Threats are cheaper, and anyone with a theological hair stuck across his ass can issue them. Excommunication, on the other hand, involves the slow grinding of bureaucratic machinery in conditions of utmost secrecy. Ultimately, both threat and act can be equally effective in winning press coverage, but a mere threat has the added environmental benefit of reducing the necessary paperwork.

Q. *They can't excommunicate everyone, can they?*

A. Group excommunication is the latest vogue. Using management techniques of which Carnegie would be proud, they've improved excommunication productivity tenfold by issuing sweeping judgments of excommunication netting hundreds and sometimes thousands of people. Individualized justice has never been a big concern for ecclesiastical courts, so the loss of precision and rigor in the group-excommunication model hasn't bothered the Vatican a whit. Examples:

- 1990: The African-American Catholic Congregation and its leader, George A. Stallings Jr., for advocating for female priests and the use of birth control.
- 1996: All members of Call to Action, a Catholic group in the Midwest that advocates for marriage of priests, increased work to combat poverty, female priests, and inclusion of gays and lesbians.

- 2003: St. Stanislaus Kostka Church parish of the Archdiocese of St. Louis, for asserting fiscal autonomy and hiring its own priest.
- 2006: All scientists engaged in stem cell research.

✂- - - - - - - - - - - - - - - - - - cut here - - - - - - - - - - - - - - - - - - - ✂

Walking the Excommunication Walk

I tried to contact some of those who have recently been excommunicated to talk about the experience. Here are two stories with very different ends.

Father Ed Cachia and the Will of God. Father Cachia, the pastor of St. Michael's Parish in Cobourg, Ontario, wrote a newspaper article calling for the Church to establish a dialogue with women who felt called to ordination, and, reportedly, for admitting to celebrating masses with female priests in the United States. In a follow-up interview, Father Cachia said the ordination of women could be

> the beginning of a new and awesome change in the life of the Church. [It] would bring dialogue to help people sit down and as human beings work out our differences. These women would like to talk about this, and Rome is not giving them a chance. Rome believes these women are only after power. My experience is very different. I am edified by their spirituality, compassion, and love. They wash the feet of others and are very humble in service. They are rooted in faith, willing to suffer consequences. For them, this is no cheap stunt or meaningless event. By closing the doors of debate and dialogue on women who feel the call of being ordained priests and deacons, the Church is perpetuating violence against these women by saying: "You have only to pray, pay and obey; we have no time to dialogue with you."

Refuting the claim that Jesus chose only men as his disciples, Cachia pointed out, "Jesus only chose Jews, too."

In November 2005, Cachia lost his job for these and similar statements. The bishop of Peterborough, Ontario, announced Cachia's excommunication on the following Palm Sunday. Responding to the announcement, Father Cachia said:

> My statements that the Church should speak respectfully and should re-establish dialogue with women who are called to ordination are what I believe to be true. For me, this is the truth regardless of whether the Church agrees with me. To force me to retract my statements would be to force me to lie. The choice I was given was to lie to the people or lose my position in the Church. If we sacrifice our principles and integrity to save ourselves we have sacrificed everything. I lost everything: my home, my job, my benefits, my pension, and my security.

However, Jesus calls us to stand by our convictions even to the point of suffering. Father Cachia then started his own church called Christ the Servant at a local United Church in Cobourg. He reportedly told the press, "I never in my whole lifetime ever dreamt it would come to this. . . . I really believe that, if I am following the will of God in all this, the Lord will not abandon me. He will not let me down."

Apparently, however, the Lord *did* abandon him. Cachia has since quit Christ the Servant and met frequently with his bishop in an effort to rejoin the fold.

Father Marek Bozek and the Parish Rooster. In 2003, the parish of St. Stanislaus Kostka refused to cede control of its assets and property to the Archdiocese of St. Louis. Archbishop Burke removed the parish's priests, thereby depriving the congregation of communion, baptism, marriage, and funerals — an attempt to induce "spiritual and sacramental starvation," according to Bozek. Rather than knuckle under, the parish hired Bozek to replace the fired pastor. After a year-long process of spiritual discernment, Bozek accepted the position on December 2, 2005.†

Burke accused Bozek of the "ecclesiastical crime of schism" for encouraging the parish to accept his priestly ministry. Within three weeks and without any process whatsoever, Burke excommunicated Bozek while the latter was vacationing in Peru. Burke accused those parishioners who accepted sacraments from him of committing mortal sin. The archdiocese also reported Bozek, a native of Poland, to immigration authorities.

Neither Bozek nor his parish backed down. The *Chicago Tribune* reported that one parishioner, a lapsed Catholic, described her reaction to Bozek's ministry this way: "I feel like I've got more spirit, more hope. It makes me feel closer to Christ. This church has brought me back to my roots. In a roundabout way, Burke has helped this parish."

Bozek himself said: "I could imagine Jesus saying to me: 'Kids could not be baptized. Parents died, and you did not come to me.' I didn't want to be told to move aside because I was not courageous enough. . . . [Burke] sees the church in terms of regulations, not human lives and human suffering. Doing this, he really breaks people's hearts and people's souls."

In 2005 and 2006, Bozek attracted more people to his Christmas Mass than the archbishop who excommunicated him. In an e-mail, Bozek wrote that before the schism, "the Parish rooster [sic] listed about 250 households. Today there are more than 600 registered households in Saint Stanislaus. [The v]ast majority of them are so-called 'outcast' Catholics, or people who for various reasons felt alienated from or marginalized in other Roman Catholic parishes. They all have found a spiritual home, free of judgment and politics." Bozek acknowledged that the parish "has been blessed with many gay, lesbian, bisexual, and transgender parishioners, and they provide us all with a beautiful witness to God's grace present in all our lives."

---

† "Discernment" is the long, slow process of deciding what God wants you to do. Overused in the Catholic Church, it has gotten to the point where bishops have to discern whether to take their morning bowel movement. See also "inertia" and "excuse to do nothing slowly."

Hearing this story gave me the same sense of renewal as the parishioner at St. Stanislaus Kostka. Hell, I felt jealous. Not just because Father Bear-Daddy had not purchased a parish rooster for Saint Anthony Shrine, but also because excommunication seemed like a backhanded blessing. If you could get yourself excommunicated by B16's unloving hierarchy, you could wear it as a moral stamp of approval. And besides, after getting a *latae sententiae* (with soy milk) from a Capuchin like Seán, Starbucks would never look the same again.

Not being a woman presented a bit of a problem. Without enduring a great deal of body sculpting and pancake makeup, I couldn't just go and get myself ordained. How do you go about getting excommunicated in the comfort of your own living room?

Three Easy Steps to Excommunication

Step 1: Cross Archbishop Seán

For fifteen years, Shirley Gomes served as a eucharistic minister at a church where she had married and raised her family. When she ran for state representative, someone tipped the church's pastor that Gomes might be prochoice. He fired her from the lay ministry and told her she should not be receiving communion until she renounced her views. Noting that her male opponent in the race had stronger prochoice views but had attracted no interest from her pastor, Gomes appealed to then-bishop Seán to be reinstated. Following a private meeting with Gomes, Seán supported the pastor's decision to fire her and his belief that she ought not be snacking on communion wafers. Denying the Eucharist isn't the equivalent of excommunication, but it's heading in the right direction.

Step 2: Don't Sin in Silence

In affirming priests' obligation to deny communion to divorced Catholics who remarried, J2P2 required both that the divorcée "obstinately persist" in sin *and* that she or he make "the situation of grave sin" manifest.

In other words, the Church only held the Eucharist hostage for public disagreements. Polls consistently showed that the majority of American Catholics holds views on birth control, ordination of women, and priestly marriage similar to those for which the Church excommunicated Fathers Callan and Cachia, Call to Action, and others. Catholics have always been notoriously more liberal than Protestants on gay marriage. Yet the excommunication of this majority doesn't appear imminent.

So what do we make of the requirement of manifestness? It's the ecclesiastical equivalent of "Don't Ask, Don't Tell." Take the example of Leah Vader and Lynne Huskinson, the Wyoming lesbian couple. (Let's pray they have a son and name him Darth.) After years of taking communion at their church and appearing in its parish directory, Leah and Lynne committed the sins of (A) announcing their engagement and marriage in the local paper; (B) sending a letter protesting a bill that would outlaw same-sex marriages to their legislator, which was read on the House floor; and (C) being interviewed and photographed by the local paper with ashes on their forehead in observance of Ash Wednesday.

As soon as the story ran, Leah and Lynne received a letter from their pastor, sent at the direction of Bishop David Ricken, that barred the couple from receiving communion. The Associated Press reported the couple's priest as saying, "If all this stuff hadn't hit the newspaper, it wouldn't have been any different than before. . . . The sin is one thing. It's a very different thing to go public with that sin."

Catholic life as it is truly lived is much messier than the rules acknowledge, so pastoral responses tend to occur on the sly. When my brother and his wife — who lived in sin for three years before getting engaged — were preparing for marriage, they participated in a pre-Cana program at their local church. The program spiritually prepares them for married life. They listened to lectures, discussed Bible passages, and met individually with the priest.

The priest asked my sister-in-law about herself, her beliefs, her willingness to raise Catholic children, and other pleasantries. As he was closing, he posed the following question: "Do you have any reason to believe Bruce will not be able to perform the husbandly duties necessary to allow you both to accept children from God, if He so wills it?"

"Oh, God, no!" my sister-in-law said. The priest thanked her and asked her to send in my brother. The priest posed all the same questions to my brother, ending again with the one concerning my sister-in-law's ability to get the job done sexually. My brother's affirmative endorsement was equally enthusiastic.

The priest then called them both in and announced that they had successfully passed the pre-Cana test, and their marriage would go forward as planned in the Church. They thanked the priest and prepared to leave.

"Oh," said the priest, "one last thing."

"Yes?"

"That last question, about whether you know about any sexual dysfunction? The correct answer is *not* 'no.' It's 'I don't know!'"

Step 3: Dare to Trust Your Co-Catholics' Maturity and Reasoning Capacity

Nearly every excommunicant trusted his or her fellow Catholics' moral reasoning abilities and gave them credit for having a clear conscience and a robust faith. The Church, on the other hand, has little faith in the faithful. It treats Catholics as if their faith is timid, and they are children easily led astray. It presumes that the faith of the people is so weak that it requires protection from scandal and unorthodoxy.

B16 and I know the same people — Catholics discern silhouettes of the Virgin Mary in the icing on their breakfast pastries and parade garish plaster saints through the streets while passersby hurl rosary beads. (Or is that Mardi Gras? I always get confused.) At Saint Anthony Shrine, when Father Myron accidentally spilled a half-dozen communion wafers, he and Her Highness cracked heads trying to retrieve them and then fought over who would have the honor of consuming the soiled Host. These are people whose faith needs protecting? Their faith looks pretty robust to me.

The Church's attitude toward the faithful is not only infantilizing, it's downright dangerous. According to testimony by bishops in the court cases arising out of the pedophile priest scandal, one of the reasons for keeping the accused priests' sins hidden was to avoid "scandalizing the faithful." Ironic, no? What actually scandalized the faithful was the attempt to avoid scandalizing the faithful. Years after the scandal broke, Saint Anthony Shrine's annual appeal contains bold language stating that all donated funds stay with the Shrine and do not go to the budget of the archdiocese. The friars implicitly recognize that the people's faith in God and most priests is intact; it's their faith in the Church's leadership that has rightly faltered.

A Lovely Day for an Excommunication

I had "grave sin" down pat. Scott and I were still engaging regularly in the sin that cries out to heaven for vengeance. Our debauched gay lifestyle went something like this:

1. Come home after work on Friday night.
2. Open bottle of wine.
3. Prepare butternut squash "boats," candied beets, and pepper-rubbed steak topped with a fig reduction.
4. Endlessly bicker about whether the black leather sleeper sofa I purchased without permission is a complete abomination.
5. Agree that at least we can agree on the pew.
6. Set table and light candles.
7. Eat.
8. Watch the latest Netflix DVD.
9. Fall into bed exhausted at 10 P.M.
10. Engage in a little sin that cries out to heaven for vengeance.
11. Sleep.

Serving as Satan's full-time handmaiden was out of the question. He would have fired my ass in a heartbeat. As Scott will attest, I can't so much as boil an egg, fold laundry, or clean up after myself in the kitchen — let alone turn down the Evil One's sheets.

Making my sin manifest was my weak point. Sure, I had come out to the Three Hale Marys, Tony Cinnabonini, and Fathers Francis,

Myron, and Bear-Daddy. The chancery had received a deluge of my letters to Archbishop Seán and Reverend Kick-Me. The cameras caught me prancing around the Massachusetts State House during the rallies for gay marriage.

Yet no denunciations came my way. It was quite disappointing. My dreams of tightly wound parochial-school-trained albino monks sacrificing me on the altar and burying the corpse in the secret passageway between the friary and the nunnery of the Poor Sisters of St. Clare didn't come true. Bringing to life my best fantasies of near-martyrdom — in which I snatched the assassin's bullet out of the air midflight, held its metal jacket to my lips, and blew it cool while staring down my assailant — proved impossible.

In April 2004, the Archdiocese of Boston gave me a chance to correct the problem. Through its lobbying arm, the Massachusetts Catholic Conference, the chancery made available a video to play in place of a homily. ("We interrupt our regularly scheduled Mass to bring you this brief political announcement. . . .") This was the video that pitted senior citizens against gay couples and drove Jean Marchant toward ordination. An Associated Press story that appeared in the *Boston Globe* reported that the video "says civil unions 'discriminate against the poor and needy' and will hurt the economy by paying out Social Security survivor benefits."

This article compelled me to dash off a letter to the *Globe* condemning the video for such silly and legally inaccurate propaganda. The consequences of this manifestness were immediate. Anonymous, irate Catholics left messages on my home answering machine accusing me of being a liar and a pervert. The inbox of our Romentics Web site brimmed with nasty messages (cc-ing the *Globe*).

I began to look both ways for stalkers and nutjobs when exiting my condominium. The division between manifestness and martyrdom had narrowed. Where was my trusty parish rooster when I needed him? He would have pecked the bastards to death.

XI

Living on the Liturgical Edge

To really understand the good Samaritan story today, you must replace the good Samaritan with the good Muslim. The good queer. The outsider, when all the establishment people walked on by.

— Andrew Sullivan

The Good Queer

 HE COBBLED SQUARE at Boston's Old State House was full of clean, hot young products of the parochial school system who had probably never masturbated in their entire lives. They accosted passing strangers and bribed them with offers of free pizza. A priest descending the stairs with the grace of a prom queen shook my hand and bade me welcome. An elderly nun in a blue habit guarded the sign-in sheet. She looked poised to critique my penmanship with a wooden ruler.

"E-mail, too!" she demanded shrilly. It wasn't optional.

Beyond the nun stood a spare friar dressed in the usual brown robe with knotted cord. A silver cross hung from his neck to his waist, and he wore a square gold ring on the third finger of his right hand. (*Mixing gold and silver? Naughty.*) Before my brain could register what I was looking at, a small, energetic bald man in a suit and too-thin tie seized my hand and shook it warmly.

"Welcome. Have some pizza," he said. "His Eminence is about to begin."

The other men in the audience wore pocket squares and tie pins in an old-school Irish lace-curtain way you would never mistake for gay. Elegant colonial seafaring paintings hung on the walls. At regular intervals, the subway passing beneath the State House caused the room to shake. At the sight of the wide pine floorboards, the real estate agent in me began assessing an asking price.

Archbishop Seán took his place at the podium not eight feet from my front-row seat. He was wearing unfashionable square glasses. His hair and beard had mostly gone white, but a little gray remained in his neatly trimmed mustache. The hood of his brown robe revealed a quilted lining that I found touching.

O'Malley's voice was deep but gentle, without a hint of frivolity. Gray, maybe — gay, no. He kicked off with a well-worn story. Before becoming archbishop of Boston, Seán had visited a church on Martha's Vineyard. The church had stained glass windows that read, each word on a successive panel: Go — and — sin — no — more. But because it was summer, the pastor had opened one window to catch the sea breeze, changing the admonition to read: Go — and — sin — more.

The assembled crowd guffawed and made clear that, whatever sins they might have committed, failure to appreciate the archbishop's sense of humor was not one of them.

H'O'Malley?

I know you're dying to know: *Is he or isn't he?*

In the interests of full disclosure, I have virtually no gaydar. Having come out late, I am a sorry excuse for a homosexual. I have the Gay Voice, but no clue when it comes to symbols, signals, intentions, indications, gestures, winks, signs, bitchery, double entendres, and twilight lives. I have trouble distinguishing Prada from Payless. 'Nuff said.

Anyway, back to our regularly scheduled dishing — *is he or isn't he?*

- *Wears a brown dress.* This cuts two ways: it is a dress, but the Franciscan robe is hardly going to cut it during Fashion Week. (Neutral.)
- *Loves opera.* His sister's favorite childhood memory is Seán bringing her to *Madame Butterfly.* (Homorific.)
- *Believes in the power of architecture.* In 1999, O'Malley blamed church architecture for the decline in prayerful silence before Mass, noting that churches no longer looked like churches due to the "suburbanization of the new Jerusalem." (Homorific. Not since Nick Gaetano's paintings for Ayn Rand's books has art had so much power.)
- *Navy blue socks, brown habit.* His own sister outed him on this fashion faux pas. Maybe he can get a braided leather belt to match. (Straight.) Bonus: For the 2007 World Series, Seán switched to red "sox."
- *Theater major.* In his teens, the Brown Bag reportedly was "active in theater" at Saint Fidelis Minor Seminary, a feeder school for students considering joining the Franciscan order. (Homorific.)
- *Fatty diet.* According to newspaper reports, "A steaming bowl of chowder or a heaping plate of pasta are O'Malley's favorites when he goes out to eat." As we gays all know, carbs = grave sin. (Straight.)
- *Hates MTV.* In 2004, Seán publicly denounced MTV as "poisonous." Not gay, not straight, just Sean without the fada — old. (Neutral.)
- *Doesn't like to touch girls.* On Holy Thursday, clerics traditionally wash parishioners' feet in imitation of Christ, who washed the disciples' feet at the Last Supper. Seán refused to touch any girlfeet, demanding men only. (Super homorific.)
- *Nickname.* Seán used to be known by the nickname "Shags" when he first grew his beard. The name reeks of beer farts and fantasy football. (Super straight.)

Final verdict: A draw.

"We are not at church to be entertained," Seán said. "Mass-going makes sense when we know how to pray." He extolled silence for its many gifts of grace and told us that the gift of the Spirit was bestowed in the context of a worshipping community.

"Many people see Catholicism as the Church of No," Seán said. "No this, no that. But it is a Church of Yes. Yes to God, yes to life, yes to the beatitudes. Religion is not intended to be used to manipulate people but to humanize them."

But that's how you use religion in politics, Seán — to manipulate, nay, intimidate. Isn't that what excommunication is all about? I monitored his speech and mannerisms obsessively, trying to mine useful clues. *There must be more*, I thought. *There must be a code, secret signals I'm not seeing. Seán is no soaring demagogue. He's not a natural charmer.* The weird intensity of my feelings made me think that if I wrote him another letter, a marshal with a restraining order would show up at my door.

Seán continued, "The *authentic* practice of Catholicism humanizes people."

Murmurs of assent rose from the crowd at this backhanded reference to an *inauthentic* practice of Catholicism. Seán and his audience clearly had divided the sheep from the goats. A gay, irreverent porn writer? They might as well have given me cloven hooves and tattooed 666 on the back of my head.

"We must accept the call to discipleship," Seán said. "We must not only love our neighbor, but also the stranger and our enemy." The weight Seán placed on the word *enemy* made clear that he was referring to all of us inauthentic Catholics.

At the end of Seán's speech, I raised the question that started me on this book. "Archbishop Seán, what should a Catholic do with the anger that develops at those whose views are diametrically opposed but whose good faith must be credited in an era where fury is the medium of discourse, political and cultural?"

Seán flashed me a look full of patience and experience and then said, "If we're always expressing anger, then we'll never change hearts."

Before I could follow up, someone else asked, "How do we answer lapsed Catholics who have switched to another faith where they say they are more comfortable?"

Seán answered, "The more we discern the riches of our faith, the more able we are to respond. People who dismiss the Church often make the mistake of failing to look at its doctrines globally in relation to each other. To take the teaching in an isolated way does violence to it."

Introspection and guilt blocked out the rest of the Q&A. If I had come to express anger and get excommunicated, how could I hope to change hearts? Was I just taking the Church's teachings in an isolated way?

Archbishop Seán took a position at the top of the stairs as we filed out. It was the perfect opportunity for the leper's kiss. My mind struggled to find the right words. In my head, the confrontation took this form: "Archbishop Seán, I'm a proud gay Catholic in a long-term, monogamous, spirit-filled relationship. The anger about which I questioned you is the anger I feel toward you. You make me angry. Do you have any advice for how I should deal with that anger, you bastard?"

Even as I put my question together, that phrase, "long-term monogamous relationship," rankled. As if my complaint would be less legitimate if I were a big whore. *All are welcome*, I reminded myself. *It wouldn't be any different if I were Ward and June's fun-loving son.*

This internal debate, coupled with a childish reluctance to profane a priest, hijacked my gay voice. My speech came out like this: "Please-tomeetyoummmmm." The line moved on. Before I knew what had happened, I was out in the street, and the archbishop was behind me.

What happened? Excommunication appealed to my instinct for martyrdom. It was a chance at another minute of fame, as interest in gay romance novels cooled. It also sounded cooler than philately or making religious dolls.

The cause was familiar from conversations with priests: I feared getting tossed out. I feared becoming a stranger. I feared losing the experience of the Spirit. I feared losing Father Myron, the Three Hale Marys, the G-L Spirituality Group, Ye Olde Piety Show, and the skeptical little old ladies showering me with praise. What I really sought from Seán was excommunication lite. Excommunication with a seat belt and training wheels. Not the real thing.

After work, I stopped by St. Anthony's and sat in the back pew. Relief and exhaustion washed over me. My eyelids drooped. The combined odor of incense, sweat, candle wax, cedar, wet feet, and floor polish filled my nose. Restless sighs escaped the faithful. Perhaps a tear rolled down the cheek of the plaster virgin. It was so easy to believe in a great big miracle, so easy to say, "Lord, I am not worthy. Only say the word, and I shall be healed."

That night, at home, I engaged in an act of self-love that makes masturbation and YouTubing look like works of charity. I Googled myself. An obscure site informed me that my surname derives from the Latin *ponte fractus*, which means "broken bridge." In contrast, the word *pontiff*, commonly used for the pope, derives from the Latin *pontifex*, "bridge builder."

Myriad interpretations suggested themselves, but the one that kept coming to mind was that my quest would not only fail to build bridges — through baldness and otherwise — but doom the few not yet burned.

Tuesdays with Anthony

Tuesday at the Shrine meant retrieving three-inch-thick brass discs about twice the circumference of a hockey puck from the back room of the sacristy. Each puck functioned as an oversize locket, containing a chunk of the body of Saint Anthony of Padua himself. After each Tuesday mass, the eucharistic ministers stood on the chancel with a purificator in one hand and a brass puck in the other. One by one, the parishioners approached and bowed their heads.

Why Tuesday? Why not Wednesday? Or Thursday? Or the second Saturday in June? Because Saint Anthony's friends brought his body to the friary at Padua for burial on a Tuesday. Those who prayed for Anthony's intercession on that day reaped miracles, rewards, and other spiritual bonus points. Ever since, the devoted have tuned in on Tuesdays, hoping lightning will strike twice.

A shortage of ministers forced me to serve as a relic holder on one Tuesday. A line formed in front of me. I smiled inanely, wanting to greet the parishioners, congratulate them, or perhaps perform some liturgical dance. Some parishioners kissed the holy puck. Others bussed cheeks as if greeting a socialite. Some only touched the puck with their fingertips. Before the next parishioner approached, I wiped the puck "clean" with my purificator.

Mary Flanagan approached the puck, closed her eyes, and looked beatific. As she pursed her lips, a voice spoke loud and clear, as if from on high:

This is idolatry.

The voice belonged neither to God nor Mary. It was Gram's. I was channeling Gram. Had Gram a chance to observe all this puck-kissing, she'd have had a field day. A hundred Catholics grubbing after a lock of hair of unproven provenance would have engendered in her a fit of high-Protestant protestation and renewed visions of tunneling priests.

No one in my family ever went out of his or her way to lock lips with a bone fragment. No doubt parochial school kids better understood the practice, but it smacked of voodoo — as if Saint Anthony's DNA had the power to transmit magical vibes, but only if you came within inches. Call it the germ theory of spiritual contagion.

My Baltimore Catechism gave the following explanation:

> Q. *Why do we honor the relics of the Saints?*
> A. Because their bodies were temples of the Holy
>   Ghost and will one day rise from the dead to eter-
>   nal glory.

Well, of course — body temples. That clears the whole thing up.

Wouldn't the modern Church prefer to hide relic worship away and pretend it doesn't exist — like a crazy spinster aunt, a flamboyantly homosexual archbishop, or, for that matter, a pedophile priest?

Father Daniel Hennessey, vocations director of the Boston archdiocese, explained that reverence for relics dates to the early centuries of Christianity. In the days of Roman persecution, many Christians were killed because they refused to renounce their faith. According to Father Hennessey, "Christians would gather around the mortal remains [of the early martyrs] in order to remember the love by which these martyrs witnessed to Christ and to be strong in their own faith and courage in the face of possible martyrdom for themselves."

After the Romans stopped persecuting Christians, believers transferred the remains of martyrs to sites where churches were to be built. In fact, for hundreds of years, the Vatican actually required that every church house a relic under its altar, along with a certificate of authenticity from Rome. No relic, no certificate — no Mass, no way. The altars of eighteen European churches house the foreskin of Jesus, known as the Holy Prepuce, which has the power to make sterile women fertile. I am not making this up. Christ must have been terrifically popular on the biblical version of ManHunt.net if his manhood was sufficiently large to supply eighteen separate sites with skin.

The rules regarding altar relics changed after Vatican II. Nowadays, with O'Malley closing and consolidating churches, the archives of the archdiocese overflow with used relics from over 170 saints: bone fragments, scraps of cloth, and fabric soaked in a saint's blood.

But these were the B-list relics. Even in the twenty-first century, certain relics outrank others, and the archdiocese was playing host to a particularly famous specimen, the kind of relic that had its own paparazzi: the sacred heart of Saint John Vianney, curé of Ars.

Stealing the Sacred Heart

Saint John Vianney, a diocesan priest in France, had a great talent for reading the hearts of penitents. Surviving on only a few hours of sleep and some boiled potatoes, he regularly spent fourteen to eighteen hours a day in the confessional. Tens of thousands of Catholics, including bishops and aristocracy, sought spiritual counsel from him. To accommodate the worshippers, France built a special railroad link from Lyon to Vianney's hometown. They even printed holy cards bearing Saint John's picture, the spiritual equivalent of baseball trading cards. "I'll give you one 1430 Joan of Arc for three 1858 Saint Johns, an 1820 Mother Seaton, and I'll throw in a Holy Prepuce to boot!"

Venerating relics earns you indulgences, which, in simplified terms, are like getting time off for good behavior. Each indulgence reduces your stay in purgatory and hastens the journey to heaven. As an accomplished porn writer with a body more like a carport than a temple of the Holy Ghost, I set aside my skepticism. A little sacred time with the heart of a power confessor could do me no harm.

Spiritual Generally Accepted Accounting Principles (GAAP)

I make my living chasing after people who cook the financial books, but we all know that the most deceitful accounting takes place in our moral ledgers. We debit ourselves a few points for sins and credit ourselves for good deeds. Saintly intercessions and indulgences boost the bottom line — graces, too. From time to time, we petition that certain sins count against those who led us astray, and we seek to transfer credit for others' good works to our own account. During most quarterly periods, I operated in the spiritual red, taking a huge advance against my moral allowance and suffering the most usurious terms of repayment.

Like a Wal-Mart with limited supplies of the latest Xbox offering during Christmas season, the cathedral was mobbed. The line of penitents reached from the altar to the doors. And the crowd didn't — or didn't exclusively — consist of kooks or religious wingnuts, either. They appeared to be normal folk of immoderate faith. There were more old people than young, but ages ranged from single to triple digits, and at least two twenty-somethings, wearing designer jeans and untucked oversize striped shirts, would have been at home at Google headquarters or a Coldplay concert.

In the narthex, the cathedral's foyer, a stern blue nun handed me a flyer that informed me that Saint John's body had been exhumed after he was beatified. This practice, a canon law tradition, allowed for identification of the body as well as documentation of a potential miracle — in particular, whether the potential saint's flesh had decomposed. The Church viewed bodily incorruptibility as a sign of moral incorruptibility. Thus, a preserved body supported sainthood.

Despite the passage of years, Saint John's body had been entirely free of decomposition. The French therefore decided to cut the saint's heart out of his chest.

Wait. *What? Why on earth would they do that?*

The blue nun's flyer did not elaborate, but the absence of explanation or justification suggested this act should be attributed to Gallic whimsy. *Those crazy Gauls!*

Personally, I pictured three or four dignified Frenchmen in berets gathered around a fresh hole in the ground. The saint's coffin sits off to the side, its lid tilted at a precarious angle. The Frenchmen stare down at the saint's corpse. The gravedigger leans on the handle to his shovel. As a group, they cross themselves and eat some Brie. The gravedigger smokes a Gauloise Blonde.

"*Eh, Jacques, regarde!*" says the gravedigger. "*Il est bien préservé, n'est-ce pas?*" (Hey, Jack, check out how well preserved he is.)

"*Mais oui,*" Jacques says. "*Qu'est-ce qu'on va faire?*" (What should we do?)

"*Dit le curé.*" (Tell the priest.)

"*Merde! Que le curé aille se faire foutre!*" (Screw the priest!)

"*Oh la la! Alors, faisons une autre pause de Brie et Gauloise.*" (Well, we might as well take another Brie-and-Gauloise break.)

"*Bonne idée!*" (Good idea!)

The Frenchmen break out a jug of wine and a baguette and insult each others' mothers for a while. When they finish, the gravedigger jumps up and inspects the corpse.

"*Quel dommage! Il paraît que quelqu'un a déjà volé le prépuce.*" (Too bad. Looks like someone already got the foreskin.)

The Frenchmen confer and drink more wine. After they finish another jug, the gravedigger again stumbles to his feet.

Brandishing the Brie knife, he shouts, "*Je sais ce qu'il faut faire — à la place du prépuce, découpons son coeur!*" (I know what to do! Instead of the foreskin, let's cut out his heart!)

OK, maybe not, but you come up with a more plausible explanation.

From that day of Brie and Gauloise forward, the heart and body were preserved in separate receptacles in the saint's hometown. The body stayed put, but the saint's extracted heart gallivanted to Rome for canonization in 1925 and was touring again eighty years later.

A case like an antique mantel clock housed the heart. The case sat at the foot of the chancel under a domed ceiling 120 feet high. Like a set of peacocks, five extremely French men surrounded the antique mantel clock. Each wore a plumed hat, white gloves, and a white sash, each with a different colored cape pinned neatly at his lower back. They exuded Gallic dignity.

The long, orderly line of pilgrims snaked down the center aisle. Four wooden prie-dieux (individualized kneelers or prayer benches) formed a semicircle around the reliquary. Father Hennessey directed traffic. When one worshipper rose from a prie-dieu, Father Hennessey directed the next in line to take his place.

Entire families approached en masse. Some of the kids knelt on the floor. A small boy refused to kneel because he was too short to see over the prie-dieu. Each worshipper handed a rosary, saint's medallion, or one of the blue nun's flyers to one of the white-gloved Frenchmen. Like a holy game of hot potato, that Frenchman handed the offering to the next Frenchman, who handed it to the next Frenchman, who laid it for thirty seconds on the reliquary — apparently long enough for the object to soak up a spiritual taint. Holy hot potato was repeated in reverse, from Frenchman to Frenchman to Frenchman to American devotee. Many of the pilgrims prayed during the process with closed eyes; others watched the progress of their offerings from Frenchman to Frenchman with an ill-concealed distrust of Gauls.

A basket for offerings sat in front of the relic. Devotees left both dollar bills and bits of paper with requests for intercession.

Asked to speculate as to what the pilgrims were asking for (aside from time off for good behavior), Father Hennessey said, "They'll ask Saint John Vianney to intercede with God for the Archdiocese of Boston, that the Lord might send to us more men who are called to be ordained priests."

Why do you need a relic to ask for that? Why not just pray and leave the heart in France, where it belongs?

"It's tangible," he said. "Relics are important in Catholic religious practice, not as talismans or good-luck charms, but as reminders of the saints' holiness and as encouragement for others to emulate the saints' behavior."

"Think of Elvis Presley," another priest suggested. "People get on eBay and they'll try to get belongings or artifacts from Elvis . . . because having something of his makes you feel close. For Catholics, having a relic in our presence . . . inspires us because this relic is from the body of a person whose body and soul was for God."

As it turns out, this priest hit the nail on the head: at any given moment, eBay auctions dozens of pieces of Jesus' actual true cross. Many other relics would be available had the site not banned the sale of human remains.

"Seems like idol worship," I suggested.

"It's *veneration*," Hennessey clarified in an interview, "not worship. Worship is for God alone."

"And Jesus and the Holy Spirit."

"God in *all* His aspects," Hennessey said.

The heart itself was brownish with a hint of pink in the middle. No evidence of gel or formaldehyde suggested chemical meddling. The holy absurdity made me want to participate in the spiritual burlesque.

I saw myself snatching the heart from its case, tucking it under my arm like a football, and sprinting down the center aisle. Dodging pilgrims and leaping pews, I sprinted out into the morning light, wildly squandering indulgences. The five Frenchmen chased me with drawn swords and capes flying, seeking to cut out my heart. We ran past the gay urban knickknack emporium where Mary sang her show tunes, past the gay gym where muscle boys spilled out onto the sidewalk to cheer, jeer, and pick up some fleet-footed priests with wandering eyes. We made a hard right turn at Twig, the flower shop, and ran down the Pride parade route, complete with Mardi Gras beads and go-go boys, past the home of the Gay Men's Chorus and the Fenway Community Health Center's AIDS hospice.

Waking from this vision of giddy irreverence, I wondered what the shuffling pilgrims were thinking. They seemed models of piety and goodness. Their faith was palpable and dense, their humility humbling.

Asked whether he regarded the saint's well-preserved heart to be a miracle, Father Hennessey said, "I'd call it an extraordinary reality."

Gram was going to have a hard time accepting the subtle theological shadings that separated veneration from worship, miracles from extraordinary realities, and divine foreskins from the secular variety.

Perhaps because the glory of Saint John's heart had blinded me to his presence, I hadn't noticed that Seán had his own smaller line of pilgrims on the opposite side of the sanctuary. He couldn't compete with the day's headliner.

Joining Seán's line, I told myself I would be firm but kind. I wouldn't lose my temper or my voice. Words wouldn't fail me this time. I'd make elegant and compelling arguments leavened with humor and plainfolk wisdom. I'd confess my homosexuality. I'd point out that there are other vocations besides the priesthood and hetero marriage, other callings — including lectorhood.

"Whaddya gonna do, Seán?" I pictured myself saying. "Cut my heart out? You're not even French!"

At these words of wisdom, Seán would fall down like Saul on the road to Tarsus. He'd repent and rededicate his remaining years to serving as chaplain to the *Queer Eye for the Straight Guy* production set.

When I finally reached the archbishop, his handlers were tugging gently at his sleeves, reminding him of another appointment. He looked weary and stoic. Around his neck hung a reliquary in the shape of a cross.

"Whaddya got in there?" I asked to break the ice, instantly regretting the chatty tone.

"It's a piece of cloth stained with the blood from the stigmata of Saint Padre Pio," Cardinal Seán said. "I got it as a gift."

"Cool." *Cool? Oh, my God. What was I doing?*

"Saint Pio was a Capuchin, too," Cardinal Seán added, beaming as if he, too, might bleed from the feet and ankles someday.

One of the handlers interrupted. "Time to go," he said. "Will you excuse us? Sorry."

"Wait!" I said. I blurted out something confused and long-winded about how the Church's interference in the politics of the gay-marriage fight was demeaning the Church and depleting its resources and gifts, etc.

The handlers drew His Excellency away, blinking rapidly. Had he heard me? A moment later, Elvis had left the building.

"It's my Church, too!" I called after them, weakly repeating this claim to the old man behind me wearing a Red Sox jacket. The man scolded me as if I were one of his naughty children. Not only had I cock-blocked the archbishop, but I'd spoiled his whole spiritual day. He spouted hellfire and the usual panoply of sins, yet tacitly his scolding acknowledged that I still belonged to the great big Catholic family.

The following Tuesday, I returned to Saint Anthony Shrine.

"How's the heart?" Mary Flanagan asked.

"Weird and wonderful," I said.

She laughed softly, as if I'd confirmed her suspicions.

"What brings you here today?" Father Bear-Daddy asked. "It's not Friday yet, is it?"

"I thought I'd volunteer for relic duty," I said.

My discomfort with the brass pucks had evaporated. The show of faith — even blind faith — in St. John Vianney had moved me. The sacred heart was no holy prepuce, but a deep sense of transcendent tranquillity infused the devotions to it.

As the parishioners approached the Saint Anthony relic, their lips moved, citing the cares and worries for which they sought intercession, perhaps praying safe return of sailor sons and warrior daughters from the war in Iraq.

XII

The Empire Strikes Back

If only holiness were measured by the volume of our incessant chatter, we would be universally praised as the most holy nation on earth. But in our fretful, theatrical piety, we have come to mistake noisiness for holiness, and we have presumed to know, with a clarity and certitude that not even the angels dared claim, the divine will for the world. We have organized our needs with the confidence that God is on our side, now and always, whether we feed the poor or corral them into ghettos.

— Charles Marsh, *Boston Globe Magazine*, July 8, 2007

Speaking of Relics

N 2005, I PROSECUTED a criminal securities fraud case against a local lawyer. Defense counsel, a small man with a Napoleonic ego, was an excellent lawyer. Frequently, he wounded our witnesses' credibility on cross-examination. Each time he did, he adjusted his package.

It became routine. Every time he believed he had scored points for his client, all eyes went to his crotch. Sure enough, package adjustment followed. Eventually, the jury no longer listened to him. Instead, they just watched his crotch. Package adjustment? Score one for the defense. No package adjustment? A win for the prosecution. Adjusting his jock substituted for substance. (Ultimately his package failed to impress; the jury convicted his client.)

The same phenomenon played out on the political stage. Gay issues became Archbishop Seán's big spiritual package adjustment. Whenever Seán was on the defensive — because of parish closings or

pedophile priests, for example — he'd lobby politically against gays.
The highlights:

• January 16, 2004: Mails a glossy four-page brochure to a million
Massachusetts Catholics, urging them to help pass a constitutional
amendment banning gay marriage. (Number of glossy brochures sent
to Catholics concerning the pedophile priest scandal = 0.)

• February 2004: Telephones at least one Catholic legislator who
had not yet announced his position on same-sex marriage and urged
that legislator to "vote with the Church." O'Malley instructs other
legislators that they have an obligation to cease receiving communion if they vote "against the Church." (Contrast to his position in
October 1994, when he opposed retail stores' being open on Sundays,
but told voters they needed to become informed and vote their con-
sciences.)

• September 1, 2005: Writes to pastors of the archdiocese "to encour-
age parish cooperation in the campaign" for collecting signatures for a
citizen petition for an amendment banning gay marriage. Permits pastors to collect signatures at parish masses "or to insert copies of the signature petition in your parish bulletin."

• September 21, 2005: Sends letter to Massachusetts Catholics announcing the archdiocese's support for a political organization devoted
to collecting signatures to put an amendment banning gay marriage on
the ballot. The letter explicitly encourages the collection of signatures
after masses and at parish events.

• November 23, 2005: Issues a statement suggesting that Catholics
have a duty to condemn the behavior of their homosexual brothers and
sisters and that such condemnation constitutes an act of love: "If we
tell people that sex outside of marriage is not a sin, we are deceiving
people. If they believe this untruth, a life of virtue becomes all but
impossible. . . . Calling [homosexual] people to embrace the cross of

discipleship, to live the commandments, and at the same time assuring them that we love them as brothers and sisters can be difficult. Sometimes we are told: 'If you do not accept my behavior, you do not love me.' In reality we must communicate the exact opposite: 'Because we love you, we cannot accept your behavior.'"

Read that passage again: a life of virtue is "all but impossible" if you engage in sex outside of marriage. In other words, sexual sin trumps everything else. You could be Mother Teresa herself, but if you allowed another sister under your skirt, hellfire had you for eternity. The archbishop's current vicar general, Richard Erickson, personally suggested that I should take comfort in this particular statement of Seán's love.

• May 5, 2006: Prints letter to Massachusetts Catholics in the archdiocese's newspaper urging them "as soon as possible" to contact their legislators with "personal visits, phone calls, and emails" to urge them to put an amendment banning gay marriage on the 2008 ballot.

• June 30, 2006: Issues statement attributing gay people's desire for equal marriage rights to an "exaggerated sense of entitlement" motivated merely by "personal wants."

• October 22, 2006: Issues statement in which we learn for the first time that the issue that concerns him is not same-sex marriage (what a relief!), "but whether the people have a say."

• November 14, 2006: Ditto.

• December 21, 2006: Sends personal letters to every legislator, urging them to vote to put an amendment banning gay marriage on the 2008 ballot.

• December 29, 2006: Issues statement reiterating the content of the December 21 letter.

With great fanfare, Archbishop Seán signed a petition urging Congress to pass an amendment to the federal constitution banning gay civil marriage. Over and over, the Brown Bag, his lobbying arm, and VoteOnMarriage.org dishonestly repeated a smokescreen that was patently untrue but calculated to win votes: For thousands of years marriage has been the same, a union between one man and one woman.

Thousands of Years, My Ass: A Short History of Matrimony

- The Old Testament describes marriages consisting of one man and many wives.
- Marriage became a sacrament in the twelfth century. That means it *hasn't* been a sacrament longer than it *has* been a sacrament.
- Until the nineteenth century, marriage constituted a contractual relationship concerning property. The husband had dominion over his wife and her property. Marriage assured the orderly uniting and passing on of family fortunes. It had nothing to do with personal relationships.
- As late as 1917, the Church described the role of marriage as procreation and a safe vessel for men's nasty sexual urges. Only in 1930 did it first decide that the unity of spouses was also important.
- On October 29, 1951, Pope Pius XII (the only pope to invoke papal infallibility, to put forth the dogma of the assumption of Mary) suggested, for the first time ever, that married couples could engage in sex in ways that did not lead to conception provided they used no actual contraceptives.

Although he preached chastity, when it came to same-sex marriage, Seán proved promiscuous, even wanton. So long as you stood against it, he wouldn't turn down an opportunity to join hands. He shared stages with right-wing nutjobs Mitt Romney, Concerned Women for America, and the Family Research Council, whose spokespeople said, among other things, that the "truth of homosexuality" meant a lifetime of AIDS, syphilis, and early death. Several of O'Malley's early statements against same-sex marriage were also signed by the then-bishop of the Diocese of Worcester, Massachusetts, who subsequently left his post in disgrace after being accused of molesting boys years earlier.

Although it had closed sixty parishes due to financial pressures, the archdiocese spent $911,000 on "community relations," including gay marriage opposition, of which half a million went to its lobbying organization, the Massachusetts Catholic Conference (MCC).

Holy Mathematics

Ed Saunders, executive director of the MCC, told me he couldn't provide even an approximation of how much went to opposing gay marriage, though he helpfully conceded that the MCC spent $400 for a spot on EWTN. I performed the following calculation based solely on the January 16, 2004 mailing:

1,000,000 brochures x $0.157 per piece nonprofit standard mail rate = $157,000.

That wasn't so hard, was it, Ed?

The political mobilization was nearly unprecedented. The closest historical echo came from the 1940s, when the archdiocese registered voters, rented billboards, paid for radio advertising, and had priests urge a no vote from the pulpit against a measure liberalizing the state's restrictive birth control law. ("Birth control is against God's law; vote no on Proposition Two.")

Seán's single-minded focus on gay marriage made me feel unfairly singled out. Where was the speech advocating a law forcing non-Catholics to donate to the poor? Why was Seán not seeking a law banning birth control for everybody or making birth control users ineligible for civil marriage? Why wasn't the Church going after civil divorce, clearly at odds with sacramental marriage, and far more of a threat to heterosexual marriages?

Marauding Lesbians Snatch Boston's Children

Seán's opposition to gay marriage didn't squelch my spiritual uplift from the sacred heart of Saint John. No, that happened when he targeted the most vulnerable children in the commonwealth. On February 28, 2006, following the recommendation of Archbishop Gabriel Montalvo Higuera, the papal nuncio to the United States, Seán banned the archdiocese's social service agency, Catholic Charities, from placing orphaned children with gay parents. Not two weeks later, he ordered Catholic Charities out of the adoption business entirely.

Keep in mind, Catholic Charities had placed just 13 children, out of 720, with gay parents. That's less than 2 percent. But rather than tolerate these placements, Seán decided that the archdiocese would help no children at all in the future.

Why? Archdiocesan officials referred to a 2003 statement from the Vatican's Congregation for the Doctrine of the Faith. The Rat wrote "allowing children to be adopted by persons living in [gay] unions would actually mean doing violence to these children, in the sense that their condition of dependency would be used to place them in an environment that is not conducive to their full human development." According to the Rat, placing children in gay households was therefore "gravely immoral."

The clearest proof that lesbian parents are not doing violence to their children is that none has ever chosen me as a godfather. But even if you believe that straight parents provide a better atmosphere for raising children than gay parents, that was not the appropriate comparison. The question was not whether a child got straight parents or got gay parents; it was whether the child got gay parents or *none at all*.

Archbishop Seán believed it was better to leave the kids with no love at all. Indeed, in a 2006 interview, a *Boston Globe* reporter gave O'Malley three chances to disavow, nuance, or more fully explain B16's "violence to children" comment. Each time, O'Malley held the party line, saying the teaching "would not admit of dissent."

The Language of Love

Dear Reverend Kick-Me:

What's up with Seán's language problem? It seems odd that a man who speaks 13,000 languages fluently has difficulty translating the exact philosophical and theological language of the Church into everyday concepts that (A) people can understand and (B) right-wing nutjobs won't be able to use gratuitously and unjustly against us.

Leper kisses,
Scott

Kick-Me left me a phone message in return, saying an old dog can't learn new tricks, even if the old tricks drive people away from the Church in droves: "The Archbishop tends to use formal language, probably because he has been so long in a theological setting. He's unlikely to shift toward colloquial or conversational language. It's more of a personal preference and not something he has taken on lately."

Not every prelate stays inside the theological comfort zone. Francis Cardinal George of Chicago stated that the "concern that language can make it difficult to welcome people is one I share. The Church speaks, in moral and doctrinal issues, a philosophical and theological language in a society that understands, at best, only psychological and political terms. Our language is exact, but it does not help us in welcoming men and women of homosexual orientation. It can seem lacking in respect. This is a pastoral problem and a source of anxiety for me."

To me — and seven members of Catholic Charities' board who resigned in protest — the archbishop's decision regarding adoption caused unspeakable cruelty. It contradicted the scriptures I read from the ambo of Saint Anthony Shrine. A profound sense of spiritual dislocation and estrangement washed over me. That O'Malley would insist on rules that — like B16's description of gay adoption as a form of violence to children — fell so far outside reality as to mark a spiritual ghost town, population zero, boggled the mind. As one priest said, "The Church used to be the biggest supporter of adoption. . . . Its stance [on gay adoption] is a vivid example of the sickness in the Church right now. . . . It's not based on good theology, not on Gospel; it's based on pure oppression."

The archdiocese hosted a gathering of clergy at Boston College at which Archbishop Seán invited priests to come to an open mike and ask questions. Father Butterballino asked for some pastoral advice. "How would I present to the people in my parish what you just said [about gay marriage and adoption] in light of the fact that in my parish are gay and lesbian couples who are committed to each other, who are faithful churchgoers, and are raising their children in the faith? How do I tell them what you just said?"

"Preach the truth," said Archbishop Seán. "Tell them what the Church teaches."

Father Butterballino described his reaction to me a few years later:

> I was so angry. I wanted to scream out, "Do you have any idea what it's like to be in a parish?! Do you know who these people are? Do you know what their lives are like?" How sad that, walking out of the [Q&A session], I should get clapped on the back by so many [priests] thanking me for what I had done. And all I did was ask my bishop a question for some pastoral advice, "How do I do that?" And I got nothing. Nothing. . . . I didn't say, "I disagree with you." I just said, translate that for me for my people. And it was clear he couldn't do that.

Surely puppetry was to blame. Surely some evil force was pulling O'Malley's strings — a group of wooden, tone-deaf political bullies at the MCC pushing him into ugly, graceless pronouncements of which no mother could ever be proud. I wanted to gather the bishops around and say: Guys, how about some kinder, gentler package pulling? How about some more honesty? Run it by me first — I'll review it gratis.

You don't have to change your fundamental opposition; just say it with love. For example, instead of attributing gay people's desire for equal marriage rights to an "exaggerated sense of entitlement" motivated merely by "personal wants," you might acknowledge that love motivates their commitments to others. Instead of calling gay adoption "gravely immoral," you might characterize it as "not ideal." Don't lie about the history of marriage, and don't conflate civil marriage, recognized by the state, with sacramental marriage, recognized — at least since the twelfth century — by the Church. Have facts on your side. The Church could do better. O'Malley could do better. B16 could do a lot better.

Make Your Own O'Malley Homily Kit

Archbishop Seán took the Vatican's paperwork reduction initiative seriously. He so excelled at recycling that you could predict exactly when Seán would throw the Flannery O'Connor story about how boring but compelling the Mass is into a homily or when he would drop the next firecracker about same-sex marriage and the mendacity of the homosexual lobby.

In fact, you can build your own authentic Archbishop O'Malley homily from scratch in nine easy steps:

Step 1. Begin with funny story. (Choose one.)

(A) Martha's Vineyard "Go and sin more" story
(B) Call from receptionist to Fanny Cardinal Spellbound story. (R: "There's a man at the door who says he's Jesus Christ and wants to speak to you. What should I do?" C: "Look busy.")
(C) Story about JFK's 1963 visit to Ireland, during which a general amnesty of the local jail was pronounced. When officials discovered the jail was empty, the constable rounded up townspeople the night before the visit in order to have prisoners to release.

Step 2. Sprinkle anecdotes throughout. (Choose two or three.)

(A) Namaan the Leper, who refused to follow Elisha's instructions because they weren't sufficiently bombastic.
(B) Soccer team in Andes air crash who survived by eating the flesh of their dead friends. (Analogize to Christ offering his body.)
(C) The conversion of Saint Francis, who began kissing lepers.
(D) Aleksandr Solzhenitsyn complaining that men have forgotten God.
(E) Don Quixote, whom people thought crazy but who was actually more sane than others because he saw what was noble, important, and good.
(F) Mother Teresa pushing a wheelbarrow containing dying man filled with maggots.

Step 3. Add some deep reflections on marriage. (Choose two.)

(A) Let the people vote.
(B) Gay people have an "exaggerated sense of entitlement" motivated merely by "personal wants."
(C) Gay marriage is a "national tragedy."
(D) "The institution of marriage has been the same since time immemorial: one man and one woman."
(E) The Massachusetts Supreme Judicial Court "blithely" swept aside the true meaning of marriage.

Step 4. Insert clever theology. (Choose one.)

(A) "The Eucharist is God's invention."
(B) "The Gospel tells us to be fishers of men, but too often we become keepers of the aquarium."

(C) "Christ is the bridegroom, never the widower. He does not exist separate from the Church."

(D) Technology is wonderful, but we have lost our sense of sin.

Step 5. Note the persecution of Church in the culture of death.

Step 6. Reflect on obedience and show a deep respect for the conscience and maturity of the flock. (Choose one. Now.)

(A) *Quodcumque dixerit facite.*

Step 7. Remark on the constancy of Church teachings. Disregard the Assumption, Immaculate Conception, the divine appointment of kings, sacramental marriage, the innateness of homosexuality, etc.

Step 8. Insert joke about *Da Vinci Code* and Mrs. Jesus Christ.

Step 9. Sprinkle with a blessing. Bake five minutes.

Serves thousands.

News Flash

Here's the article I wanted to see in yesterday's *Boston Globe*:

Cardinal Seán Pushes New Measure to Strengthen Marriage

BOSTON, Mass. — Today Cardinal O'Malley announced that the Archdiocese of Boston will back a petition drive for an amendment to the Massachusetts Constitution to ban divorce. Noting that divorce constitutes a grave threat to marriage in that it tends to end it, O'Malley promised that churches across the Commonwealth would give parishioners a chance to sign the petition. "The legalization of divorce is a national tragedy," Cardinal Seán said. "Divorce is contrary to the constant teachings of the Church and to God's plan. Divorced people have an exaggerated sense of entitlement motivated merely by personal wants and that doesn't consider what is good for children and society." O'Malley added, "People have redefined marriage as if it were merely for the entertainment and benefit of adults, but it is really about the children. And the best place for raising children is a family with one mother *and* one father. That's what those children are going to get, or we'll ship them off to a Romanian orphanage, goddamnit."

As O'Malley put his signature to the petition, he added, "By the way, the Church's political efforts should not be construed as discrimination against divorced people. Even divorced people have human dignity worthy of respect. They're big quitters, nonetheless."

Then I woke up and put aside the bottle of rubber cement. It was time to face facts.

How Great the God That Made an Asshole Like You

Father Bear-Daddy paled when it came to enforcing the rules. Far more potent and poisonous are orthodox Catholic bloggers, a strange subculture of Pharisee snitches linked in a self-approving Internet circle jerk. They take their chief pleasure in life from spying on parishes and denouncing perceived liturgical deviants to the local ordinary. These people got beat up even on the parochial-school playground.

Rather than Christ, they worship rules, canons, laws, edicts, and the General Instruction of the Roman Missal — the official playbook for saying Mass. According to the league of snitches, liturgies everywhere didn't count because jazz friars like our Father Justin strayed from the game plan. The snitches frequently twisted their knickers in a knot over:

- holding hands during the Our Father
- children on the chancel during consecration
- ingredients in the holy wafer recipe
- glass vessels for the sacred species instead of metal
- priestly handshaking during the exchange of peace

But for our snitchery, the bloggers intimated, renegade Catholics would be making burnt offerings, worshipping golden calves, proclaiming our allegiance to Gaia, and maybe even permitting gay folks on the altar.

Quodcumque Dixerit Facite

Vatican II expressly rejected the rules-based, strict-obedience model of Archbishop O'Malley and the league of snitches: "[Christ] fulfills his prophetic office not only through the hierarchy who teach in his name and by his power but also through the laity. He accordingly establishes them as witnesses and provides them with an appreciation of the faith and the grace of the word so that the power of the Gospel may shine out in daily family and social life." Accordingly, among those venerated as saints are those who dissented from then-current Church teaching and stood up to episcopal bullying:

- Mother Théodore Guérin: a nun who lived in Indiana in the mid-1800s and whom B16 canonized in 2006. Her own bishop expelled her from her convent, demanded that she resign as mother superior, banished her from Indiana, and forbade communication with her fellow nuns.
- Joan of Arc: burned at the Church's request in 1431, canonized by B15 in 1920.
- Thomas Aquinas: the Church questioned his writings when they first appeared, but canonized him fifty years after his death.

- Mother Mary MacKillop: a nun excommunicated by her bishop in 1871, reinstated by Pope Pius IX the next year, and beatified by J2P2.

Even B16 used to believe in the primacy of conscience over rules: "Above the pope as an expression of the binding claim of Church authority stands one's own conscience, which has to be obeyed first of all, if need be, against the demands of Church authority."

Sometimes the snitches escape the blogosphere and make undercover forays into real life. Throughout the history of the Jesuit Urban Center, self-appointed spies took to its pews, seeking liturgical improprieties and sermons on gay topics. Reverend Kick-Me told me that certain gay-marriage foes canvassed every parish and reported back to the chancery those that refused to make petitions available or preach in sufficiently fire-and-brimstone terms about the evils of gay people in love.

The Protestant Catholic Church

Rules-based snitchery has become a peculiarly American phenomenon. As one priest put it:

We are an American Protestant church calling ourselves Catholic. When something comes from Rome we follow it. In Italy, they thank the leader for the dead letter and the guidance and they do nothing. They work it out pastorally. . . . That goes on at every level. I remember on Vatican radio after some pronouncement condemning homosexuality, the question was, "How are you going to deal with [a] gay couple?" The answer was, "You've got to work it out, because better for them to be together than to be going to bars."

Several people who had done missionary work in Latin America told me that priests routinely took concubines and had children. My parents, who spent four years as medical missionaries in Africa in the late 1990s, reported that married priests were

> the norm, not the exception. As another American priest told me,
> "It's only here that we take celibacy seriously."

The anonymous meanness of the snitches' blogs reveals an un-Christian bearing that does more damage than a little offhand, new-age religion in a homily. But sympathy and compassion for another's errors don't make for interesting blogs; the snitches want nastiness, not virtue. Every time I read one of these blog entries, I wonder how the authors call themselves human. I shake my head and think, *How great the God that made an asshole like you, how vast His creativity*.

Unintended Consequences

Archbishop Seán's spiritual package adjustments had an effect he never intended. His words encouraged snitchery that threatened my physical safety. On Ash Wednesday, 2004, a group of zealots staked positions at the Shrine's front door. They accosted those arriving for ashes and pressed flyers on them, promoting a book called *Defending a Higher Law: Why We Must Resist Same-Sex Marriage and the Homosexual Agenda*.

Excerpts from *Defending a Higher Law*

- Criminal law should be used to punish private homosexual acts, because homosexual acts are "intrinsically evil," whether public or private.
- Any association that "promotes" homosexuality should be outlawed because the purpose of such an association is "evil," "illegitimate," and "proscribed under natural law." (Anybody see any First Amendment issues?)
- "We will show how the [homosexual] movement has a worldview based on a false morality and a neo-pagan mystical eroticism that is completely opposed to a Christian worldview and natural law."

Father Bear-Daddy several times demanded that the zealots leave. After each request the pamphleteers moved away, but then sneaked back to their original positions. Father Bear-Daddy then stood next to the zealots, telling people to whom they offered a flyer that it was anti-Catholic and anti-Franciscan. Father Bear-Daddy also put a garbage can in the lobby with one of the flyers pasted to its side and a sign that said, "Deposit here." Finally, Father Bear-Daddy called the cops.

"If we put 'All are welcome' on the door, then all are welcome. At the same time, we have zero tolerance for those who harangue, scream, and shout, or disrespect what this place is. Jesus entered into relationships with people — and through those relationships lives changed. He didn't insist that this and that must change first," Father Bear-Daddy explained.

Despite Father Bear-Daddy's fierce defense, the Snitches grew emboldened. They regularly trashed announcements concerning the G-L Spirituality Group. They scribbled hell and damnation on them and shoved them into Saint Anthony's "bread box," a receptacle for donations for the hungry.

On Valentine's Day, 2005, the director of evangelization at the Shrine received a bitter voice mail. The caller requested that she tell Father Bear-Daddy that "they" would be coming for him, that Father Bear-Daddy would know who "they" were, that he was a disgrace of a priest, that he had no balls, and that *she* had no balls. (A few seconds later the caller conceded parenthetically, "Of course you have no balls.") The caller urged Father Bear-Daddy to "go back to Rhode Island where all that vermin and filth come from." The caller appointed a specific Sunday mass three weeks later as the day on which "they" would show up.

"Did they?" I asked.

"No," she said, "but we hired a police detail just in case."

Over the next few months, someone regularly marked up the Shrine's weekly bulletins with words like "Repent!" and slipped them under the door of the director's office. The penmanship pointed to parochial school. Neat and clear, the writing in places had torn through the page from the force of the writer's rage.

"Go join the Unitarians and their female bishops!" one defaced bulletin read. In the margin next to the notice of another G-L Spirituality Group meeting, another said, "Tell them the truth!"

"I'm afraid someday someone will show up and be . . . well, *disruptive*," Mama Bear confessed. Sure enough, a few weeks later, a scary, silver-haired gentleman showed up at the G-L Spirituality Group meeting with a small Dunkin Donuts coffee in his hand and a lot on his mind. He pulled out a breviary. His lips moved frantically as he read.

Bigotry Mad Libs

Like teenagers who think they have invented sex, every bigot thinks that he has just invented hatred. History, however, shows that bigotry relies on a script. Each generation fills in the blanks with its own villains. Indulge in the following:

_____ engage in blasphemy, immorality, cruelty, and acts of a "subversive nature." The _____ lecherous engage in "continuous acts of unspeakable depravity." Their practices involve all sorts of personal vice. Good people should not be duped into believing _____ is harmless and indifferent. In fact, the _____ have turned _____ into a "moral cesspool" with their "vile propensities." Accordingly, a committee will root out depravity of this kind in _____.

Pop quiz! Circle the letter you think applies to the paragraph above:

(A) Snitches condemning the gay lifestyle.
(B) B16 letting loose in the Vatican and forming a committee to root out homosexuality in the seminaries.
(C) None of the above.

If you chose "C," you win. That paragraph reflects Protestant Boston condemning Irish Catholics in the eighteenth and nineteenth centuries.

Each member of the G-L Spirituality Group introduced him or herself and said a little bit about why he or she was there. When it came to him, the gentlemen and his breviary remained silent.

"And your name is?" I prompted.

"Bill," he barked, then looked down into his breviary.

"OK. Welcome, Bill."

Then we tore off our clothes and engaged in a raucous orgy right there on the second floor of the Shrine.

Actually, we read and discussed Archbishop Seán's address concerning the importance of the Eucharist.

Bill's face expressed his overwhelming disappointment. *What, no lust, no recruitment of children, no roasting of human fetuses?*

He stormed out.

For God's sake, I thought, *don't you have more important things to do, like protesting* The Da Vinci Code *or* Harry Potter? *Get a drink — or a hooker or something.*

More Bigotry Mad Libs

In the blanks below, write in the names of the groups you hate. Go on. Give it a try.

> We must educate our brethren on the threat that the powerful and well-funded _____ movement poses to children, marriage, and freedom. _____ groups spend tens of millions of dollars every year to market and normalize their aberrant lifestyles. It's time for good Americans to stand up and resist the demands of this lobby and counter the lies upon which it is built. Most Americans remain ignorant of the tremendous threat to freedom and morality that this radical ideology poses to society. The insidious _____ propaganda has seduced people into believing it's all a matter of choice, not right and wrong. Little by little, the _____ desensitize the public and push acceptance of their immoral lifestyle. The _____ demonize taxpaying Americans and threaten our troops' effectiveness abroad. We must be vigilant in our schools and government offices to make sure the _____

don't get a foothold, and we need to defend our children against their advances.

See, didn't that feel good? Now go to www.SinceMyLastConfession .com for absolution.

What We Look Like

The upcoming wedding of Scott's brother Rory and his fiancée Jezebel filled me with dread. Father Pamplemousse, the backwoods cracker priest they imported from a small town near the Canadian border where Jezebel grew up, would froth about homosexuals and the evils of gay marriage while Rory and Jezebel nodded with smug satisfaction that Truth had been proclaimed and that people like themselves still existed who believed in God and family values, which confirmed for them all the happy choices they had ever made in their whole lives.

Father Pamplemousse proved to be a breathtakingly queeny, roly-poly cleric who had obviously sublimated his sexual desires into gustatory desires. Rory and Scott were standing in the sacristy, tweaking their tuxedos and nipping at the unconsecrated wine, when Scott compared the half-naked Christ on the crucifix to his own performance in a production of Terrence McNally's *Corpus Christi*.

"I have much better abs," Scott boasted. "People should worship *me*."

At just that moment, Father Pamplemousse appeared at the door. Hearing Scott's comment, he threw back his head and laughed — a jolly cleric untroubled by blasphemy.

Gram and I sat together and watched the Catholic kookery unfold. *So that's what we look like! Automatons pressed into ill-fitting rental tuxes and twice-worn suits making empty, thoughtless gestures, jerked from knees to feet to ass and back again like puppets*. At the alleluia, Father Pamplemousse's voice cracked. The entire congregation dutifully repeated the error. We shuffled forward in the communion line as if we were headed to work in a gulag. Rory bowed too low. The old woman should have removed her doily and let her hair hang free. Father

Pamplemousse should have preached with a less gay voice. The service should have been deeper, less obvious, more meaningful. *Don't pay the least attention to these Catholics, Gram. Or to me. We can be better than we seem, honest.*

Gram, of course, saw what she wanted to see: idolaters, pedophiles, priests off to the nunnery, and too many books in the Bible.

See that? See that? That's not bread anymore, that's the Lord! Did you see it change? Hand quicker than the eye and all that, huh? I wanted her to acknowledge the Living Presence, to worship it — to become Catholic.

What's that you say, Gram? Can you have a taste? Oh, no, sorry. Only we can eat the Eucharist — B16's strict orders.

A few nights later, after a family dinner, Scott and Rory argued all night about religion. Bitterness and booze fueled the conversation. Scott could see only the Church's bad works, its condemnations.

Embracing oppression, Jezebel chimed in, "Everywhere people shit on the Church — especially you!"

"Oh, boo-hoo," I said. "You want oppression and persecution? Try being gay. No one's feeding Christians to the lions anymore, but people are still killing homosexuals for being who they are."

The dispute raged on into the night through paper-thin walls. Scott's mother butted into the argument to forestall fisticuffs. She insisted her son would be happier and less angry if he found God.

Scott said that he *was* happy, and normally not angry. But it was apparent both statements were lies. Correcting himself, he said, "It's not godlessness that makes me unhappy. It's the way you people who say you believe in God act and talk."

That Flushing Sound Is Charity Going Straight down the Drain

Scott and I learned by accident that my brother and sister-in-law — Mikaela's parents — had voted for George Bush in the 2004 election. The announcement came at a dinner party months after the fact. With a Cheshire cat smile, my brother said: "This is a Bush household."

My jaw dropped open, and he repeated: "This is a Bush household."

His wife sidled up behind him and slipped her arm over her shoulders. They preened.

My brain whirled. I bit my lip so hard it bled. It was all I could do not to stomp out.

His wife pressed the issue. She wanted to complain about John Kerry's flip-flopping, the Democrats' lack of ideas, and a hundred other complaints.

"We need to stop talking about this," I muttered. It was inconceivable that — in front of my boyfriend — they could express support for a man as antigay as George Bush, a man who expressed support for a federal constitutional amendment banning same-sex marriage.

"But —"

"We need to stop talking about this *now*."

My anger exploded in the safety of our car an hour later. I railed against my brother and his wife. I called my sister and railed to her. When I got home, I let loose with my poison-letter-writing habit. It was two in the morning. There was no light in the room except from the screen of my laptop.

Dear Bruce (I wrote):

Fuck you.

I stared at the phrase for a few minutes. I had trouble coming up with anything more. The phrase seemed so perfectly to capture my feelings, as if the words had been invented solely for my use on this very day, and all other uses prior and into the future were purely accidental and necessarily inapt.

Nevertheless, I continued:

I could not go another minute letting you get away with staying inside your tiny, claustrophobic breeder's cocoon. You have fucked me, you Judas.

I stared at the words. They seemed of reasonable biblical wrath, and I continued on in much the same vein for about ten single-spaced pages ending with a promise: *I'll remember this. I'll remember it forever.*

Out of habit (and out of truth), I started to type "l-o-v-e" as the closing before my signature. Then I stopped. Shaking with rage and indecision, I stared at the finished page. Send it? Don't send it? Drive back to Bruce's house and murder him in his sleep?

I tore the pages from the printer and thrust them in Scott's face. Sitting on the pew, he read the letter and remained silent for a long while.

"Well?" I demanded.

"Don't be a hypocrite," he said.

"What? Are you taking their side? Who'd *you* vote for?"

"How do you think I feel about your participation in the Catholic Church? You even give money to them! This is no different."

I reminded him about the good works the Shrine does. For the hundredth time, I touted the Shrine's autonomy and the fact that the proceeds of its collected baskets never reached the archdiocese.

He shook his head. "Don't you think your brother can find excuses for Bush, too? He'll say he voted for Bush despite the antigay thing, not because of it. Just like you say about the Catholic Church."

"That's not the same thing at all," I fumed, full of irrational resentment. We argued all night, a reprise of the fight Scott had had with Rory and Jezebel. At dawn, exhausted by the battle, we stared at one another, each of us wondering how he could possibly have less in common with the other, and what capricious bastard first came up with the idea to thrust us together for His own amusement.

XIII

The Super Colon and the Scandal Of Faith

Loyalty and obedience are good values, but obedience to my parents when I was three and they told me don't ever cross the street without holding Mummy's hand, there's a reason behind that. And the reason is not just "because I said." But if I'm thirty years old and I still have to wait for Mum and Dad to hold my hand to cross the street, perhaps I haven't understood the meaning behind the message.

— Father Richard Lewandowski, Diocese of Worcester, Massachusetts

The Success of Snitchery

 UIBBLING ABOUT WHETHER to put one or two scoops of wheat in the holy bread batter doesn't constitute most people's idea of a good time. So it might have been easy to dismiss snitches like Bill the Breviary as just more Catholic kookery — *Oh, those wacky snitches, don't mind them* — except that their penchant for stealth and deception over face-to-face dialogue mirrored the Catholic bishops' standard operating procedure.

Consider Father Walter Cuenin's story. Testifying before the Massachusetts legislature, Cuenin questioned the propriety of a proposed constitutional amendment to ban same-sex marriage. *The New Yorker* quoted him saying that the front rows of Catholic churches should be reserved for divorced people and gays. He received an award at a gay pride ceremony from the Pride Interfaith Coalition for his work for justice. At his suburban parish, he regularly acknowledged his gay parishioners from the pulpit, referenced pride in his bulletin, and baptized the children of gay couples. He also signed a letter calling for the removal of Archbishop O'Malley's predecessor, the panderer Cardinal Law.

Cuenin's activities made him a favorite target of the snitches, who smugly claimed to be sending letters to Rome asking, "How could you allow this man to be a pastor?"

In fact, Cuenin never preached against Church teachings. Instead, he raised questions, and one of his homilies might go something like this:

> The archdiocese is asking Catholics to vote for the amendment banning same-sex marriage, so you should pay attention to the archbishop's letter. At the same time, people are finding that gay couples' adopting children seems to be a good thing. Take a couple of gay guys who adopt children from Romania. You don't have to favor same-sex marriage to think those children are better off with a pair of gay parents than in a Romanian orphanage.

But when O'Malley took over from Law, the situation soured. On July 8, 2005, Bishop Lennon, the vicar general of the archdiocese, wrote a letter to various snitches reporting that Archbishop O'Malley was "very disturbed" by reports that Cuenin had encouraged parishioners to participate in gay pride: "Please know that the archbishop is very disturbed by the information that you, along with others, have sent to him regarding this event and the involvement of Father Cuenin. He wishes to assure you that he is in the process of addressing this whole matter."

"Addressing" soon followed. O'Malley summoned Cuenin to the chancery and asked him to resign from his post. Rather than cite his homilies or legislative testimony — or give no explanation at all — Seán helpfully suggested a few excuses Cuenin could offer his parish, none of which had the benefit of being true.

Cuenin refused the invitation to lie. Shortly afterward, the archdiocese hired a forensic auditor to review the books of Cuenin's parish. The auditor soon "discovered" what the parish's normal auditor had blessed for years: the parish paid for a leased car for Cuenin's use. The parish finance board had approved the lease, but the archdiocese now disallowed the arrangement. For this manufactured impropriety, the archdiocese removed Cuenin from his church in late September 2005.

The Church addressed the "problem" of womenpriests using the same backroom approach. In 2007, the womenpriests persuaded a pastor at Saint Peter's Lutheran Church in New York City to rent his church to them for an ordination. Shortly before the scheduled ordination, a Roman Catholic nun named Sarah Butler got wind of it. Sister Sarah had once written a paper in favor of women's ordination, but she traded teams in the off-season and became a Sambo-style apologist for the Church's refusal to open the conversation to the possibility of ordained women. B16 regularly points to Sister Sarah, tells her to dance, and says, *See, even women don't want to be ordained!*

Sister Sarah visited RomanCatholicWomenpriests.org and saw the announcement of the New York ordination, checking it against the online calendar at Saint Peter's. Instead of calling the pastor directly and expressing her dismay, Sister Sarah e-mailed the nearest Roman Catholic priest, claiming the ordination would "do very serious damage to the relationship between the Catholic and Lutheran (ELCA) churches." As a result of Sister Sarah's sleuthing, two weeks before the ordination, the presiding Lutheran bishop told the pastor at Saint Peter's that he was risking an "international incident" that might have ramifications for Catholic-Lutheran relations. The pastor promptly canceled the contract and disinvited the womenpriests. It was the first time since the Reformation that a Lutheran bishop has taken direction from the Roman Catholic hierarchy.

Within days of averting this potential international incident, B16 reasserted the primacy of the Roman Catholic Church. He approved a document that expressed the view that other Christian communities were either defective or not true churches and that Catholicism provides the only true path to salvation. So much for the spirit of comity and ecumenism that Sister Sarah was worrying about!

My own low-octane brush with the Church's underbelly occurred when I called Father Kick-Me to determine the archdiocese's opinion on gay godparenting. On learning that I was writing this book, he closed our conversation with an oblique but unambiguous shot across my bow. He recounted the story of George Spagnola, a diocesan priest. According to Kick-Me, Spagnola had launched a public protest against a parish closing. Prior to the protest, Spagnola's former male partner (Spag, as he liked to be called, had taken a short vacation from his vow of celibacy) warned that the publicity would likely expose their relationship. Spag foolhardily persisted. He cheerled a protest that garnered extensive media coverage. Three days later, Spag's relationship came to light. He lied that it had been his only relationship — only to be exposed again. Ultimately Spag faced accusations of molesting a child. "The number of people at the second protest was down to about ten," Kick-Me said smugly. "And they were very sullen-looking."

Kick-Me's invocation of Spag's story implied that I, too, should watch my gay ass. Did I really want to make a public spectacle when I had so much to hide? I decided my best course was to launch a preemptive strike. You heard it here first. I:

- murdered a gerbil,
- insisted on my own personal Christmas tree and expected a second set of gifts to surround it,
- threatened the sanctity of marriage,
- failed to recycle my public speeches,
- fried bugs under a magnifying glass in the sun,
- coveted throat lozenges,
- derefrigerated strawberries,
- built more tunnels than bridges,
- self-Googled,
- YouTubed,
- served as Satan's handmaiden,
- wrote dirty stories,
- indulged in non-FDA-approved pharmaceuticals,
- experienced a little sexual tension in conversation with Father Bear-Daddy, and
- held Mama Bear's process-oriented comments against him.

Not having taken any in the first place, I didn't stray from any vows of chastity.

Less Holy

The more the Church defaulted to veiled threats or underhanded action, the more the defensible Church shrunk in my hands, and its spirit slipped out between my fingers. Instead of putting honesty first, the Church offered the pretextual firing of Cuenin, retribution against him and the fifty-seven other signers of the letter demanding Law's resignation, and MCC's dumb show that it couldn't even begin to estimate how much it spent opposing gay marriage.

Why the bullshit? Why the unerring instinct for the untrue? If I couldn't trust the Church on such simple matters, why in God's name would I trust it with my salvation?

My outlook grew less holy. I feverishly collected articles about gay couples oppressed by the Church and contacted them to learn their stories. I subscribed to antigay Catholic blogs and engaged in senseless online warfare. I ran into a group of friars shopping in Downtown Crossing, Boston's low-rent shopping district. With plastic sacks curled round their wrists containing their meager loot, they looked shabby and unbecoming, like the cast-out remnants of a once-powerful family.

The year's bad news piled up like a judgment:

- Mary Flanagan slipped on the wet stairs of the subway, and her hip and collarbone shattered on impact.
- Francis the Franciscan Friar announced he was leaving Saint Anthony Shrine for a parish in Virginia.
- My ex-girlfriend's elderly mother — whom I had loved dearly — signed a petition in support of an amendment banning gay marriage.
- Solely to spite me, B16 made Seán a cardinal, rewarding his loyalty with a red hat.

What next? Mikaela murdered? Scott crushed in a freak pew accident? Gram drowned in the lake? What meaning was I supposed to extract from these events? That rage and persecution would drive me from the Church began to seem like destiny, my loss of faith as inevitable as death and taxes.

> *Help me understand, God. Are you trying to remind me of learned helplessness? Are we two-and-three-quarters times around the chapel with the Devil at hand? You enjoin us to see you in others, but this is the God I see in Cardinal O'Malley: a cheap, mean bastard with a vicious sense of humor. Is this who You are? A God who takes the Church to which I was born and perverts it beyond recognition, so that my heartbreaking pride turns to embarrassment, so that I am forced to explain, mitigate, excuse, and justify? My Lord, for Your sake, give me something to work with here. The lives of the saints are so yesterday.*

My prayers streamed at maximum bandwidth, a drone as loud and steady as city noise. More prayers went up to heaven than ever before, whether in good times or bad, bald times or gay. My steady prattle must have kept Him up nights, prompting Him, no doubt, to question why He didn't do me and Himself the favor of killing me off in my sleep. *If I should die before I wake,* indeed.

Then the archdiocese turned on the goldfish. Two days before the last class at one of Boston's parochial schools was to graduate, O'Malley closed the school in the dead of night, worried that parents would occupy the school the way they had occupied closed parishes. The children showed up the next morning to find padlocks on the doors. They begged to be allowed to recover their belongings left inside, including several bowls of goldfish. The archdiocese, however, was not falling for this clever ruse, for these so-called childish tears. Saint Anthony may have preached to the fish, but Archbishop O'Malley and his minions let them go belly-up.

Selling Holy Rocks

At the annual street fair in honor of Saint Francis, card tables and concession stands lined the sidewalks beneath a giant inflatable saint.
Nurses from the Shrine's Wellness Center were testing blood pressure.
There were free hot dogs and pizza and fresh goldfish. The last of the
religious-goods stores not driven out of business by the Internet set
out a table of rosaries, medallions, and Jesus action figures. Friars
drifted about two by two. Retired priests from the friary across the
street had parked their wheelchairs on the sidewalk and waved benev-
olently.

Lost in resentful meditation, I stalked up and down the block,
cursing this pathetic, dying Church with its repressed sexuality and
barbaric beliefs in black magic and the healing powers of thousand-
year-old chips of bone and foreskin. *May it dissolve into goofy obscurity,
its churches, run by rule-worshipping Teutonic automatons and professional scolders, destined to become museums rather than living vessels of the
Holy Spirit.*

I wanted to bust open the case of religious dolls in Saint Anthony's
lobby and stick pins through them until somewhere a cleric screamed.
I wanted to crash a conference of cardinals, knock miters astray, and
snap crosiers over my knee. Most of all, I wanted to bind the goldfish-
murdering archbishop with his own rosary beads and thrice-knotted
cord. My fury was so hot that everywhere I looked, it started fires.
Nuns jumped out of my way. Children wailed.

At the far end of the block opposite the hot-air Francis stood the
"Super Colon," an inflatable walk-through intestine infested with
polyps, cancers, STDs, and all kinds of other colonic mishaps. The
chief of the Wellness Center, a diminutive nun with a shock of snow-
white hair and a gorgeous Irish accent that reminded me of my
mother, offered to show me around the Super Colon, but I brusquely
assured her that I was reasonably familiar with the geography.

Mama Bear and I took our places at the G-L Spirituality Group
table, set up next to the colon by a nun with a sense of humor. Pam-
phlets explaining the group and its ministry as well as dozens of book-
marks and prayer cards to Saint Anthony littered the table. Stones

served as paperweights to keep random gusts from scattering homosexual literature to the masses like tickertape at the Macy's parade.

Several people picked diffidently at the literature. They really wanted the rocks. "Where did these come from?" "Did you get them from the Holy Land?" "Have they been blessed?" "Are they for sale?"

Mama Bear and I exchanged glances. Father Bear-Daddy would never know if we converted the stones to cash. Anyway, the group needed the money. How else would we keep ourselves in multigrain bars and juice boxes? Just before we consummated the sale, a woman marched up and demanded to know whether we were "condoning this stuff."

"Sales of holy rocks under false pretenses?"

"Homosexuality." Then she quoted Corinthians at me.

I mumbled something about the primacy of conscience.

She pressed, "You *are* telling them the truth?"

I mumbled something about the Super Colon.

"Father Tom told me they're teaching lies here at the Shrine," she said. "About *them*." She tapped a piece of our literature that featured a photo of a smiling homosexual.

Determined to radiate benevolence, understanding, and goodwill, I pasted on a frozen and toothy grin that you could have lifted from my face with a spatula. "I'm one of 'them,'" I explained.

Not surprised, she had obviously assumed my sinfulness, even if she didn't yet know what form it took. She in turn confessed to me her own divorce and her son's multiple adulteries.

"I never judged," she said, "but I told him the truth, and now he has come around. God is good."

She asked for my name and took my hand. She promised to pray for my conversion. I returned the favor. I said I hoped her heart would heal, her boy would make her proud, and God would see fit to convert her thinking on what, precisely, the truth was.

As she walked away, resentment flooded back into my heart. "*Corinthians!*" I muttered. "Corinthians also tells women to cover their heads. Where's your headscarf, bitch?"

I glanced around for support, but Mama Bear had completely dematerialized at the first sign of conflict.

"Where the hell have you been?" I demanded when he returned.

"Washing my hair," he said, flashing an innocent smile.

"You're as bald as I am."

"To get some more Saint Anthony prayer cards," he said, placing three more cards next to the two hundred already on the table.

"You're a bastard."

"I already did my time with one of the lunatics before you came," Mama Bear said.

My right hand tightened around a holy rock. I ached to strike Mama Bear in the temple. There would be no witnesses, and I could hide his body in the Super Colon.

The Cock Crowed for the Third Time

Having walked into a glass door, Father Myron was suffering from a hand wound and dizzy spells. It hurt to see someone I knew and loved grow old before my eyes. I wanted him to stay the way I knew him. To cheer him up — and me — I invited Myron to lunch.

When the food arrived, I dug in, but Myron stayed my hand. "We'll say grace," he murmured.

"Of course we will," I said. "Right after I shoot myself for being such a godless ingrate."

The conversation turned to gays and marriage. Myron's gentle spirit had always struck me as queeny, so it surprised me when Myron began to rant, "Marriage is a sacrament. God created it. It's man and woman. If you didn't have man and woman, there would be no human race at all. So God planned that. And that's what it is. . . . I would like to have the marriage amendment put on the ballot and let the people vote."

I tried to interrupt.

"Let the people vote!" he repeated, slamming his wounded fist down on the lunch table so that our plates jumped.

I tried to take Myron's coming-out to me as a same-sex marriage opponent with the same grace with which he accepted my coming-out as a gay erotica writer. It was hard. In fact, it was all I could do not to stiff him with the check.

Soon after, I attended another same-sex marriage rally. I passively

took out my fury with Father Myron on the assembled crowd, counting missed opportunities to do good as if they were sheep putting my
soul to sleep:

1. An antigay activist was struggling down the steps of Boston
   Common with her stroller, while her husband took care of their
   two other children. An impulse to help her quickly gave way to
   bitchery: *Let Myron give you a hand!*
2. A bitter gay activist confronted the antigay crowd, shouting that
   they all had gay people in their families. I reached out a hand to
   lead him away from the engagement, but immediately dropped
   it. *Fuck it*, I thought. *They deserve this lunatic. Myron can intercede
   if he likes.*
3. An antigay older couple thanked me for letting them pass
   through a doorway at which I had arrived first, but I couldn't
   muster so much as a "You're welcome" in response. *Screw you,
   I'm fresh out of graces — Myron took the last one.*

As if the parish rooster had crowed for the third time, I remembered
the best definition of sin I have ever heard: Sin is a failure to love when
you have the capacity to do so.

My experience of going to Mass changed entirely. Incense now
smelled like moldering garbage. The brass bell sounded like trashcan
lids clanging together. The Book lost its music. Chewbacca remained
a bright spot of pure courage, but also a reminder of inexorable, de-
generative forces at work in the world. For the first time in my life,
opening the lectionary and reading the Bible filled me with fear. No
doubt some elderly Myronic party-line friar would use these passages
against me.

"You are reading to people," Father Abraham once told me, "not
to a ceiling, not to God. He knows the words already: they're His.
Each time you look up during the reading, make contact with a different pair of eyes. Don't sweep the room with your gaze like you would
your back porch. Find an actual person. Just one."

Every pair of eyes looked inhospitable, disgusted, judging — or
asleep. The judgments were various:

You don't believe what you're saying.

You don't love Jesus.

You would be more reverent if you had real faith.

Your belt doesn't match your shoes.

This last judgment reminded me that there was at least one more homosexual at Saint Anthony Shrine besides me. But hell hath no fury like a fellow homosexual who doesn't want to be out. Scorpions and black widows are more friendly. This one sniffed, his lip curled, and he buffeted me with waves of disapproval far stronger anything Scott Whittier had directed my way in our recent fights.

"Then I sent Moses and Aaron, and smote Egypt with the prodigies which I wrought in her midst."

My eyes caught the gaze of an ax murderer keen to smite me.

"The Egyptians pursued your fathers to the Red Sea with chariots and horsemen."

This time, it was a baby rapist.

"I sent the hornets ahead of you."

A little old lady, her gaze as sharp as a bee sting.

After Mass I approached the priest, a friar with whom I had never served.

"Sorry, Father," I said. "I should have cleared the dishes at the end, right?"

"Yup."

"I'm not normally a eucharistic minister," I explained, feeling considerably less than extraordinary. "I'm just filling in for Mary Flanagan, so I'm not used to the rules."

He gave me an icily unforgiving look, as if he were going to report me to Father Bear-Daddy. I yearned to tell him that he mispronounced "Girgashites," and his socks didn't match, and he needed a makeover. Silence wisely prevailed.

Father Bear-Daddy asked me to jot down reasons for insisting on a relationship with the Church. I wrote:

10. I don't cut and run.

9. I can save the goldfish.

8. I like big Catholic words.

7. Guilt

6. Learned helplessness

5. I want to be the center of attention.

4. I have an abiding love for all the world's godchildren.

3. Mental illness

2. Delusions of grandeur

He read through the list with pursed lips. "The number one reason?"

"That I'll be ignored."

> Q. *Anthony of Padua, patron of lost things, my cause is
> what appears to be lost. What shall I do?*
> A. That's Saint Jude's department. Next!

Dreaming Julia Roberts

I hoped to be the Julia Roberts character at the Saint Anthony Shrine pro bono legal clinic. I imagined showing up wearing hot legal briefs that exposed my shapely legs. The clients would be righteous, progressive, faultless, and pure enough to make Mother Teresa blush. Crooked landlords would fall. Greedy companies would spend billions to clean up their environmental messes. High-powered teams of nasty defense lawyers would beg for mercy.

Within a few weeks of launching the clinic, my dreams of being Erin Brockovich with a rosary and a tonsure came face to face with reality. The legal advice center attracted mostly lunatics and lonely people. Forget Perry Mason. What the clients most craved was what I wanted as a gay man: to be taken seriously by a person with an unjudging ear.

One afternoon, a big-hipped, bearded white guy in filthy sweats made an appointment. He called me "brother" right off the bat. His voice overwhelmed the tiny room. He said he had a formal education, but he sprinkled too many five-dollar words into Boston Irish street lingo otherwise so pure that I longed to learn it as if it were the language of my long lost tribe.

"My name is Seamus O'Dooley," the client said. "My daddy's name was also Seamus O'Dooley." From a Target bag, he dumped a smothering pile of documents on the table between us. He showed me copies of two ten-year-old wills meant to show that he had been screwed out of his inheritance, a rap sheet long as a roll of toilet paper, his First Communion certificate, and the restraining order he had obtained against some former roommate.

He rifled through his pile of sacred relics until he located two articles torn from an ancient *Boston Herald*. Each pictured an old man passed out and slumped sideways near the fence surrounding the Boston Common.

"That's my daddy," he said. Sure enough, the caption referenced one Seamus O'Dooley.

"Sorry to hear it," I said grudgingly, reluctant to lend my ears to one more pity party without a resolution in sight, when my own pity party was raging.

He said a teacher had framed him with accusations of violence. This incident sent him spiraling. His father had taught him to smoke dope, and he had multiple convictions before he was sixteen. Then he cleaned himself up and found Jesus. He had a chance to go to an evangelical Protestant college, but he had no money on account of having been screwed out of the inheritance.

"My whole life went downhill from there," he said.

It was the Church that did it, right?

He blathered about Section 8 housing, getting digitally raped by a cop who frisked him for marijuana, and a former male landlord who accepted sex in lieu of rent.

You can tell me. It was B16, right?

"Oh, I can tell you some things," he said. "I can tell you stuff you wouldn't believe. Cops, hah!"

Vatican cops? The Swiss Guard?

Every story came with a specific address.

Thrown out of public housing? 224 Dorchester Avenue.

Digitally raped? The alley behind 623 Shawmut Street.

First taste of smack? Loading dock of 66 Charles Street by the Common.

What happened at the chancery, 2121 Commonwealth Ave.? They killed your goldfish, didn't they?

He told me about a slip-and-fall claim, adding that he was now ready to sue the lawyer handling it. Everyone was cheating him. He tried to enroll in a mental health program, but when he told them he would rather have a white counselor than a black one, they refused to serve him.

I admitted that I was just posing as Erin Brockovich. I couldn't actually help him resolve his legal problems, for which the statutes of limitations had passed years before.

He quickly gathered his relics.

"Mr. O'Dooley, not all is lost," I said. "I'll call you on this last issue, this restraining order you want expunged."

"No, brother," he said. "If you can't help, you can't help."

Then he disappeared. He had come to Saint Anthony Shrine for assistance, but the tabernacle lay empty, the pages of the lectionary were blank, and the homilies full of false promises. Outside the Shrine, none of the people among the rush-hour crowd seemed unhappy. They brayed about their knockoff Kate Spade handbags and lobster-covered Hub of the Universe sweatshirts. They brandished pictures of a shrinking polar ice cap, ultrasounds of fetuses at the local abortuary, and a portrait of Lyndon LaRouche that looked as if he had been preserved and stuffed by a drunken taxidermist with a cruel sense of humor.

I turned back to the Shrine and knelt in the dark, trying to pray for Seamus O'Dooley — without success. I couldn't begrudge him a word. I might as well have been in a polyp-filled Super Colon as in the bowels of a Catholic church.

Simple Words with a Dozen Syllables

Real life streamed by, and every hard fact or solid circumstance rendered my religious life less real. At Gram's camp in rural Maine, where hi-speed Internet was still a pipe dream and video choked bandwidth, we abandoned YouTube and sailed unchecked into campfire conversation with Scott's extended family. Politics, religion, abortion, extramarital sex, and cholesterol — the land mines detonated. Scott's shirt frequently came off so he could show off his abs to his blood relations. He and his female cousin flexed for the camera. Gram laid out the breakfast table, took her morning swim, and emerged from the kitchen hours later with eight mason jars of pickled brake greens and another of asparagus. She had cleaned every surface, including beneath the refrigerator, though she refused to say how she moved it herself.

Minor household disasters regularly ensued. Scott's four-year-old second cousin announced, "I have to pee," which actually meant, "I have already peed and am now standing helplessly in a puddle of my own urine waiting for an adult to hose me off." Scott's Uncle Wayne cheerfully sought ways to fleece us city boys. Jezebel took pictures of everything, which often proved necessary in the morning for those pesky blackouts.

Gram inspected one of these photos, and then, smiling wickedly, she held it out toward me. "Your best profile," she said.

The photograph showed me bent over a cooler, fetching a beer and exposing my backside. If I had had a Super Colon, it would have been dead center.

Rory and Jezebel's Catholic fervor had cooled. They were prepared to admit, for example, that Father Pamplemousse was "a gay," now that the good father had quit the priesthood and taken to selling auto insurance. They acknowledged that they had known he was gay at the time of the wedding, but something had kept them from admitting it.

"His being gay would have diminished your wedding?"

"N-n-n-n-n-n-n-n-n-n-n-no," Jezebel said. But the word had a dozen syllables.

"You didn't want Scott to have all his antireligious beliefs confirmed?" I asked.

"Maybe," Rory conceded. "Scott wants to make everything gay."

"Maybe you weren't ready to concede the hypocrisy of an antigay Church led by gay men, so your day could be pure?"

I went to another mass in rural Maine with them. A beautiful college kid on summer break took the collection. He had thick, straight brown hair that ended in ringlets at the back of his neck and gorgeous green eyes. As he worked his way through the crowds, he showed two smiles. One was coy, involved lots of eyelashes, and gave him two dimples. The other smile, mischievous, he used on a friend. The boy held the collection basket too long in front of his friend, even though it was obvious his friend had nothing to give.

When the boy reached me, I tried to catch his eye. He closed up like an oyster, swallowing even the possibility of a smile. Not unlike God Himself, Who offers one smile to some, but a different, closed look to people like me.

What do you want of me, God? You want my Super Colon? It's yours. My holy prepuce? My right arm? Another body part? Be my guest. Just give me a sign here, for Your sake! Throw me a bone.

The homily and prayers of the faithful passed with nary a word about intrinsically disordered, perfidious homosexuals, but just when it seemed the Lord had finally heard my petition, the priest announced that the Knights of Columbus stood ready in the narthex with a sheaf of petitions seeking a ban on gay marriage in the federal Constitution. Je-RU-salem!

After Mass I asked Rory and Jezebel, "How do you guys deal with gay issues in the youth groups you lead? Has a student ever linked from Jezebel's MySpace page to our Romentics gay romance site and been scandalized?"

"We told one of the students that Rory had a gay brother," Jezebel said.

"Other than that," Rory said, "we haven't discussed it."

"If it comes up," Jezebel added, "I'll tell them the truth."

"What does that mean?"

"I'm supposed to teach what the Church teaches, but I don't agree with the Church on this and a few other things." She refused to divulge what the "other things" were. "So I would tell them what I believe. I would describe our relationship to you guys, how you are at least as normal as other relationships we have known."

"The bar for normal is not that high in these families," I pointed out, laughing bitterly.

Jezebel readily acknowledged it.

"So why are you not affirmatively speaking up?" I asked. "Why aren't we all speaking up?"

Jezebel shrugged. It was the same old story. My straight Catholic acquaintances would say: "I have no problem with your being gay, but those other Catholics . . ." They saw themselves as enlightened, but had zero faith in their peers, who, they warned us, rejected homosexuality out of hand. Therefore, went the syllogism, there was no sense in speaking up.

Back at camp, I made a beeline for the bathroom. I gave the stuffed-loon doorstop a good swift kick. The sign over the toilet, which read, "Closing the lid . . . will not cause brain damage," took on new meaning. Stating what you believe to be the truth won't cause brain damage, either.

The face in the mirror was as guilty as anyone's.

Here's my confession: I lied in the prologue of this book. When Father Francis told me that the Church's teaching on gay marriage was cruel and that was why the friars didn't preach it from the pulpit, I wasn't in fact encouraged that the brown robes stood on my side. Their cowardice disgusted me. *Why aren't you speaking out, not merely remaining silent? Why do you lack courage?*

But my eagerness to belong allowed the cowardice to pass. Homosexuality had never made me feel ashamed, but this puppyish eagerness to pass haunted the dark corners of my psyche. Now — in the middle of Gram's camp — it had finally put its mitts firmly on my soul. That's the power of Catholic guilt. You can seem perfectly happy and well-adjusted, and forty years later you remember a childhood shame so acute that you spontaneously combust, sell your worldly goods, become a recluse, and herd goats in the Central Andes for the rest of your life. I had all but packed my crosier.

XIV

Confessions of a Crossover

Man is least himself when he talks in his own person. Give him a mask, and he will tell you the truth.

— Oscar Wilde

Confessions of a Crossover

 RESISTED THE ONSET OF GAYNESS with the tenacity of a tongueless Jesuit missionary grunting Hail Marys as a Mohawk scraped off his skin. The argument in my head went something like this:

Q. *Are you gay?*
A. Don't be ridiculous! I'm captain of the football team!

This brilliant reasoning carried me straight through to my second year in law school. It defeated such inconvenient counterfactuals as oral sex with male high school friends and the porn video catalog I found by the side of the road and treasured for years. Such things never happened. "Experiment" spilled from my lips as if it were an Act of Contrition. "This is not happening," I told myself. "This *never* happened" — the same phrase I used after bottoming for the first time.

No one's kind when you come out at twenty-nine.[†] Potential lovers patronizingly drawl that they will not date you because you need at least a year's worth of random sex before you're ready for a relationship. Other gay men, who discovered their orientation in the womb, sniff at your years as a closet case. When you carry on conversations with people who knew you as straight, you discover that the word *boyfriend* has about thirty syllables. And you don't know how to react when a scary troll pins you to the bar, shoves his tongue in your mouth, and insists with tent-revival fervor that effeminate men just skeev him out.

Serves you right, I told myself, backhanding the spittle from my lips. *That's what you get for being a crossover.* Crossovers — religious, sexual, or otherwise — deserved no respect in my mind. But with the prospects for gay Catholicism fading and prayer all but impossible, I packed my crosier and hopped over to the non-Catholic side of the fence.

The Religious Crossover's To-Do List

❏ Joke with the Hale Marys that you're trading them in for younger, Episcopalian models.
❏ Consult Gram concerning nonidolatrous worship.
❏ Ditch your Saint Anthony medallion at the door.
❏ Distinguish true faiths from false ones.
❏ Read Sufi poets.
❏ Call for a free Book of Mormon (Warning: they deliver in person).
❏ Lose a few books from the Bible (Judith, Wisdom, Tobit, Sirach, etc.).
❏ Board up tunnel between the rectory and nunnery.
❏ eBay copy of *Lives of the Saints*.

[†] Coming out is the process by which you realize that everyone you thought to be completely oblivious has been humoring you for years.

> ❏ Do your crunches in the morning to get ready for the hot Protestant boys.
> ❏ Set aside your preconceptions. Then do it again.

Once You Go Black

The only service I attend the morning of Gay Pride is the service of mimosas on a silver tray on my roof deck. However, because Pride followed dead on my decision to cross over, I announced to Scott Whittier that I was going to attend the thirtieth annual ecumenical service sponsored by the Pride Interfaith Coalition. Scott announced in turn that he was going to get another boyfriend.

Founded in 1818, Union United Methodist Church is one of Boston's oldest black churches. Little boys in starched shirts, men looking like a convention of funeral home directors, and regal women in cutthroat competition for the gaudiest hat typically surround it on weekend mornings. The Interfaith service was the first time I actually went inside. Shabby velvet cushions from that first service back in 1818 covered the pews. Their seams had popped, and the stuffing was sticking out. The carpets and prayer books looked equally worn. But for all their wear and tear, the music ministry made it new and brassy, rollicking and alive.

The service kicked off with a warm musical welcome with extended solos by the organist, pianist, and trumpet player. A female rabbi blew the shofar. Episcopalians and Methodists swapped "high-church low-church" inside jokes. A member of Dignity read scripture with gender-neutral language. A female chorus sang Gregorian chant. The ecumenical celebrants looked like the premise for a racist joke: a rabbi, a dashiki-clad minister, and a young white minister walked into a Methodist church.

Troy Perry, a gay man raised Baptist, who subsequently founded the predominantly gay Metropolitan Community Church, delivered the sermon. "Turn to your neighbor. Say, 'God bless you. You are in the right place.'"

When I turned to my neighbor, a powerful religious hangover from the Church's pre–Vatican II ban on attending Protestant services said, *No, you ain't, brother — not the right place at all.*

Reverend Perry riled the New England crowd with a sermon of great length on healing and hope, in which Perry himself was a major character. White, northern, and predominantly Catholic, we weren't quite sure how and when to punctuate Perry's sermon with amens. It wasn't because we weren't willing; the amens swirled in our souls. But our timing needed work. Stray amens went off at odd moments, so that you couldn't tell what exactly was being blessed or affirmed.

Several times, Reverend Perry even had to request amens when they didn't spontaneously follow appropriate lines.

"Amen? Amen?" we called out.

Perry commented, laughing, that he had never heard amen spoken with a question mark.

For a while, it appeared we might escape the passing of the collection basket. But rather than announce in typical Catholic style, "Today's collection will be for the support of curing knock knees among friars of the Order of Perpetual Motion," a separate speaker gave an entirely new homily devoted solely to the topic of money. This second speaker, a Massachusetts legislator who tirelessly championed gay marriage, induced me to drop forty bucks in the collection plate. Only an hour later, at the Gay Pride cash-only block party, did I come to my senses. It felt like my pocket had been picked. A beer short, an hour late — isn't that how the saying goes?

United Church of Vegetables

After Union United, I wanted an experience that involved fewer amens and wallet-thinning collections. Physically much larger than Union United, the Church of the Covenant occupied a block in Back Bay, one of Boston's wealthiest zip codes. I imagined old-school Protestants inside, upright, stern, unemotional — with the numerals 666 tattooed at the hairline.

In stark contrast to Union United, the sanctuary at Church of the Covenant was nearly empty. In fact, I had sat down before I realized that the service was already in session. The ritual was as unstructured as if they had just made it up on the spot. Freelancing abounded, and the population was alarmingly vagrant. People leapt up mid-ceremony and visited with neighbors. One man ambled up to chat with the liturgical director during the sermon.

The vagrancy unnerved my Catholic soul. We tend to plunk down on our knees as soon as we arrive, and we don't move until summoned to communion. Period. Lightning would strike us dead if we ever approached the altar unless we were carrying a collection basket or communion wine.

In the pew ahead of me, a little girl was clutching a carnation and a stuffed dog. She brought the dog with her during the service as she went around with the collection basket. People signed the dog with a felt-tipped pen, but no one ever explained its purpose.

Some strange Protestant rite from the Reformation, I decided.

A young, earnest minister speaking in a dead liberal monotone delivered the sermon. It lasted eons. Any friar worth his salt could have fit a half-dozen haiku homilies into the same space. Occasionally the earnest minister asked rhetorically: "What do you think?"

The performance was deeply unsatisfying. The priest was supposed to tell *me* what to think, damnit. That was his job, after all.

A wave of people swept toward the altar to offer celebrations and concerns, until virtually half the church was up front. They began with birthdays. Then someone mentioned the transformations that caused politicians to change their votes regarding gay marriage. Then Father's Day got a plug. Then thanks for memorial flowers. Then thanks for the generosity of those who gave money to support a delegation to Congo. Then the story of a teenage daughter's departure for Nicaragua for two summer months, including delayed planes. Then a young man announced that he was celebrating his own tenth anniversary of coming to the Church of the Covenant. "Thank you," he said, "and please pray for my sister-in-law." Sunday-school teachers. A married lesbian couple who were leaving the congregation and moving to western Massachusetts came to the altar for a group hug from the Nicaragua delegation.

Finally, everyone returned to their seats. The collection plate passed. Scraps of paper of all kinds filled it, and they weren't all green. *No wonder they couldn't even afford a decent statue of the Virgin*, I scoffed. *You can't repair a roof with a thanksgiving note or a request for prayers.*

The mean part of me kept score of the defects in the UCC service, using the miniature golf pencils attached to the back of the pew:

- No space between the scripture lessons
- No call-and-response
- No thanks to God
- No garish Virgins — of the marble variety, anyway
- No votives
- Healthy goldfish
- No bloody crucifixes
- Nothing to eat, not a single wafer to be had

While I was tallying up the score, vagrancy overtook the service entirely. Everyone — my friend Richard, the liturgy director, the girl with the ritual stuffed dog, the anemic pastor — visited, hugged, chatted, and offered one another best wishes for the trip to Nicaragua.

Unbeknownst to me, the service had ended. There was no procession, no sending forth, no "This Mass is ended," nothing whatever to signal our freedom. By the time I recovered and started hugging complete strangers, half the attendants — approximately seven people — were already clawing at the potluck table.

"Why so few people?" I asked my friend Richard.

"Oh, we take summers off. Not much goes on here."

"Summers off from God?"

"By the way," he said, dodging my skepticism, "if you want meat, you've got to bring it yourself and eat in the corner while looking shameful. It's a congregation of vegetarians."

That was the last straw. A church that took time off from God and eschewed garish Virgins was one thing, but vegetarianism lay beyond the pale. I prayed to God to send me a religion like He sent Joseph Smith — one that was fully formed, replete with stone tablets, and tithing-based, so I wouldn't have to rely on putting fraudsters in jail or writing memoirs to earn a living.

DisCouraged

After spending so many Sundays with Protestants other than my boyfriend, I decided to spend some quality time with Courage, the Vatican-approved Roman Catholic group for gay men. Courage emphasizes lives of chastity, and I had nothing to lose. The way things were going with Scott, I was already pretty much a celibate.

Tracking the group down proved almost impossible. Visitors to the Oval Office cope with fewer security procedures than Courage employed.

I called the archdiocese and reached a lovely lady in the Office of Spiritual Direction.

"I'm looking for Courage," I said. I might as well have asked for the Department of Burnings at the Stake.

"I don't think that exists anymore," she said.

"But they have a Web site," I explained. "It lists this number."

"Oh. OK. I'll check around and get back to you."

She never did.

So I turned to a snitch with whom I occasionally sparred on the Internet. "Alice, I'm having a conversion experience. How do I get in touch with Courage?"

Pleased but skeptical, Alice provided contact information. A couple of e-mails to Courage failed to elicit a reply. One more try, I vowed, then I will declare myself officially disCouraged.

An anonymous reply signed "Boston Courage" followed my third attempt. Further e-mail exchanges gave me a name: "Dan."† Dan supplied me with his phone number but offered no information concerning the meetings, as if afraid to commit this dangerous information to writing.

---

† Daniel was a Franciscan brother and martyr who was beheaded and his body mangled when he refused to renounce his faith.

On the phone Dan sounded like John Ratzenberger, the actor who played Cliff the mailman from the TV show *Cheers* — but with a more authentic Boston accent. Gruff but friendly, he told me the name of the church where Courage met, but he could not remember the street, which I had to look up myself.

The Courage group was hanging out in the parking lot like a bunch of high school thugs when I arrived. We descended into the basement and formed a circle of folding chairs. Courage meetings take their format from programs like Alcoholics Anonymous. After the opening prayer, the members introduce themselves, first names only, and read aloud the five goals of Courage, which primarily involve neutralizing SSA.[†] Then a member presented a meditation on one of the twelve steps, followed by other members offering their own reflections on the step. Those with a "burning desire to share" could take the floor next, and the meeting closed with a Hail Mary, as if the group was trying to land the airplane of their celibacy in the storm of their sexuality.

Ten men had come, about average. Dan, a lumbering man with the amused air of someone who has learned to laugh at the cruel God who turned him gay, wore Coke-bottle glasses. "Ewald" wore a yellow golf shirt and Wrangler jeans — both visibly ironed — and his face betrayed an eagerness to be just one of the guys.[‡] Ewald was the kind of guy who took religiously his mother's admonitions to wash behind his ears and wear clean underwear every day because you never knew when you were going to be in an accident.

The only other newbie gave the name "Ben." Classically effeminate in a computer-nerd sort of way, he had grown a thin beard to cover his chinlessness. He claimed to be a crossover, both a convert to Catholicism and, more dubiously, a veteran of girls.

As Ewald gave a presentation on the day's step, I focused on Ben. The name had to be a pseudonym. *Why Ben? Short for Benjamin, a*

[†] SSA is "same-sex attraction." Courage discourages use of the terms *gay* and *lesbian*, which, in their view, involve a lot of parades.

[‡] Ewald is the name of a pair of martyr brothers, one fair, one dark, one of whom was killed by the sword and the other torn limb from limb.

martyr? Or Benedict? Maybe he was a big pope-aholic? Or could it have been Ben-there, done that, referring to the gay lifestyle?

I had come to the meeting equipped with only my actual name. It hadn't occurred to me to take on a saint or martyr I had always wanted to be. Fernando seemed a little over the top. *But I could have been a Crispin*, I reflected. *Or a Justus. Then if I became a member of the Supreme Court, they would call me Justice Justus. How odd that only one of my siblings — the one born in Ireland — got a saint's name. We American-born children got nothing. Scott? Who ever heard of Saint Scott? The Pearly Gates were going to pose a serious challenge without a proper saint to pull strings for me.*

When my reverie ended, the whole circle of celibates was looking at me expectantly. Uh-oh.

"It's your turn," Dan said.

My turn — right — to reflect on the step about which Ewald had been eulogizing for the past ten minutes, a step about which I knew nothing. In fact, the whole staircase was a mystery to me, except for my vague notion it involved lots of apologizing, soul-searching, and making amends at some point. It was surprisingly tricky to find some honest middle ground that did not imply condemnation of homosexual activity or endorse the concept of SSA as a twelve-steppable offence.

The arrival of Courage's chaplain got me off the hook. Full of bonhomie and casual charm, Father John was a man's man — forty years old, movie-star handsome, a strong handshake, and a tough South Boston accent. He looked a shade too cool for school, but proved warm and genuinely interested. A lot of the celibate boys surely developed serious crushes on him.

The Church really is determined to torture these guys. They couldn't have chosen a little ninety-year-old eunuch as chaplain? Instead they assign this virile stud?

Father John, who insisted he doesn't suffer from SSA, later admitted to me that when he first became chaplain, he had feared getting hit on. He thought, What happens if they fall in love with me and I feel all weird? "I used to call people faggots," he confessed.

But he said the phobic feelings had disappeared: "It is what it is. I don't care what people think or say. There's a clear understanding that the love I have for these guys is platonic, like Jesus would have with his disciples. They know I am looking out for their good. I have affection for these guys."

The ten men told no dramatic, self-abasing rock-bottom stories. Masturbation, of course, posed a chronic problem for Courage members. Ewald confessed to "looking at pictures I shouldn't have been looking at."

According to Father John, these guys suffered primarily from fear of rejection and low self-esteem, not loneliness: "It's hard for them to see themselves as lovable or having worth."

When the hour-long meeting ended, Father John said to me, "Good night, brotha. See you next time." I half expected to bump chests or knock fists with him.

Then "Demetrius," a thickset sixty-year-old in Bermuda shorts and white sneakers, shook a packet of brochures from a crumpled brown bag that probably once held a bottle of bourbon.[†] He said he had been coming to Courage since 1990 and had been "out of the lifestyle" since 1981. He invited me to consider the materials and take them home with me.

My Favorite Courage Quotes

- "It is therefore easy to see how the homosexual relation fails as a totally human relationship."
- "People who have successfully integrated homosexual desires with their personalities . . . are rare indeed."
- "Here one sees the sterility of the homosexual relationship in which there is no family and no family history." (Does Gram know she doesn't exist?)
- "Finally, homosexual actions have no meaning in themselves. They can mean whatever the person wants them to mean." (Sounds good to me.)

---

† Saint Demetrius was a martyr who was speared to death in the public baths.

- "[The homosexual] must come to realize he is powerless over homosexual acts." (Only if your master says so. Sir.)
- "Frequently the friendship of a priest becomes a source of strength to the homosexual in his loneliness." (I bet!)

Asked whether all the depictions in the media of happy gay couples raising children and getting married in Massachusetts raised doubts in some Courage members' minds, Father John said, "When they are honest, yeah. . . . [But] only a few guys question, 'I wonder if same-sex marriage is for me.' Most don't believe in it. We don't make apologies for Church teaching. The guys support that."

In our discussion, Father John mentioned same-sex couples, one male and one female, who had spontaneously embraced chastity and reduced their romantic unions to friendship while continuing to live together happily and in harmony with the Church's teachings on sexuality.

"I'd love to meet them," I said.

"Oh, uh, they don't live in Massachusetts."

I suspected the truth was, the couples only existed on whatever planet Father John went to when overdosing on the pain medication for his old football injuries.

Father John didn't attend my second Courage meeting, and a palpable sense of struggle and misery took hold. Dan was having trouble praying. Demetrius expressed the shame he felt as he got older: "Everyone else is getting married, and they look at you and they know something is wrong with you. When you were younger, you could get away with it, make excuses." Ewald bitterly noted that certain straight people were called to chastity, but he had no choice in the matter. Ben admitted that it was a relief not to have to make choices, saying, "You don't have to try to figure out God's will for you." Their alienation from their sexual identity was compelling — but also obscene, like watching a little girl with a box knife cut herself.

Unchurching

My energetic frustration was turning to enervating despair. Everything seemed inexplicable, cross-eyed, ass-backward, and upside down. Mother Teresa might be able to handle a fifty-year-long dark night of the soul, but I — in the words of Lloyd Bentsen and my friend Tim — was no Mother Teresa. *Let them all go to hell*, I thought, and a voice answered: *There is no hell*. Another voice echoed: *Hell is here, hell is now*.

Salting my wound, the Rat issued a statement barring priests with "deep-seated" homosexual tendencies from seminaries. Gay men, intrinsically disordered, were unable to relate even nonsexually to both men and women, explained at least one bishop — reasoning that suggested that the seminaries would turn away the huge population of ordained priests who were gay if they were to apply today.

Two American bishops spoke out. William Skylstad, president of the U.S. Conference of Catholic Bishops, wrote: "There are many wonderful and excellent priests in the Church who have a gay orientation, are chaste and celibate and very effective ministers of the Gospel. Witch hunts and gay bashing have no place in the Church." Bishop Matthew Clark of Rochester, New York, assured his gay priests, "We deeply value your ministry." To gay men discerning whether to enter the seminary, he gave welcome, promising, "We treat all inquiries fairly. Yours will be no exception."

Most bishops, including O'Malley, said nothing. "No comment," according to newspaper reports, which Father Kick-Me confirmed.

Screw Seamus Heaney, I thought. *I am going to disavow words like* thanksgiving, host, communion, *and a whole bunch of others besides.* I swore never to crack *The Lives of the Saints* again. I vowed to content myself solely with secular saving ministries. Was it too late to become an EMT?

Outside the Shrine, a homeless man sat on the sidewalk with a giant Bible open to a page that never turned. It looked as if he had made it this far and then stopped, unable to understand or move past what lay before him, plain for all the world to see.

At home, Scott was falling precipitously out of love with me. We were keeping separate calendars. We were engaging in separate YouTube sessions. Garbage and dirty clothes piled up. We fought over whose turn it was to replace the toilet paper. Necessity forced Scott to break first. He returned from the store with a single roll on which he placed a sticky note that read "For Scott W's beautiful ass only." We had transformed our condo in the largest intact Victorian neighborhood in America into a latter-day gym and frat house — without the casual sex.

One night, Scott was lying on the pew. Having broken a rib while skiing, he clutched a pillow to his chest just beneath his chin like a little boy hugging a teddy bear. He had read somewhere that hugging a pillow reduced the pain from coughing. His eyes had become slits. Raw hostility hit me the moment I walked through the door, as if I were responsible not only for the sins of the Catholic Church but for all the coughing he might endure.

That weekend, at a friend's wedding, Scott and I had a meltdown in front of straight people, whose prior approval of our relationship had made me want to shout "anal dildo" and "crabs." We were like a couple of show poodles gone wrong.

A few weeks later, in January 2007, the Massachusetts legislature considered whether to put an amendment banning gay marriage on the 2008 ballot. More than two-thirds of the legislators had announced their opposition to the amendment, but the antigay faction needed only 50 votes to succeed. Sure enough, we lost — 134 votes against, 62 in favor.

Shortly afterward, the Jesuits announced the closing of the Jesuit Urban Center, the ultra-gay church. The order's provincial cited the high costs of maintaining the building but made no effort to reestablish the ministry in a cheaper rent district.

The personal, political, and spiritual news seemed inextricably mixed. Praying Hail Marys to keep an airplane from crashing looked positively sane compared to my frantic efforts to keep the Church holy for gay people. The questions raced through my head: *Why am I doing this? Why chase the cardinal? Why go to Mass? At least the goldfish know they're not welcome.* Wanting something — anything — from O'Malley felt far too much like unrequited love. It was far too much like being a gay teenager falling head over heels for his straight best friend, filled with an inarticulate yearning but lacking the vocabulary to capture what he dreamed.

I reminded myself over and over to love Seán. I ransacked my Brown Bag dossier for positives. Like a mantra, I repeated: *He hates cats. He loves languages. He hates cats. He loves languages. Tastes great. Less filling.* I repeated it until I was blinking stupidly, smiling inanely, asking for spare change, and hanging around airports in bright orange robes chanting, *I love Seán. I love everyone.*

Gram would have looked at me kindly, slipped an extra ace from her sleeve, and said, "Well, you *are* gay, after all."

I wanted to be someone else. Every once in a while, I crossed over, just for a sense of relief. A new acquaintance at the Shrine mistook me for an actual Catholic — a good one, pious and loving, likely to make a good husband and father and to wear a brown braided belt with navy shorts dotted with pink and green golf bags or whales. After checking my left hand for a ring, that new acquaintance suggested I might want to meet her daughter. And in truth, I had nothing against meeting the daughter — perhaps for a joint mani-pedi. So I played with her misconceptions. I talked knowingly of nights up at 3:00 A.M. with crying infants, parochial schools, the high cost of diapers, and sundry other factoids I had absorbed from spending too much time with godchildren and straight people. These strange sessions of make-believe became a dirty pleasure.

The auguries were ominous. At Gram's camp, a hummingbird plucked a struggling insect from a spider's web. A robin's nest spilled an egg, which split and cooked to the sun-baked pavement near Gram's back door. Everything was going to shit.

One night at my parents' house, Mikaela was gumming a frozen waffle. As I made polite conversation with Mikaela's mother, cocaptain of the Bush Household, Mikaela toddled around the kitchen. Already conscious that she was different, she sought out others similarly wounded. Her grandfather's thumb, which he had smashed in his youth and which had healed strangely, fascinated her.

When the basement door near the entrance to the kitchen stood completely open, it nearly touched the wall opposite. Mikaela managed to wedge her head between door and wall. Trapped, she screamed. It was the third way of destroying herself Mikaela had devised that morning.

Despite her terror, Mikaela had retained a firm grip on the waffle, which, once free, she calmly resumed eating — a reflex that would serve her well when she started drinking martinis and had to backflip while still holding upright the miraculously unspilled glass. Why the hell did she need a gay godfather if she already had this trick down cold?

It was time to leave the Shrine and let go of my spiritual waffle. Shortly before I announced my decision to the Marys, Father Bear-Daddy, and the G-L Group, Father Bear-Daddy's brother, the director of human services at the Shrine, called. He invited me to join yet another advisory committee, this one overseeing the Shrine's human services, including the legal clinic, wellness center, programs for kids and seniors, résumé-writing workshop, Lazarus Center, and dog-blessing during Saint Francis Week.

"Well," I said, "the thing is —"

"I know you're busy," Father Bear-Daddy's brother interrupted. "I know you already do a lot for us, but before you say no, I want to tell you a little about some of the other programs."

"I don't want to hear about friars blessing household pets and issuing certificates to pet owners commemorating their blessed pets' blessedness," I said.

"No, I was going to mention that we've really been having a lot of success with the seniors program, and we got all the kids outfitted for school, and of course we buried three abandoned babies last week —"

"What?" *Did he just say . . . ?*

"Three abandoned babies. Just last week. The medical examiner brought them. One was abandoned in the streets. One was killed in a car accident — they delivered him dead, and the mother wanted nothing to do with him. One overdosed on cocaine in his mother's womb. We shut down the Shrine, and all the friars and the nuns and the music ministry said a private Mass for them, and then we went out to the graveside and laid them to rest together, side by side. Someone's donating a headstone that we'll mark Baby Anthony, Baby Jessica, and Baby Claire. So, anyhow, can you help us out?"

My brain said no, but my goddamn gay voice said: "When do I start?"

XV

Gay Voices before Mine

That raving deinstitutionalized stranger who proclaims that he is Jesus Christ? He is Jesus Christ, in a form that's particularly difficult to see.

— Seán Cardinal O'Malley

The Celestial Skywriter

LAME IT ON LECTORS' BREAKING HIPS, moving away, and falling from grace. The Shrine was running short on lectors, so Father Bear-Daddy had ordered a new session of lector boot camp. The appointed day was a cold, rainy September Saturday, a day of spiritual low tide, when all the bilge water, wadded Wal-Mart bags, used hypodermics, and other spiritual detritus washed up on the beach of the soul and lay exposed for the sand flies to pick at, children to collect for Mommy, and crazy old cranks with metal detectors to sift through.

Mama Bear summoned one of the new lector candidates to the podium. He supplied a passage from the Letter of Paul to the Galatians: "Now the works of the flesh are obvious: immorality, impurity, lust, idolatry, sorcery, hatreds, rivalry, jealousy, outbursts of fury, acts of selfishness, dissensions, factions, occasions of envy, drinking bouts, orgies, and the like."

Despondent, I checked off the fleshly sins one by one. Impurity? Yup. Fury? Check. Selfishness? Absolutely. This thoroughly depressing catalog made me want to go back to Dignity, put on a cardigan, and hear that I was 99 percent good.

"What do you hear?" Mama Bear asked.

My own spiritual doom. How the hell did I get myself into this mess?

"What do you hear?" Mama Bear asked again.

The lector candidates offered a hundred answers:

"Too fast." "Too slow." "Wrong emphasis." "More feeling." "Needs some liturgical dance."

Mama Bear said, "What do you *hear*? Don't tell me about technique."

A quiet murmur passed through the group. A few tentative hands went up, and then fell. The candidates had become a class of preteens in a sex-ed class.

"What do you hear? What *messages* do you hear?"

For the first time, we focused on the meaning of the words we heard, the content, rather than just the delivery. This was unfamiliar territory. The Church has never encouraged its adherents to read the Bible. *The Lives of the Saints* was fine, but Lord knows the faithful couldn't handle actual scripture. Even we lectors of many years standing didn't consider the Word too closely.

"I hear a God who wants us to integrate the corporal works, the works of the body, with those of the spirit," said Martina, a lector candidate I had recruited from the G-L Spirituality Group.

Mama Bear nodded approvingly. "Now that we have heard the message, we can proclaim it. One must be a good listener before one can ever be a good reader."

"Listening?!" Scott exclaimed after I mentioned this revelation to him. "What a novel concept! You might want to try it someday."

No sooner had the words left his mouth than I knew Scott had spoken my own private commandment direct from the Lord: *Sit down in that pew, quit your bitching, and listen, for My sake. With all that beseeching, horse trading, dealmaking, and yammering about Hale Marys, friars, wookies, fraudsters, and godchildren, you skipped the most basic prayer of all: listening.*

Divinely scolded into brokenness, I dragged my sorry, wounded ass over to the pew as directed. Sullen as a child, I asked God, *Listen to what, exactly?*

Something inarticulate, something beautiful, something to love. Mikaela's crying, Father Myron's sermon, an emphatic belch — anything at all. I've been saying it since day one: This is not about you.

How about, I proposed, *I go back to Dignity, what's left of the Jesuit Urban Center, and all my gay spiritual forebears, and really pay attention this time, swear to You, cross my heart, hope to die? I'll find the good in them.*

And the Almighty said, *It's about time you heard a gay voice besides your own.*

At the Feet of My Forebears: A Short History of Gay Catholics

In the beginning was a gay cardinal. You heard me: the Brown Bag stands in the shoes of a big nancy queen. You may think this statement is merely wishful thinking, born of two sources:

1. my new easy-listening conversion experience, and
2. gay people's tendency to lay claim to just about every person who forms America's cultural inheritance: Michelangelo, Mychal Judge, Elton John, Rosie, Bert and Ernie, the Seven Dwarfs, Albus Dumbledore, and Shakespeare.

What actual evidence is there that William Cardinal O'Connell, who presided over the Boston archdiocese for the first half of the twentieth century, was a 'mo? Glad you asked. Consider the following facts:

- O'Connell wielded a jaunty gold-headed cane.
- He drove a Pierce-Arrow.
- He liked fine wine.
- His staff included a coachman, valet, and music master.
- His Renaissance palazzo had its own private golf course.
- He took fabulous vacations: O'Connell kept a winter home in the Bahamas and a summer home in an upscale beach resort, Marblehead, Massachusetts.

- O'Connell's lifelong "traveling companion," a bachelor, wrote years of letters to O'Connell, which were burned upon his death.
- He never went anywhere without his two black poodles.

My gaydar may be weak, but even I can connect these big pink dots. Short of catching him in flagrante delicto with a Broadway showboy, it was hard to garner more incontrovertible evidence. O'Connell makes Father Bear-Daddy look straighter than Captain Handsome.

✂ - - - - - - - - - - - - - - - - - - - cut here - - - - - - - - - - - - - - - - - - -

Ten Ways to Detect a Gay Catholic

Use this handy clip 'n' save checklist. Bring it to Mass and pick out the homosexuals. Which of the following traits or behaviors do you observe? Check all that apply:

- ❑ Passion for Gregorian chant (Chant is to gay Catholics what show tunes are to secular homosexuals.)
- ❑ Swooning when the pope reinstated the Latin Mass, a favorite among liturgy queens
- ❑ Swooning when Captain Handsome joins the choir
- ❑ Guilt as visible as a camel's hump
- ❑ Hip scars from liturgical hula accidents
- ❑ Pained expression, as if suffering an obstructed bowel, at yet another antigay proclamation from the cardinal
- ❑ Gay voice
- ❑ Super Colon
- ❑ Compulsion to rearrange lilies after Easter Mass
- ❑ Broadway-style bitchery
- ❑ Always seeking lead role in the passion play
- ❑ Wearing more makeup than the statue of the Virgin in the vestibule

❑ Celebrating a nonconforming Sabbath (i.e., Fridays)
❑ Using the expression "The show must go on" in connection with the Holy Sacrifice of the Mass

- - - - - - - - - - - - - - - - - - cut here - - - - - - - - - - - - - - - - - - ✂

Notwithstanding Cardinal O'Connell's ascendancy, my gay Catholic forebears didn't generally fare well before Vatican II. As one gay priest put it, "Look at the language of the Church fifty years ago. We were called pederasts and we belonged in the lower reaches of hell."

A few reasons for hope presented themselves nonetheless:

- In the 1960s, the Church first distinguished between homosexual persons and homosexual activity and began loving the gay sinners (though still hating their sin that cried out to heaven for vengeance).
- In the 1970s, Boston's Cardinal Cushing reportedly gave two priests permission to say Mass for the "exodus community," an assembly of alienated Catholics including divorced people, those who had children out of wedlock, criminals, and homosexuals.
- Around the same time, this same audience started Interfaith, Sunday-evening house masses in a Boston apartment.

A veteran of Interfaith described the services this way:

People sat around the coffee table on the floor. . . . It was a very intimate liturgy. . . . Maybe 50 percent of the time the homilies were dialogue homilies. The priest would throw out a topic, say some words on it, and then throw it open to anyone in the room who wanted to give personal comments on it. Sometimes that was very powerful, what they had gone through, things you didn't know about them, what their experience with the Church had been. Quite often, there would be, you know, a lot of tears. It was very intense. At that point, I was living 45 miles outside the city, and I never missed it.

Many of the Interfaith regulars also had a hand in the early days of the Boston chapter of Dignity, founded in 1972 at a gay bar called the Randolph Country Club. Priests from many religious orders and a few active diocesan priests led Dignity's weekly services, which for a period of time took place at Saint Clement's, a Catholic church. A straight religious brother at Saint Clements took it upon himself to disseminate information about Dignity.

A Dignity veteran told me,

> The people who were involved [in Dignity] felt the righteousness of the cause. There was no doubting, there was no groveling, no "Maybe we deserve this," or "Maybe we're OK." Everything was a flat-out [affirmative] statement, and that's how I felt, too. . . . I know people struggled for years, "Me oh my, oh poor me." I never went through that. . . . I never felt that I was an awful person. The only thing I felt unfortunate about being gay was [that until Dignity] I didn't have a place where I could share how I felt about myself and my relationship with God.

By the 1980s, weekly attendance at Dignity liturgies had reached 300 people, and once a month a Dignity member sponsored a more intimate Saturday home Mass of his or her own design. As another hopeful sign, the Church's social service arm, Catholic Charities, adopted an employment nondiscrimination policy that covered gays long before Massachusetts ever passed such a law.

Marianne Duddy, now executive director of the national Dignity organization, told me, "You've got to remember, there was a real climate of fear back then."

Knee-jerk skepticism filled my head. *Fear? Fear of what? Had the members of Dignity experienced a severe outbreak of static cling from all that hugging? Was there a horrible gluten emergency? Did you admit someone to membership who was only 98 percent good?*

"The police were still raiding the bars back then," Duddy noted. According to her, members went by first names or adopted aliases to avoid having to rat out fellow Dignitarians to the BPD. "They would publish names in the papers, and there were no employment protections back then. You could get fired."

Because of this fear, going to Dignity in those days was like entering a gay bar for the first time. Or like showing up at Saint Anthony Shrine that first day for lector training. Nearly every aged Dignitarian told me some version of the following story about his or her first Dignity meeting:

> I was twenty-one years old and living with my mother. I found a parking space on the street where I could see the entrance [of Saint Clement's]. Then someone pulled out of a space, so I parked even closer, right in front of the door. I watched people go in. About a minute before it started, I finally forced myself to go through the door. The main sanctuary was completely dark. Where did all the people go? The only light came from a winding stone staircase that led down in the basement. All of a sudden, a man grabbed me by the elbow. He asked, Are you looking for the Dignity Mass? It's downstairs. He propelled me down to the basement. All I could hear was laughter. I thought: *That's not what people do before Mass!* I panicked. I thought, *No one is going to find me. Maybe they'll find my car. . . .*

In fact, what they typically found was a community even more tightly knit and friendly than the hug-fest I attended thirty-five years later. The priests dressed in street clothes and only put on a stole for the consecration. The kiss of peace was the standard greeting. The post-liturgy social hour routinely resulted in thirty or more Dignitarians heading off to dine together at local restaurants.

Even bomb threats couldn't scatter them. After a 1982 *Boston Globe* article about Dignity, the sound of boots in the hallway interrupted a Dignity liturgy. Right before the homily, Dignity's president stood up and said, "I don't mean to alarm you. The Boston Police are here, but they're here as our friends. There's been a bomb threat called in. The [caller said] there's a bomb timed to go off during the Dignity liturgy and blow up all the faggots. You can leave if you like, but the police are recommending that we stay because the person is probably watching."

Two mothers got up and left. More than two hundred people stayed put.

According to Duddy, "People were looking at each other, and you could tell they were thinking, 'Is this real? Are we going to die? Is something awful going to happen?'"

Asked why they did not leave, another Dignitarian explained: "If I was going to die, why not die here? This was my real family. I felt closer to them than to my cousins."

An arsonist targeted Dignity's office two years later. These tales made my despair over the closing of the JUC, a lifeless Easter Mass, or a lost vote in the Massachusetts legislature look silly. The closest I had come to open flame was when our rooftop grill flared on a particularly choice T-bone. Behind all the hugs and consolation, Dignity had dignity. These were people I would be proud to count as my own and number in my prayers at bedtime.

I sought out more Dignity elders, gathered at their feet, and begged them to tell me stories about the old days in the archdiocese, when heroes wandered the earth, dragons flew, and we jousted with archbishops for sport. This wasn't about me, and I was goddamn thankful for it.

Hail, Holy Queen

On the feast days of Catholic saints, interminable processions parade through the narrow streets of the North End, Boston's Italian neighborhood. The Italian faithful hoist Our Lady of Leche to their shoulders so the Irish faithful can say oh-la-la at her exposed breast. (The Boston Irish get truly incensed about uncovered breasts.) These parades proceed so slowly that they seem to take one step back for every two steps forward.

The archdiocese adopted the same rhythm in its treatment of gay Catholics. In 1977, for example, it expelled Dignity from Saint

Clement's Church. In 1979, the archdiocese declared that its priests were no longer authorized to serve at Dignity services. In the 1980s, the archdiocese made a point of refusing to take Dignity's money. Dignity took a collection and sent the proceeds to the archdiocese. Every year, the check came back. It became a game to see how large a donation it would take before the Church allowed itself to be bought.

The AIDS crisis marked a temporary cessation of hostilities. Ignorance about the disease made many people, including priests, frightened to engage those dying of the disease. Churches refused to have funerals for the afflicted. Priests refused to administer sacraments. Even at Dignity, questions arose. What was safe and what was unsafe? Could HIV-positive men drink from the chalice? If a man was sweating, what would you do at the sign of peace? Could you kiss him? Touch him?

One old-school Dignity member said to me, "When one of my friends came to me and told me he had been diagnosed, I fell into his arms sobbing, saying, 'You can't die. I don't care what you have. I want to hold you.' But if he had not been one of my friends? Well, I probably would have kept him at arm's length. We just didn't know."

The ignorance had a spiritual cost. One priest who had never before had much contact with gay people described his first encounter with a dying AIDS patient this way:

> It was 1983. I was in the hospital anointing someone who was dying, and they called me to anoint someone dying of AIDS. I was dressed in my collar. The patient saw me and said, "Get out of here. I hate priests!"
>
> "Why?"
>
> "I'm gay. My priest told me I'm going to hell and a no good piece of garbage. I asked another priest to anoint me. He stood in the doorway and said, 'I'll give you a blessing from here.'"
>
> "That must have been painful. I'm sorry," I said. We talked for a while and then I asked, "Do you want me to anoint you?"
>
> He said yes.

When I got close, I saw his head was sweating. I had heard that you could get AIDS through bodily fluids. I thought to myself, *If I touch his sweat, I could get AIDS.* But I didn't want to be like that other priest. So I took a deep breath. *OK, God,* I said, *it's important to do this. If I get it, I get it.* I didn't heal that patient. But he sure healed me.

Even Cardinal Law responded to the crisis, albeit in the Church's typically underhanded, secretive way: "[He] did a lot of work with people with AIDS," Duddy told me. "Quietly, of course, going late at night, but really listening to people, spending a lot of time. People found him really comforting and very much with them."

In addition to Dignity, another familiar gay Catholic name served as a bright spot in dim times. As the AIDS crisis took hold, the Jesuit Urban Center at the Church of the Immaculate Conception reached out to its urban neighbors, who, during the 1970s, had become pre-dominantly gay. For the next twenty-five years, the JUC hosted Tuesday dinners to give people suffering from AIDS a chance for fellowship and conversation as well as a meal. The JUC buried scores of gay men, including those whose families and home parishes had abandoned them. Parishioners participated in the AIDS walk and later marched with a JUC banner in Boston's gay pride parade.

A series of Jesuits led the JUC community. Homilies often began with jokes about skimpy Pride costumes. Many JUC members fondly recalled a particular Marian devotion in which the gay Jesuit presider processed during the opening hymn from the back of the church to the altar. When he reached the microphone and the music stopped, he joked, "I always feel a little nervous when I walk down the aisle and they are playing 'Hail, Holy Queen.'"

Brokeback Lent

Already known for homilies that touched on gay topics, one Jesuit homilist managed to work *Brokeback Mountain* into his pre-Lent sermon:

I suspect many in this community have already seen *Brokeback Mountain*. If not, see it; if you have, see it again, and . . . let this Lent be a Brokeback Lent. Let yourself feel genuinely dreadful at just how little you accept God's invitation to be yourself, to be honest, to live more freely, to love more passionately, even to be prepared to die for those whom you love.

Within hours of the Brokeback Lent homily, the presider received over a thousand messages from all over the world, including death threats, with copies to Cardinal O'Malley, the Jesuit provincial leader, and J2P2.

Weeks later, the presider introduced himself to the cardinal's secretary, Reverend Kick-Me, whom he had never before met.

"Oh, you're the *Brokeback* priest!" Reverend Kick-Me exclaimed.

"And you're the poor schmuck who had to read all the e-mails," replied the presider.

Milk and Cookies

On October 30, 1986, the Rat issued the "Halloween Letter," a statement urging all Catholic bishops to oppose every legislative effort, at every level of government, that could be construed as providing equal rights under the law for gays. The targets of this initiative included not just opposition to gay marriage, civil unions, and domestic partnership benefits, but also ordinances targeting discrimination against people in the workplace on account of sexual orientation. As a result of the letter, all Dignity chapters across the United States that had not yet been expelled from Church property were given their walking papers.

Despite his earlier work with AIDS victims, Cardinal Law vigorously enforced the Rat's mandate. According to Marianne Duddy, Law "had a powerful lobbying arm. It really delayed our getting civil rights. He threatened legislators [and] did a lot of damage to public-health funding and youth education around HIV transmission. He even worked to oppose allocating money for youth suicide prevention."

In 1998, Dignity members sought a meeting with Law. They gathered at the chancery. "It started off strange," Duddy recalled. "He had the nuns bring us milk and cookies. It was like an after-school special — so weird, and such a hierarchical, traditional nun-bishop kind of thing. Then he started lecturing us, doing the whole party-line thing.

"Someone in our group said, 'We came to talk with you, not to have you talk at us. How about if we each tell you a little bit about us, what our lives are like and then we can talk?' It cut him off. We talked about who we were, what we were doing with our lives, how long we had been involved with Dignity, how we grew up Catholic. He was getting it. He was very empathic."

Shortly afterward, Law wrote an editorial in the archdiocesan newspaper condemning antigay violence. He addressed ministry to AIDS patients in the bulletin at the cathedral. But the papal nuncio promptly showed up at the chancery and told Law to get back in line.

Being a bishop means never having to say you're sorry, I imagined him saying. *Now, where's that damn nun with my milk and cookies?!*

Need a Catholic Priest? Ask the Lesbian Jew

As if passing a tarted-up Our Lady of Leche from one set of shoulders to another, other gay Catholic heroes stepped in to take up where Dignity left off. It was early 2002. Vermont's civil unions had taken effect, and the conservative crowd in Massachusetts (all six of them) in concert with the snitches launched the first campaign to amend the Massachusetts Constitution to prohibit gay marriage.

Holly Gunner, a New York–born lesbian Jew, asked herself, What's the competition got that I don't? The answer: the Catholic Church and a claim that kids are better off with straight parents.

Gunner assembled world-class pediatricians to address the latter issue. The former proved more problematic.

"I knew nothing about the way the Church worked," she admitted, "but I knew the legislature was around 70 percent Catholic. A bunch of Quakers and a few rabbis wouldn't do."

Gunner heard about three potentially helpful priests and set to work persuading them to join the cause. Fathers Walter Cuenin, Tom Carroll (director of the JUC), and Rich Lewandowski (a pastor in the Diocese of Worcester) all agreed to testify before the Massachusetts legislature against the proposed amendment. Their carefully crafted testimony didn't contradict Church teaching on sexual morality, but instead questioned the proposed amendment's justice and fairness. Lewandowski's approach was typical:

> I believe it to be imperative that both the Church and the state do all in their power and join forces whenever possible to assist couples in strengthening the bonds of marriage. . . . House Bill 4840, while promoted as a "defense of marriage" constitutional amendment, does nothing to protect or help marriage. . . . It fails to address the divorce factor. . . . In fact, this amendment infers [sic] that multiple marriages and countless unions are just fine as long as these bonds are of "only one man and one woman" at a single time. Also, by stating that "any other relationship shall not be recognized as marriage or its legal equivalent, nor shall it receive the benefits and incidents exclusive to marriage," it excludes same-gender relationships and family units from affirmation and societal support. This does nothing to protect family life. It only weakens it. My fear is that House Bill 4840, rather than honestly supporting marriage and family life, might be used to encourage unjust discrimination against gay men and lesbian women and their committed relationships and the children in those relationships.

The three priests caught the Catholic Church flatfooted. Weakened by the scandal, the Massachusetts Catholic Conference did not produce a single witness to testify in favor of the bill. The next day, the headline in the *Boston Globe* read, "Three Priests Oppose Ban on Gay Marriage." The proposed amendment died.

A new amendment came to a hearing in 2003. Cuenin was unavailable, and Gunner knew she couldn't afford to go from three priests to two, so she sought the help of James Keenan, a prominent Jesuit theologian at Boston College. Making a distinction between "the Church's theology of chastity as it applies to sexual relations between gay and lesbian persons and the Church's theology of justice as it applies to all persons, regardless of sexual activity," Keenan noted that "the Church does not by any extension endorse the unequal or discriminating treatment of those whose sexual practices she condemns." He testified that there were therefore no Roman Catholic theological grounds for support of the amendment.

This time, the MCC had assembled its own trinity of witnesses to testify in support of the amendment: Gerry D'Avolio, Daniel Avila, and an older parish priest. Each claimed that Catholic teaching on sexuality required a vote for the amendment.

When the MCC finished testifying, a Catholic legislator named Chris Fallon rose and addressed the priest. "Father, I'm confused. I'm a good Catholic. I go to church every Sunday. I went to parochial schools my whole life. And you're telling me that for me to be a good Catholic and follow Catholic teaching, I should vote for this amendment. But I just heard three priests tell me that to be a good Catholic and support the Church's social justice teachings, I have to vote against the amendments. And one [sic] of the three priests is a Jesuit, and we all know Jesuits are smarter than anybody. Father, what am I to do?"

After the laughter, the proposed amendment again died.

How Did the Church Punish the Renegades?

Good question. You're catching on to how the archdiocese operates, forgoing transparency in favor of secrecy. First, the priests each received loads of hate mail from the snitches, including fellow clerics. Lewandowski told me, "I received a number of letters, mostly unsigned, and e-mails. I was given access to some Web sites that were pretty nasty. . . . One [priest] . . . from the Archdiocese of Boston called and left a message . . . something to the effect that I am one with Satan."

Cardinal Law called Cuenin and told him he had misread the text of the amendment. Cuenin politely disagreed and offered to talk it over. Law broke seven appointments to do so and then resigned in disgrace because of his role in the scandal. O'Malley ultimately forced Cuenin to leave his parish, though the chancery denied that Cuenin's testimony was the problem.

The day after the testimony, the MCC issued a scathing attack on Keenan and Lewandowski that concluded, "The priests communicated their personal opinions to the committee under the false guise of authority to the detriment of the integrity of the public hearing process. In our opinion, the manner of participation in the hearing by these priests on April 28 was a disservice both to the Catholic Church and to the Massachusetts legislature." The MCC also faulted the priests for not asking the MCC's permission to testify. *The Pilot*, official newspaper of the archdiocese, published an article that called Keenan nasty names.

None of the four priests holds the position he held at the time of the testimony. Ostensibly their removal had nothing to do with the notion that any of them was one with Satan. In fact, no reason has ever been offered for the removal of Lewandowski, Keenan, or Carroll. Must be pure coincidence.

Luckily, fellow clerics came to the support of the four priests. One sunny Sunday afternoon, 300 priests marched on the chancery, chanting "Power to the priests!" They ceremoniously burned their scapulars and stoles on the chancery steps. They strung up an effigy of Bishop Lennon on the Boston Common. Jesuit scholars worldwide signed a nearly unanimous letter vindicating Keenan. Hunger strikes were announced. At over 60 percent of Massachusetts parishes, the pastor held a moment of silence in solidarity with the oppressed priests. Posters of Ché Guevara appeared on the walls of the nunnery of the Poor Sisters of Saint Claire (and on the walls of the tunnel between the convent and rectory). Masked men in clerical garb rolled Cardinal Seán's black sedan (Massachusetts license 80) over in the street outside the State House and put a torch to it. Mobs ransacked the editorial offices of *The Pilot*. A half-dozen renegade seminarians serially mooned Cardinal Seán's bedroom window at the Cathedral of the Holy Cross.

Well, not so much. None of this happened. Let's just say that the Mohawks wouldn't have found much to eat in the chests of the local priesthood.

A proposed amendment to ban gay marriage came before the legislature a third time in late 2003, around the time the SJC had recognized same-sex marriage in Massachusetts as a constitutional right. As always, two steps forward, one back: none of the priests would testify, in part because the bishop of the Archdiocese of Worcester was to speak.

The tables turned. Now the only Catholic voice at the hearing was the Church's. Worcester's bishop delivered the Church's views with ringing clarity: "To redefine marriage itself or change the meaning of 'spouse' . . . is to deny the unique public value of the spousal bond between a man and a woman." In a subsequent letter to the editor of several newspapers, Reilly added that gays "do not possess the right to have a same-sex relationship treated as a basis for entitlements."

That amendment proposal ultimately went on to victory in 2004. Halftime score: gay people 2, Church 1.

But the Church had won the most recent battle and had momentum on its side.

Back-Room Heroes

To make it to the ballot, amendment proposals must win approval by two successive legislative sessions. So while Scott and I were singing "You're a Grand Old Flag" and not engaging with Mr. Sodomy and Pastor Bob, Gunner and her fellow lobbyists were working feverishly inside the State House to get legislators to defeat the amendment on the second round.

They operated on a simple principle: You've got to learn to be a good listener before you can ever be a good legislator. They handpicked citizens from the legislators' districts to meet with their representatives and tell their (gay) life stories. Almost weekly, Gunner called PFLAG or a lesbian parents' playgroup and placed a request for voters the way you'd place an order for fast food at a drive-through:

- Find me a working-class lesbian couple, preferably in the helping professions, who have lost their health care. Adoptive children and a horrible disease would be a big plus.

- Find me a conservative heterosexual father who struggled to make peace with his lesbian daughter but now is sponsoring the daughter's wife's conversion to Catholicism.
- Find me a senior lesbian volleyball player who's a former nun and primary caregiver to her devout Catholic mom.
- Find me a one-legged gay veteran with a couple of Vietnam tours, a Purple Heart, and a mean cribbage habit.
- Find me a homosexual lector-lawyer working for the government with an angry atheist boyfriend, a porn career, and a chip on his shoulder!

OK, Gunner never really asked for that last one, but I was ready to do my part had I been called on.

To win over Marian Walsh, a legislator known for her deep Catholic faith and a voting record consistent with the chancery's positions, Gunner sought a parent of a gay kid who was Catholic, went to parochial school, and lived in Walsh's district. The best the local PFLAG group could do was a shy woman who fit the description, but lived in the district adjacent to Walsh's. Walsh took the meeting anyway, and she and the mother immediately hit it off.

"You know that Catholic chatter," Gunner said. "Same schools, same nuns, oh Sister So-and-so this, and oh Sister So-and-so that."

When the meeting ended, Walsh declared she would vote against the amendment. "I think it's *mean*," Walsh said.

"Mean?"

"Mean," Walsh confirmed.

Excited, Gunner asked Walsh to use her influence to persuade others.

Walsh fixed Gunner with a steely look: "You've had a pretty good day today," she said. The subtext: Don't push your luck.

Gunner nevertheless continued to work the Catholic legislators. Despite her Jewish heritage, she was the go-to lesbian in charge of clerics. "He needs a priest," the other lobbyists told her. "Go get one." If the target legislator was a genuine churchgoer, Gunner tapped her network of friendly priests to determine whether the legislator's parish priest was gay-friendly. They scanned the church bulletins, probed the priestly scuttlebutt, and did everything but check guest lists at Provincetown bed-and-breakfasts.

Gunner and her crew no doubt used a checklist that looked something like this:

- ❏ Swishy walk to the podium
- ❏ Gold-tipped canes
- ❏ A Romentics novel collection
- ❏ Entourage including coachman, valet, and music (or perhaps dungeon) master
- ❏ Ownership of a miniature greyhound
- ❏ Subscription to *Bay Windows*
- ❏ Association with Father McSlutty
- ❏ Demonstrated talent in the primary homosexual arts — design, gardening, bitchery, etc.
- ❏ CD collection includes Maria Callas, Judy Garland, Gregorian chant, Billie Holiday
- ❏ Broadway-style liturgies

Score as follows:

0–2	Straightish
3–5	Questioning
6–8	Answering the question
9–10	Big nancy queen; sign him up!

Her efforts produced results. Gunner wouldn't comment on or identify particular pastors, but she said that many priests had quietly lent a hand in the lobbying against the amendment. Representative Paul Kujawski, who ultimately voted to defeat the gay marriage ban, said that two priests had made arguments to him against the amendment. Another Catholic legislator, Christine Canavan, said she consulted her local priest, who told her to vote her conscience — not necessarily the Church's party line.

These not-so-public clerics taking to the halls of power in defense of those of us in the street brought tears to my eyes. To all of you priests who so participated — and I mean this in the best Mohawk way — I'd like to eat your hearts.

While Gunner went about with her quiet missionary work among the Catholic priests, the Cardinal Seán political machine also kicked into high gear. Gunner persuaded a priest to speak to his legislator, and Cardinal Seán FedExed customized letters to parishes, providing contact information for the local representatives. Father Lewandowski organized a teach-in regarding same-sex marriage at a local state university, and the MCC made available the terrible dishonest video that drove Jean Marchant to womanpriesthood. Gunner provided a Jesuit to consult with a Haitian-American legislator about matters of conscience, and the bishop of Worcester announced, "Catholics, especially public officials, who willingly and with approval facilitate the legal sanctioning of same-sex unions are involving themselves in cooperation with evil."

Nevertheless, cooperating with Satan became all the rage. Other churches in the archdiocese came out as gay-friendly. Like the gay bars of old, no sign identified them, and no rainbow flag hung in the window. Instead, you've got to follow the smudges, keep your eyes peeled, and your ears open. *Listen. What do you hear?*

Maybe the Saint Anthony's G-L Spirituality Group advertises in their bulletins. Perhaps gay and lesbian couples appear in their parish directory with their children. Maybe every once in a while their pastors raise questions about the propriety of the Church's political efforts against same-sex marriage. Maybe a girl like Mikaela is brought to the altar and baptized while her two beaming mothers look on.

Spiritual Flamer

Inspired by all this gay Catholic history, I went back to the JUC shortly before they closed. It was the first time I had been back since my abortive trick with Michael days after I arrived in Boston a decade earlier. Bright multicolored bunting draped down from the roof of the sanctuary.

"For gay pride?" I asked a fellow congregant.

My comment won the kind of chilly stare commonly reserved for a small turd or the person who had failed to collect it from the sidewalk.

"*Pentecost*," he snapped righteously. "It's a representation of the flames of the Holy Spirit coming down on the apostles."

Pentecost! I hadn't even realized it — my favorite feast! It celebrates a gathering of the faithful in which the Holy Spirit filled the apostles and they spoke in different tongues understood by every person:

> They were all in one place together. And suddenly there came from the sky a noise like a strong driving wind, and it filled the entire house in which they were. Then there appeared to them tongues as of fire, which parted and came to rest on each one of them. And they were all filled with the Holy Spirit and began to speak in different tongues, as the Spirit enabled them to proclaim. Now there were devout Jews from every nation under heaven staying in Jerusalem. At this sound, they gathered in a large crowd, but they were confused because each one heard them speaking in his own language. They were astounded, and in amazement they asked, "Are not all these people who are speaking Galileans? Then how does each of us hear them in his native language? We are Parthians, Medes, and Elamites, inhabitants of Mesopotamia, Judea, and Cappadocia, Pontus and Asia, Phrygia and Pamphylia, Egypt and the districts of Libya near Cyrene, as well as travelers from Rome, both Jews and converts to Judaism, Cretans and Arabs, yet we hear them speaking in our own tongues of the mighty acts of God."

To reflect the different tongues, the JUC lectors proclaimed the Prayers of the Faithful in Spanish, Portuguese, German, Swahili, and Chinese. The homily concerned the hymn "Come Holy Spirit," sung in every Catholic church worldwide on Pentecost to emphasize universality. The presider said that Pentecost celebrated the birthday of the Church. He noted that Christ has no body in this world now except us, no hands but ours, no feet but ours.

"Let peace begin with me," he said. "Let it begin in this church. Go out and meet Christ when he comes; do not wait for Him to come to you."

Meet Christ? Hell, I have trouble trying to get a date with Cardinal Seán!

Then God said, *Shut up. Listen. What do you hear?*

Different voices, all the same God. On Pentecost, everyone was a flamer — even Cardinal Seán, the man of many tongues.

Inflame me, God, I asked. *Make my eyes as big as saucers, like a child, like Mikaela. She is who I must be, spiritually speaking.*

XVI

Acts of the (Gay) Apostles

Ours is not the escapism of some kinds of religion, nor is it the disconnected boring experience I'm afraid some Catholics remember. . . . You're always standing with the demonized, so that the demonization stops. You're always with the people on the outer fringes of the circle of compassion, so the circle of compassion can expand. You're always at the margins, so the margins once and for all disappear. And you're always with the disposable, so the people stop being disposed of.

— Rev. Gregory Boyle, Diocese of East Los Angeles

What Do You Do to Get in the Mood?

 NEW GENERATION OF WOMEN in the Bible Belt is turbo-charging the traditional Tupperware party their mothers used to throw. Instead of considering the miracle of plastic, they drink mint juleps and explore the wonderful world of sex toys.

At the G-L Spirituality Group, we, too, like to think of ourselves as hip to the newest trends. So we hosted a similar party — only we substituted prayer aids for marital aids, drank juice boxes instead of mint juleps, and nothing we were hawking required a nine-volt battery. It resulted in an entirely different kind of ecstasy.

"What do you use to get 'in the mood' for prayer?" Mama Bear asked.

The group emptied its pockets, man-purses, shoulder bags, and wallets and spilled a startling array of items on the table:

- Prayer cards (Abacus)
- Wooden statuary (me)

- A Psalter littered with colored sticky notes: red for sad, yellow for peace, blue for the Virgin (Martina)
- A rose-colored rosewood rosary made of rosettes dipped in rosewood oil (Sherwin — who else?)
- A spiritual journal (Alphaba)
- Religious collage (Mama Bear)
- Candles in the shape of Catholic saints (Job)
- A CD with the Sanctus on it (Magoo)
- Rilke's *Book of Hours: Love Poems to God* (June and Ward)
- Prayer box containing written intentions (newbie)
- *Hot Sauce* (no one, but they could have!)

Mama Bear took the cake. He showed off an entire authentic home altar torn from the bowels of a defunct church. No surprise, really — this guy had maintained a home nunnery as a preteen.

One by one, we explained what significance the objects held for us, how we incorporated them into our prayer life, and how well they worked. A current of excitement and relief passed around the table, as if prayer life was a shared vice. We all recognized our prayerful peccadilloes: *Been there. Done that. Not every prayer experience feels like what we think of as an encounter with God.*

We spoke of things many of us dared not say in our gay life for fear of ridicule. Shame transformed into pride, even defiance. To be in a room of people just like us — gay but spiritual, lesbian but a believer — gave us all a little thrill. Abacus in particular seemed to shave points off whatever sentence he had accorded himself in the hereafter, and he actually invited me to join another prayer group at a neighboring church. It probably cost his spiritual bottom line when I declined to attend. *Mea culpa.*

At the next meeting of the G-L Spirituality Group, Mama Bear challenged us with a reading from the first chapters of Genesis, concerning the creation of the world. The snitches and Mr. Sodomy point to this text as evidence that God's plan excludes homosexual love. (They take the line "God created them male and female" as a prohibition.)

"What's the overall message of the reading, and how is it applicable to gays and lesbians?" Mama Bear asked. "What do you see in this reading that's applicable?"

Alphaba, the caustic lesbian, spoke first. "I don't see anything in here. What's it say about gay and lesbian?"

Abacus pointed out the repetition of the two phrases: "God saw it was good" and "Each according to its kind." He said, "That means that all that God made — including gays — is good. And gays can be good according to their kind!"

"If we are in God's image and we are gay, there must be some aspect of God that is gay," Mama Bear added. He compared it to the Trinity — three beings in one God. He imagined gay and straight as aspects of that one being.

Alphaba stopped squirming. Occasionally, she interrupted to interject odd non sequiturs — "What translation is this?" "Where are we?" — but she was listening intently.

Job raised the idea of gay apostles, but a consensus quickly emerged that we didn't need them to be gay.

"It's irrelevant," said Magoo. "It makes no difference in how I conceive of Jesus."

Mama Bear's eyes twinkled. He had a knack for finding mayhem between the lines, playing with voices, timing, and words we thought we had exhausted. He pointed out verses that suggested God had prescribed vegetarianism for animals and man — green herbs, fruits from trees, and seed.

"Where?" Alphaba demanded. "I don't see that."

When the verses were shown to her, she let loose an appreciative gasp.

"I like meat!" Magoo confessed wistfully.

We all laughed, talking of translations, getting the words right, and using inclusive language.

"Look at this message of affirmation in Genesis, over and over," Mama Bear said. "When was the first time anyone looked at your gayness and said, 'It is good'?"

Martina, who was fifty years old, was the first to speak: "My brother did."

"When?"

"Um, last week."

An appreciative laugh rippled through the group.

"Long time to wait," Mama Bear said quietly.

We all nodded.

At the end of the evening, Mama Bear hugged me, saying, "I enjoyed what you had to contribute tonight."

I hadn't said a single word.

Pomfret's Lives of the Well-Intentioned, Reasonably Courageous, Everyday Clerics

Father Butterballino, a handsome, silver-haired sixty-year-old, had a strong brow and a slightly uneven goatee that looked like he might have tried to balance it out by shaving off a little bit on the right, a little bit on the left, more on the right, more on the left, until it was hopelessly lopsided. Frequent recourse to Twinkies had defeated his sexual appetites, and it showed.

"Just as well," he told me cheerfully. "If I were twenty years younger and a hundred fifty pounds lighter, I could get into all kinds of trouble. I wasn't a bad-looking guy, you know."

The purpose of my pilgrimage to his rectory was to listen — to hear the story of a priest who had struggled, whose actions had garnered less attention and perhaps involved less risk, and whose story did not fit squarely into a modern-day *Lives of the Saints*.

"Tell me what it's like," I asked.

Father Butterballino said he had no vocabulary for being gay as he grew up, but, he said, "I knew what pictures I liked to look at." Trapped in inarticulate yearning, he entered the seminary and was ordained. "We were sexually repressed. When I committed myself to celibacy I might as well have been committing myself to go to the moon."

Years after ordination, his sexual feelings emerged. Occasionally he was tempted to act out. "For priests," he explained, "[who] have been brought up with idea that if you are gay you are a pervert and a child molester and sexually promiscuous, and you then start sensing those same-gender feelings, you think, *I don't want to be a predator. I don't want to be this and that.* It takes a lot of courage to get over that baggage and say, Yeah, I'm gay, and I'm good. It takes a lot of courage."

He learned to accept his feelings and put a name to who he was and recommit himself to celibacy and ministry. He came out to a small circle of fellow priests after the sex-abuse scandal.

When the Brown Bag started issuing statements concerning same-sex marriage and adoption, Father Butterballino addressed them directly in his parish bulletins. For example, he wrote that to call gay adoptions "gravely immoral" and a form of violence proved only that those issuing such statements had never spent a second with gay adoptive families.

When the archdiocese asked parish priests to participate in the collection of signatures in favor of an amendment banning same-sex marriage, however, Father Butterballino was torn. For two of the three weekends Cardinal Seán requested petitions be made available in the back of the church, Father Butterballino procrastinated. Some parishioners took him to task; they wanted him to comply with the cardinal's request. Snitches raced back to the chancery with lists of nonconforming pastors, including Butterballino.

On the third weekend, he gave in and made the petitions available. He told his gay parishioners that he felt like he had no choice. "I told them 'I'm between a rock and a hard place. You know where I stand on these things. But he's your archbishop, and I am his local representative, and he asked me to provide you with an opportunity to do certain things. I find it difficult not to do that.'"

Among Butterballino's parishioners was a lesbian couple. Cradle Catholics, both named after saints, they were raising their two children as Catholics complete with parochial-school education. Let's call them Joan (of Arc) and Clare (of Assisi). Joan and Clare had belonged to the parish for nine years and were close personal friends of Father Butterballino.

Asked how they reacted, Father Butterballino was blunt. "They left the Church. I didn't blame them. If I were another age, I might make different decisions, too." A gray cloud of exhaustion passed over his face. "Joan and Clare said to me, 'For the first time we felt unsafe in our church.' And I've got to take responsibility for that. That's a great sadness for me. That I did something that made them feel that way."

Joan and Clare fled to a United Church of Christ congregation just a few blocks away and became religious crossovers.

"I felt totally betrayed," Clare told me. "I still feel betrayed about it. . . . I thought we were going to be OK, that we were going to make it through [the same-sex marriage debate] . . . which was very difficult, but I trusted that [Father Butterballino] wouldn't give any kind of sermon or preach about this. . . . I felt like I was sucker-punched . . . and I still don't understand why he felt he had to do this. . . . It was hard for me. It's still hard for me. I would love to go back to [Father Butterballino's] church. I felt like I had come home."

Joan and Clare's outrage and Father Butterballino's remorse seemed well-deserved. It was hard to find a rational basis to support his sense of compulsion. The archdiocese couched none of its communications to its pastors as demands. Reverend Kick-Me informed me the chancery never followed up on the snitches who reported nonconforming parishes. Indeed, many other diocesan priests openly announced that they wouldn't make the petitions available. Fr. Jack Ahern of St. Mary of the Assumption Church in Brookline, Massachusetts, wrote in his parish bulletin, "As is my custom, there is no signing of petitions for any initiative in the Church. Catholics differ on these matters, and we need to respect the rights of all." When a signature collector appeared at the Shrine, Father Bear-Daddy ordered security guards to escort her to the street.

Had Joan and Clare forgiven Butterballino for driving them from the Church?

"Forgive is probably the wrong word. . . . I don't know that I have something to forgive him for. . . . He's walking a tightrope in that church, he really is," Joan said. "[Father Butterballino] is very dynamic, a great pastor. . . . [He] was very good about the baptism [of one of their children] and [the children] both did First Communion. . . . [Father Butterballino] didn't treat us any differently from any of the other families."

In fact, Father Butterballino supported Joan and Clare's civil marriage and the civil marriages of other gay parishioners. He admitted, "I've been to four civil weddings of gay people. It scares the shit out of me because those are very public situations. . . . After the rite is over, whatever it is, I do some kind of prayer or blessing. If I'm called on it, I can say I was there and I performed a prayer. I didn't perform a wedding."

I asked Father Butterballino, "Why do it at all, if you're going to do it in this rinky-dink, sneaky way?" (phrased more diplomatically, of course).

"I think the Church needs to be there for two reasons," he said. "First these are Catholic people who are getting married where they are getting married because the Church won't recognize them. Second, so many times when the Church is talking about something, they just don't know."

Since the incident with the petitions, Father Butterballino reported some progress, which I couldn't help but attribute to his remorse. He came out to a member of his parish staff who had learned her son was gay. He had triumphant comings-out to select acquaintances. He even learned to be open with his parishioners that he was spending his summer vacation in Provincetown, Massachusetts, the gay beach mecca.

Sometime after Joan and Clare's wedding, one of his parishioners approached Father Butterballino and said, "You won't believe what I heard, Father."

"What did you hear?"

"I heard from somebody that lives in [the next town over] that 'those women' held some kind of wedding or something, and that you went to it."

"Is that what you heard?" Father Butterballino asked.

"Yes, Father."

"Hmmm," he said. "Isn't that *something?*"

My first instinct was to belittle these half-steps and his refusal to come out and come clean — but I tried to put myself in his shoes. After all, Father Butterballino's reticence was recognizable: it had been no different for most of us — circling the block seventeen times before we worked up the nerve to enter a gay bar, confiding in just a few people before telling the world more widely, crossing over one last time before embracing our gayness.

The half-steps he took really mattered. For Joan and Clare, the imprimatur of Father Butterballino's blessing helped reassure their children, for whom the idea of a marriage brought the unwelcome and unforeseen specter of divorce. For another gay couple, the public blessing at their wedding was as moving as the exchange of vows. They were gay men, so tears flowed freely when Father Butterballino laid his ample hands on their shoulders.

Two steps forward, one back. Father Butterballino daintily hefted his girth along the Catholic tightrope, maintaining a tenuous grip on his spiritual waffle.

Gay Voices

Scott and I were enjoying brunch one Sunday morning in the gayborhood with a friend. Our friend described an abortive attempt he had made the night before to engage a young man, whose acquaintance he had just met, in the sin that cries out to heaven for vengeance.

"You should consider yourself lucky," Scott quipped after hearing the whole ugly saga. "*I* had to go home and sleep with my boyfriend."

A woman at the next table gasped. She had just experienced an authentic gay moment. Now she could rush home and tell all the other mothers in her book group. "It was just like *Queer as Folk*!" she would gush. "They actually talk out loud about blow jobs! Over brunch!"

In reality, the moment possessed as much authenticity as breaking a wineglass and concluding you had just participated in a Jewish wedding. But it raised an interesting question. *Was* there an authentic and peculiarly gay blessing that my tribe brought to the spiritual community? A number of priests, Dignity elders, random folks, and even the Courage chaplain offered me their views:

- "We are fun-loving and campy and inject a lot of humor into hard situations." — former lay ministry committee member

- "We've been kicked around, and we bring that. I'm not sure I can say what that does for us. I guess that a lot of people who came to Jesus were those that had been kicked around." — Joan
- "Redemption. Gay people can take sustenance from the hand of the one that oppresses them." — former Jesuit priest
- "Think about how many hymns [were] written by gay people, stained glass designed by gay people, architecture." — former lay ministry committee member
- "Gay people's exuberance, their over-the-top, heart-on-sleeve, bigger-than-life feelings that are taken for granted in some cultures, but considered threatening in this cold, repressed Irish culture. In Malta, there's an arms race of village against village, parish against parish, as to who is going to have the grandest fireworks display. Some parishes actually own fireworks manufacturers. They begin planning for next year's feast the day after the feast day. Nothing like that in our culture." — Picasso (of the G-L Spirituality Group)
- "I tend to find the [gay] guys have beautiful, sensitive hearts. That can be dark, in that because they are sensitive, they get hurt easily. But it can be light — such compassion for suffering in others and a desire to alleviate suffering in others." — Father John, Courage chaplain
- "GLBT folks understand the holiness and sacredness of sexuality. . . . It is an important part of what it is to be Christian. . . . GLBT folks understand the place of body in prayer and commitment." — lesbian womanpriest
- "GLBT persons have had to learn to embrace, cherish, and celebrate the human body. From my Dignity experience, I see how GLBT Catholics bring their bodies with them to worship: singing, moving, clapping, embracing, laughing. . . . GLBT Catholics understand and live the incarnation mystery." — Dignity priest
- "The Sistine Chapel would be painted some horrible shade

of beige if it weren't for us." — G-L Spirituality Group member

- "All gays and lesbians I know have suffered, and so I think they bring a spiritual dimension that is maybe a little bit different from the suffering of their straight counterparts. A greater sensitivity to issues of injustice. A desire for a greater justice in society and the world." — diocesan priest

- "Gay people are an evolved, biologically advanced Darwinistic adaptation to overpopulation, like what happens to rats on ships. You can see it at the Museum of Science. Their sex drive shuts down. Our sex drives morph in a way that achieves the same end. . . . We're not cavemen anymore, and the concept of love has become more advanced than mere reproduction. Thus we are on a higher plane than animals who are out there grunting and trying to reproduce. Straight people want this, but they are out there shitting out babies. We're not in survival mode. We're not just breeding and putting food in our mouths. We're asking how can we make life better, not just pure survival." — Scott Whittier

My answer: inventiveness. By physical necessity, we've got to make up ways to get off since we do not use hetero tab A and slot B in the same way. (Rory and Jezebel's premarital sexual inventiveness almost made them honorary fags.) We've had to be inventive to survive persecution in a heterosexist world. Our love for and tweaking of liturgy reflects our ritual inventiveness, in which I see an aspect of God, because He, too, is an inventor. As Cardinal Seán says (over and over), "The Eucharist is God's invention."

But a nagging doubt played at me: that I wanted to be two things at once. I wanted to be both exceptional, blessed with certain charisms by virtue of being gay, and at the same time ordinary, in that I deserved civil marriage just like my straight brothers and sisters. I wanted to be a rebel within.

On account of this doubt, the most comforting answer came from a gay man at the Shrine who is civilly married to his nonbelieving husband, who told me he didn't think there was such a thing as a peculiarly gay spirituality. But he said, "I wouldn't be in the Catholic Church without [my husband]. To be loved unconditionally is to know what it means to understand who God is. And I don't think I would understand the idea of God at all if it weren't for my relationship with [my husband]."

"Does your husband know that?" I asked.

"If I told him, I think he'd be freaked out. He's a real model for me of what unconditional love is. . . . Because of him I get God in a way I never got through twelve years of Catholic school."

Back in the Saddle

Father Abraham lay prostrate on the marble. Long seconds passed. Chewbacca grunted. Aged friars, mostly retirees, kneeled in spare pews, all of which were full. The Shrine was bursting at the seams. The Passion's narrator flubbed all the proper names and betrayed a working-class accent she hid in everyday speech.

I had gone to the gym just before Mass and forgotten to bring a clean pair of underwear, so I was going commando beneath my tailored suit. When my turn at the ambo came, I felt a little sassy. Words rolled off the tongue. I said a little prayer to myself that went something like this: *I don't know what I want from You, God, if I want anything at all. I don't want to beseech You, or thank You, or seek Your forgiveness or others' salvation. I just want to stand naked before You, choked with wonder, uttering a prayer as joyful, guttural, sorrowful, agonizing, and inarticulate as an orgasm.*

We were in my favorite liturgical cycle, focusing on the Gospel of Luke, with all its outsider stories that appear nowhere else: the good Samaritan, Martha and Mary, the prodigal son, the rich man and Lazarus, the corrupt judge and the widow, the Pharisee and the tax collector, the woman at the well. All these stories emphasized ministry to the marginalized and outcast.

My mother arrived while I was reading. Her face showed traces of age, but her eyes hadn't aged a day. She looked beautiful, like the woman who arrived from Dublin at Idlewild Airport in 1964 wearing pointy Jackie Kennedy shoes.

In his homily, Father Abraham reminded us that we know the Passion story not only because it is read every Good Friday, but because we know the cross from living our own lives. His words made me think about Mama Bear, Job, Picasso, Alphaba, and all the other heroes of the G-L Spirituality Group. There are no accidental or knee-jerk Catholics among gay people. Martina did not casually drift into her devotion. Every day, every pronouncement, Abacus re-tallies the beads of his belief, the credits, debits, and bottom line. Gay people continuously ask why, and we have to keep coming up with reasonably good answers.

We suffer from uncertainty, a lack of entitlement, an acute feeling that perhaps we have been tricked, duped, snowed, swindled, cheated, and deceived. This doubt suffuses our worship with invigorating desperation. It keeps us humble, grateful even. Satirists commonly caricature people of strong faith as people whose minds are closed to all but their own beliefs. The G-L Spirituality Group members exemplified quite the opposite: that faith comes to those whose minds accept both doubt and possibility.

As one gay priest preached to a Dignity service I attended:

> The opposite of faith is not doubt or disbelief. The opposite of faith is certainty. . . . Genuine faith takes root and grows when we confront uncertainty and can embrace it and live with it and within it.
>
> Everybody who sits in this church today has wrestled with faith and its demands. It is what brought you here the first time and keeps you here. You could have chosen to stay in the closet, choose denial, silence, and invisibility. You could have rejected your religious heritage, your baptism, your call to believe and to serve. You did none of this. You did not suspend belief, neither in yourself or your God.

At the next G-L Spirituality Group meeting, two new lesbians showed up. Newly civilly married, they had been together eighteen years. Thelma wore her hair short under a man's Irish walking cap. Louise flaunted a big feminine fighting spirit, full of passion and anger. Both had a few rough edges, but they had gone on a pilgrimage to Trinity College, Dublin, to see the Book of Kells.

I explained my project with Cardinal Seán and the big wet kiss. "We're like the lepers," I said.

"Nothing wrong with me!" Louise snapped. "I'm no leper."

"I was referring to our status in society, not suggesting that we were diseased."

After considering this a moment, Thelma said, "Mother Teresa went among the lepers. Mother Teresa wouldn't have judged my being a lesbian."

Mama Bear confirmed that Mother Teresa had met with AIDS sufferers while she visited the United States and treated them as humans. She had said, "They are Christ."

"Cardinal Seán knows Mother Teresa," I said brightly. "Or knew her."

Mama Bear frowned. This was the problem with a gay spirituality group. We tossed ideas out and rapidly discarded them. Sudden inspirations and intuitions and nonlinear thinking carried us away. We couldn't stop it. We're gay people. We create. We rehab old items, or we build from scratch. We have an eye for good bones hidden by surface blight.

Louise shared the story of a colleague who complained incessantly about Stop 'n' Shop Catholics. He prided himself on being a real Catholic. He said that when he was young, his father had him regularly do the seven stations of the cross.

Louise pointed out there were fourteen stations. "Twelve years of Catholic school," she said. "I did learn *something*."

Her colleague disputed the number, until the Internet proved her right.

"Still, *I* go to church," her colleague said. "Why don't *you* go to church, Louise?"

"The Church doesn't want me," she replied.

To the group, Louise asked plaintively, "Why did he ask that? He knows I'm a lesbian." She folded her arms over her ample chest. "At least *I* know how many stations of the cross there are."

The Group's discussion frequently unleashed these pent-up reservoirs of smoldering hurt and unrequited love. *B-b-b-b-oyfriend. P-p-p-p-partner. Guh-guh-guh-girlfriend. Sppppppppouse.* Words the Group never thought they would utter under a church roof. They still seemed occasionally afraid. They still seemed like they were just taking their freedom for a test drive.

"Say it again," I suggested. "Repeat it enough times, put it in words, that's what helps. Whether it's a naughty word, or a God word, or something else entirely. I speak from experience."

B-b-b-b-b-b-oyfriend. P-p-p-p-p-p-partner. Guh-guh-guh-girlfriend. Sppppppppouse.

At first forbidden, it feels revolutionary, then secret. We imagine the party must imminently end. "They'll turn us out in the street," people at the JUC used to complain when the community got too gay. The same as Abacus way back when.

B-b-b-b-b-oyfriend. P-p-p-p-p-partner. Guh-guh-guh-guh-girlfriend. Sppppppppouse.

Repeat it like a prayer, like a benediction, like a decade of the rosary. Speak it aloud. Proclaim it on high. Use your gay voice. Take your damn pew. Amen.

Amazing Grace and Leftover Miracles

The first sign that Scott and I might overcome my Catholic fixation occurred after Dick Cheney sprayed his hunting companion in the face with buckshot. Newly cardinalized, O'Malley, who typically wore brown Franciscan robes, quipped that he was unlikely to don a red cardinal's robe — unless, of course, Dick Cheney invited him to hunt.

Scott laughed out loud when I showed him the quote. It was the first real laugh I'd triggered in him in months that wasn't tinged with caustic bitterness. A few weeks later, Scott and I spent Thanksgiving Day with his family. Gram confessed that she had finally read one of our romance novels.

"What did you think?" I asked.

"Now I know what you guys do," she said, nudging me in the ribs.

"Do?"

"In my bed."

All eyes in the room swiveled to her bedroom door except mine. A half-dozen pornographic movies played in their faces, each and every one starring yours truly.

After the meal was done, many bottles of wine were drunk, and Gram had gone to bed, Rory and Jezebel confessed that they were having trouble getting pregnant. Indeed, medically speaking, it turned out that Rory and Jezebel had about as much chance of making a baby as Scott and I did.

IVF was out of the question. They believed, in accordance with Church teaching, that the procedure guaranteed violence to the little lives in the eggs. They resisted the argument that every method of getting pregnant involves losses and miscarriages the parents often don't know about. Even for a Catholic like me, their version of my religion made me feel like a goose being prepared for foie gras.

"Let's talk about what's possible," Jezebel suggested, "rather than what we can't do." They hoped to obtain embryos from others who had succeeded with in vitro fertilization and had leftover eggs.

"You need a marketing concept," Scott suggested. "A way to get out the word."

"A marketplace, maybe," I said. "You need an eBay for embryos."

Riffing on this concept, Scott started drafting marketing materials right on the kitchen table. (He writes advertising copy for a living.)

Rory and Jezebel exchanged a grateful glance. Even I was amazed. For the sake of his newly Catholic brother, Scott put his talent behind this pitch for a cause in which he did not believe.

"We need a tag line," Scott said.

We all spewed out drunken suggestions, then came up with a logo, a Web site, and everything short of venture capital.

Suddenly, Scott held up a hand for silence. "Leftover miracles," he said, jotting it down. "Give us your leftover miracles."

Jezebel wept.

*　　*　　*

"That was very generous," I said to Scott as we got ready for bed.

He shrugged, embarrassed. "It's nothing, no big deal."

"I believe God put us together," I said.

Silence fell between us. He stared at me.

"Now, having told you that, I want to hug you," I added.

"So hug me."

"I can't."

"Why not?"

"I'm not sure if I would be hugging you as an expression of affection, a bribe, or just to stop you looking at me like that."

XVII

I See Broken
People Everywhere

The hard part is allowing myself to cease being fixated on pastors and politicians,
named individuals who either silently or vociferously wage a war against us, deter-
mined that it is God's honor that is at stake, an honor to be defended at whatever
means, however great the cost.

— James Alison

Gay People 1, Cardinal Seán 0

 n June 14, 2007, the General Court of the Common-
wealth of Massachusetts convened the last constitu-
tional convention to address the citizen-proposed and
Church-supported petition for an amendment banning gay marriage. The bad guys needed 50 votes out
of 200. If they succeeded, gay marriage would be put to popular vote
on the 2008 ballot in Massachusetts.

In a statement that was to be included in parish bulletins, the archdiocese had urged Catholics to contact their legislators to support the
amendment. O'Malley also sent a letter of support to those legislators
who had supported the amendment in the past and a second letter to
all legislators seeking additional support. On June 9, he blogged, "Marriage should not be blithely undermined by an overactive judiciary."
On the morning of the convention, Cardinal Seán got on the horn to
Catholic legislators, urging them to vote to put the amendment on
the ballot.

But the Brown Bag's moral authority had so waned by June 14 that at least one conservative Catholic legislator — Representative Paul Kujawski — refused to take his call. According to newspaper reports, Kujawski said that while driving down the highway toward the State House, "the bottom line came down to putting myself in the position of what if I was gay. How would I want to be treated?" Kujawski had decided that gay people needed his help more than the opponents did.

As Kujawski and his colleagues made their way to their State House offices, Scott and I found a place on the street outside the capital building. I hoisted a handwritten sign that read "Another Catholic for Gay Marriage" to my shoulders. When my mother arrived, I pressed the sign into her hands.

The police had divided the demonstrators so that same-sex marriage opponents stood on one side of the street, and we stood on the other. You know the dueling banjos scene from the film *Deliverance?* Substitute dueling children. Across the street, the opposition hauled out fair-haired tykes and stuck their clothes with dozens of "one-man-one-woman" stickers. On our side, gay dads boosted their adopted Cambodian offspring to their shoulders with little rainbow flags in the children's hands. The other side mustered a preteen church group with percussion instruments. The lesbian moms on our side formed a phalanx of double-wide strollers.

To their credit, our opponents kept strict discipline, fielding a unified front of mass-produced identical green signs that said, "Let the people vote." When a group of Russians showed up with more expressive handwritten signs depicting anal sexual activity and asserting direct connections between homosexuals and the Nazi party, the opposition leaders funneled them down the block to the less camera-friendly precincts.

From the Boston Common behind our opponents came a deep sound like lowing cattle. Gradually it grew and became identifiable: hymns from the civil rights marches of the 1960s. They grew louder and closer. All of a sudden, the "Let the People Vote" signs parted like the Red Sea. Carrying hymn sheets, rainbow stoles, and pocket Bibles, 250 clergy poured through the gap. The people around me picked up the refrain: "We shall overcome." The clergy streamed across the street to our side and gathered behind us, one solid chorus, until there was hardly room to stand.

My lesbian boss found a place beside me. A moment later, a ripple passed through the crowd.

"We won! We won!" someone shouted.

I leapt into the arms of . . . well, my lesbian boss, and then Scott. (Hey, it was all about proximity.)

The final tally came to 151–45. Church-backed opponents of same-sex marriage had fallen five votes short of the number they needed. Representative Paul Loscocco, a staunch Catholic who had promised to back the amendment during his election campaign just eight months before, switched his vote to defeat the amendment. According to someone who heard it directly from Loscocco, Cardinal O'Malley had called Loscocco to say that the issue was all about natural law. Loscocco interrupted the cardinal, saying, "Wait a minute, Cardinal. It's about civil rights. We're talking about civil rights." When the final vote was announced, Loscocco's wife, a daily communicant, sent him a text message that he received on the floor of the legislature. It read, "You are my hero."

Most of the demonstrators against gay marriage dropped their signs and went home. The Russians were not so easily dissuaded. They brought their stick-figure renditions of anal sex front and center. The signs read, "Not even dogs do it that way."

The governor of Massachusetts urged gay-marriage supporters to make peace with the other side of the street, but the Russians jeered, made obscene gestures, and did everything they could to drown him out. Cardinal Seán showed scarcely more grace in defeat. The four bishops of Massachusetts issued a statement calling the vote "tragic," and claiming, "Today the common good has been sacrificed by the extreme individualism that subordinates what is best for children, family, and society." They also hinted at unfair backroom political pressure and decried the supposed influence of "powerful special interest groups." Sour grapes are no substitute for the hearts of Jesuit missionaries.

But what would I have done had Cardinal Seán conceded his defeat with more grace and fewer accusations? What would I have done if he had issued a plea for reconciliation as the governor had? What if Seán had said, "Let us turn to the rest of society's pressing business — poverty, social justice, capital punishment — with the energy with which we took to the streets on this matter?"

It would have cast me adrift. With no "them" to sanctify "us," my rage would falter. *My God*, I thought, *what if I had to learn to love Cardinal Seán instead of metaphorically smacking him in the head with a baseball bat like he was a cheap piñata?*

Fortunately, I'm a bad person, so I knew I'd take the bat every time. I am Cardinal Seán's brother in rage and indignation. I am his brother in lack of graciousness. I am he, and he is me. Je-RU-salem! I was going to subtitle this book *From Porn to the Pearly Gates*, but perhaps *From Purgatory to Perdition* might prove more apt.

That night, I drove up to my brother Bruce's house to apologize for a fight he didn't even know he was in.

Why Catholic? (Part 1)

Triumph gave way to unease. It embarrassed me that the archdiocese had been so badly beaten in a legislature that was 70 percent Catholic. The Church, limping, haggard, once a moral contender, had weakened to a shadow of its former strength. A different Church, one that retained a speck of moral authority, might still have articulated Gospel imperatives that really did bear repeating: poverty, capital punishment, war, goldfish murder, the ubiquitous frat boy uniform of khaki pants and braided belts, and other objective evils.

"The whole structure has to die," a priest told me, "and it is." He cited statistics that readers of the *National Catholic Reporter*, a progressive Catholic newspaper, were on average over seventy years old. He said that the average age at a national conference of Call to Action, a Catholic reform group, was sixty-five. Indeed, by nearly every measure — Mass attendance, number of priests, political power, or bingo revenues — the Roman Catholic Church has diminished. Gallup polls showed that 40 percent attended Mass weekly in 2003, compared with 74 percent in 1958. But only 20 percent of Catholics born after 1960 report weekly Mass attendance. One priest told me, "The younger folk aren't angry. They just don't take the teachings seriously."

A task force assembled by Cardinal Seán documented the decline in the number of priests. The task force identified approximately 500 active priests in the archdiocese and projected that that number would decline to 292 by 2015. Similarly, Saint Anthony Shrine had 55 friars when it opened in the 1950s, 40 when Myron first served at the Shrine (1976–1981), and today just 16.

A smaller, weaker, broken Church doesn't distress B16, the crop of bishops appointed by him and J2P2, or the young priests ordained during their reigns. They seem happy to minister to the center rather than the margin, to exclude large portions of mankind, and to exclude the modern-day lepers. B16 has his priorities straight: host warmonger Tony Blair at the Vatican during the Iraq War and welcome his conversion to the Catholic fold, while proposing excommunication for Spanish politicians who favor gay marriage.

From a priest:

> Catholic extremism, especially in America, is a force to be reckoned with. They are represented by a cadre of bishops who basically run roughshod over the other bishops. The bishops as a conference have shown they are unable or unwilling to resist them. Any bishop who tries to speak with pastoral reason is condemned as weak on life issues.

From Father Bozek:

> I have no doubts that excommunication and withholding communion from certain persons and all groups of people is a perfect example of many bishops pushing their fanatic, reactionary agenda. Men in pink (the hierarchy) are using the most sacred elements of our Catholic faith to shamelessly promote their limited and outdated point of view, which often has nothing to do with modern, healthy theology. One does not need to be a prophet to realize that such policies

will create a church that will be more "Roman" than "Catholic." More and more Catholics will migrate to other denominations and many, I am afraid, will cut their ties with any organized religion whatsoever.

For these bishops and priests, an empty church proves they have done their job well. Only cowering jellies, helpless dogs, well-behaved eunuchs, and fantastically old people secretly relieved that they can forget about Vatican II need apply.

Reading interviews with newly ordained seminarians in the *Boston Pilot*, Father Butterballino shook his head in disgust at their pietistic sloganeering. "I'm just glad that there are so few of them."

The More Things Change

WAKEFIELD, Mass. — Rev. Ron Barker, pastor of Saint Joseph's Parish, banned Harry Potter books from the library of Saint Joseph School because themes of witchcraft and sorcery were inappropriate for a Catholic school. According to one mother, Barker "said that he thought most children were strong enough to resist the temptation, but he said it's his job to protect the weak and the strong."

Cardinal Seán, too, seemed personally broken. Shortly after his appointment, he wrote that "being Archbishop of Boston is like living in a fishbowl made out of magnifying glass." You'd think he would have shown more solidarity with the goldfish. O'Malley's father died in 2005 in the midst of the furor over same-sex marriage. People who encountered him reported a stunned, deer-in-the-headlights look. Members of the Religious Coalition for the Freedom to Marry, a group of over a thousand Massachusetts clergy of many faiths united in support of gay marriage, attended an interfaith seder at which O'Malley spoke. Reverend Kick-Me greeted the RCFM representatives and offered to introduce them to the cardinal. One of the RCFM representatives tried to chitchat about how much she had enjoyed the evening. The cardinal turned away.

The RCFM member complained to me that O'Malley hadn't passed Conversation 101: "I felt like I had to explain to the cardinal, how it works is: We say something, and you say something in return. Because there was this blank dead-in-the-water look, it went nowhere."

Another person told me, "I used to work at [a hospital], and the bishops would periodically come up. I was amazed at the difference at how he related to people compared to how Cardinal Law related to people. Law is very warm and made you feel good. And I thought Seán O'Malley was a nightmare. He didn't relate at all to the people, he was very serious. Very different . . . I was amazed at how distant he was."

So why do I cling to a broken, dying Church and its broken prelate? I continue, and the G-L Spirituality Group continues, and the pious continue, not because we seek spiritual insurance. We come because we experience something of God at the Shrine, something that moves, a whisper, a current, in a setting that both rings true and is strangely unsettling, decidedly different, where listening is active if imperfect and where acts of corporal mercy always form part of the picture. The Mass offers a chance to "acknowledge the wisdom of listening before speaking, of learning before teaching, of praying before pronouncing." 50 percent of religion is just showing up.

We don't always experience the miraculous. It's not like I can drop a dollar in the collection plate and get a spiritual snack-pack in return from some celestial vending machine. But sometimes bread and wine change into flesh and blood. I witness that miraculous change, and realize all kinds of other miraculous changes could happen, like a new Church arising imperceptibly from the suffering of the old. Brokenness is an opportunity for the Spirit to enter.

Now and at the Hour of Our Death

Stacks of first editions filled the apartment of a now not-so-Hale Mary Flanagan. Projects and artwork in process covered her tables. Yet she informed me, not without pride, that she had been amusing herself lately with trashy reality shows. She was dying. She wasn't sad, she wasn't afraid — just old.

The strangling hand of my Irish reticence locked my jaw until my inner Mama Bear emerged. I told Mary how grateful I was for everything she had done for me.

When I moved to give her a hug, Mary manufactured an annoyed expression, waved me away, and brushed off "that kind of talk." She wanted to discuss what the latest rule changes were for the eucharistic ministers so she could scoff and shake her head at Father Bear-Daddy's infinite folly. We Irish are truly a silent, cramped, maddening, and lovely people.

"What do you want, Mary?" I begged. "What can I do for you?"

"Nothing," she said, then allowed perhaps she'd like a copy of the *Boston Sunday Globe*. She tried to give me a dollar, but I dodged her. She hauled her cancered carcass up from the chair and chased me around her apartment waving the dollar, her knuckles big as marbles, her skin translucent, her head bald, but her eyes as sharp as ever.

"God's sakes, *take* it," she said. "It's not like I need a gold coin to pay my passage!"

I was on my way to her apartment when Mary died ten days later.

The funeral took place during Holy Week, the most solemn time of the year. The priests wore white, and the sanctuary lacked flowers save for the one red rose laid by Mary's sister on her casket. A waft of smoke from the censer eddied at the altar. One of Mary's friends climbed to the ambo. Unaccompanied, she sang an old hymn in Irish. The language, strange and beautiful, erased us, conjuring the smell of peat and ocean salt. Her voice wavered and broke, a harrowing sound like a bow drawn over poorly tuned violin strings. Then it gathered strength and body, the solitary voice uncowed by the church's vastness, growing, invoking something unseen and ineffable. It was easy to believe that Mary's soul had risen up from her ruined body and tarried just a moment on the way to Heaven to take possession of her friend's voice and sing with her.

My eyes locked on the useless work of the priest's hands: raising the bread and breaking it, mixing the water and wine, washing his hands for the cleansing of iniquities. Nothing made a sound, as if we had lost the audio portion of our program. There was only movement — familiar, precise, consoling, effective. It reminded me of watching Gram at work in the slanted evening light among white pines around the lake in Maine: shucking corn, snapping green beans, hulling peas, shelling pistachios, setting a table, frosting whoopee pies, cheating at cards, pouring gasoline on the fire pit, and carping about Catholics.

Being mindful of small things transformed these tiny ministries. They became bigger than themselves, more than their sum. They were calming, enthralling, instructive. It became clear why the snitches made such a big deal out of the rubrics and rules for the celebration of the liturgy. I felt, for just a moment, at one with them. The miracle was that there need not be a miracle — just a slow drip of experience. Mary would have laughed had she known that a few months after her death, Cardinal Seán sent her a letter politely wondering why she had not yet contributed to that year's annual archdiocesan Catholic Appeal fund drive — and expressing hope that she would.

O'Malley may someday end the Shrine's ministry. The chancery may fire Father Bear-Daddy or shut the group down. But other churches will welcome us, other places will allow us to convene. People everywhere reach out a welcoming hand; saints — gay and otherwise — buck the trend and speak out:

- A woman breaking her communion wafer in half and sharing it with those who have been forbidden to receive
- Father Butterballino's surreptitious blessing of gay unions
- Priests testifying against gay-marriage bans
- Bishops supporting their out clerics
- Theologians discerning truth a millennium before Church fathers

In western Massachusetts, Ann Franczyk helped found Always Our Children, a group for Catholic parents with gay and lesbian children. She approached her bishop (not O'Malley) to notify him. Within thirty seconds of meeting her, he said, "I can't condone homo-genital sex."

Well, hello to you, too, Bishop.

Franczyk took a deep breath and said, "You can make a big difference in the lives of gay people, Bishop, especially gay kids."

The bishop pushed back his chair and took his own deep breath. It stunned him to learn that kids killed themselves because they were gay.

"Have you ever loved a gay person?" Franczyk asked. "Because to love someone who is gay is never to see the world the same way."

The bishop agreed to let Franczyk start her group. Over the year, at the height of the same-sex marriage debate, Franczyk and other parents met with over twenty-five pastors, with a goal of speaking to every priest in the diocese.

All listened intently to the parents' stories. Many of the priests suggested that they had never engaged in an intellectual discussion about gay people before. Some resisted the pitch and said they viewed active homosexuals as sinners. Some said they had been reaching out quietly to gay people for a long time. Some expressed anger at Franczyk and her fellow parents for trying to start a dialogue inside a Church that had been historically so discriminatory against gay people. They seemed to be saying: *Unlike me, you can choose to leave!*

Slowly the group's efforts produced results. Priests hung Always Our Children posters in their schools and churches. They put notices of Always Our Children meetings in their bulletins. Franczyk asked one priest to recite a prayer of the faithful for GLBT people.

"You write it, Ann, and I'll read it," he responded. Here's what he read at Mass:

> *Let us pray for our gay, lesbian, bisexual, and transgender children and their families, reaching out to them with love and compassion as Jesus and His Mother would in a world which is so often afraid of what it doesn't understand. Let us pray to the Lord.*

In one parish, the pastor gave a series of Advent homilies that addressed the Church's role with respect to people on the margin. The series culminated in a Christmas homily, at which the priest declared, "As long as I am pastor, GLBT people will be welcome in my parish." He won a standing ovation.

These are small steps, discrete acts, a quiet refusal to occupy the back pew. Learned helplessness fades; we are not all shocked dogs anymore.

Re-Membering

Angela, a thin, sporty lesbian wearing a Guatemalan wool hat, ski coat, and fleece pullover, was telling the G-L Spirituality Group about her parish in the Castro neighborhood of San Francisco. Most Holy Redeemer had an 80 percent GLBT congregation, who mostly attended the 10:00 A.M. mass and had been doing so since the AIDS epidemic began.

"It was the first place I could ever go into and worship with all my parts. I didn't have to check anything at the door. I brought my whole mind, my whole body to worship the Lord," Angela said. "I didn't recognize the sacraments in my life until I came to church with all my parts."

Our ignorance of the fullness of being gay Catholics struck Angela. She, too, saw broken people. She, too, detected a sense of woundedness. Job, Alphaba, Mama Bear, me — so many of us were "dis-membered." We had left the Church emotionally, if not physically.

I nodded like a bobble doll on the dash of a Ford 150. When I first came to the Shrine, I left behind a litter of parts. Holy foreskin and severed hearts? That's nothing. I shed Scott, porn writing, Romentics, untempered fury. The Shrine could have used another lay ministry entirely, the Holy Coat-Check Girl to supply numbered tags in exchange for a few crimped bills in a jar so I could pick up all my parts when I headed out the door.

Angela suggested a solution. She had participated in a program back west called Re-Membering. "The Church is like a person with a missing limb. It needs its homosexual members. Rejoin. It needs to re-member itself." *The eye cannot say to the feet, I do not need you,* I thought. *All members of the body of Christ are important.*†

We began to plan a weekend Re-Membering retreat. "There must be lots of unstructured space to talk about the Church," Angela said. "What it really says and how to interpret that in gay life. It provides a portal, which is like a birth canal, for gay Catholics to come back."

"Just from a marketing perspective," I suggested, "I think we need to limit the birth canal analogy, if we hope to get any gay men to show up."

It would also be necessary to have someone in authority present. As Angela put it, "We need a collar in the room."

"Maybe a collar in body armor."

"People tend not to believe laypeople. They're caught up in that old-school mentality that the only source of authority in church is a priest," Angela said.

Just as I was about to riff smugly on Ye Olde Piety Show, God Himself rang a big brass gong in my head and pointed out the obvious: the Piety Show performers included me. I, too, was living with that old-school mentality. The desire to plant one on Cardinal Seán, to get him to acknowledge me, bought wholesale into the snitch model of the Church in which old men in Rome hoarded the truth and doled it out piece by piece to a thoughtless and shrinking flock, who petitioned and gave thanks for every scrap of approval thrown down.

Humiliation flooded me — for needing acknowledgement, for seeking yet again after unrequited love. *Have you ever loved an archbishop? Because to love someone who is an archbishop is never to see the world the same way.*

All of us gay Catholics ought to stop waiting for others to confer power on us. However worthless you feel, and however worthless you are made to feel, others cannot take away God's love for you or the godliness within.

"My Church," Angela said, "is right at this table."

---

† 1 Corinthians 12:21–22.

Why Catholic? (Part 2)

On seeing the announcement for the G-L Spirituality Group in the Shrine's weekly bulletin, a righteous blue-haired, middle-aged woman came up to Father Bear-Daddy before Mass while he was preparing the altar.

"Hey," she said, waving around the bulletin. "What's next? You going to have a support group for prostitutes?"

Father Bear-Daddy turned, looked at her, bit his lip, and simply could not keep his tongue in check. "Why? Did you want to join?"

False Starts and Fake Boobs: A Prayer

Catholic is the language I speak when I speak about experiences that are at once full of awe, joy, mystery, gratitude, and yearning. Confession, forgiveness, genuflection, inflection, mercies, parables, psalms, redemption, saints, signs of the cross, sins — this is my vocabulary. I never feel so authentic when I am speaking a different moral language; I never find *le mot juste*.

I come from a family of halfsies, botched starts, and conflicting impulses. My paternal aunt became a nun, left the convent, married, and now ministers to alcoholics. My uncle started life as a man but is now a woman. (We call her "Auncle.") My French Canadian side tempers my Irish half. My father was born a Protestant, but educated Catholic and served as altar boy. We take two steps forward and one back. We don't always get it right.

Gram would kill me for saying it, but we Catholics need to jettison this black-and-white Protestant notion of being saved — that one-time experience that marks a conversion. Catholic conversion is always happening now, when the ordinary speaks and we listen. Come out often, take Eucharist every day, start again. Endure transitions, translations, transubstantiation. Adopt a local view — bury a few babies, train a few lectors, pray for an archbishop you don't love enough, shake hands with a snitch, trust that He is working through others elsewhere at the same time as He is working through you, others you'd like to meet someday if only you had time.

Open the door. Sit in the pews. Bring all your parts and gifts, however homely, and hold nothing in reserve. Lay it all before God. Participate in the Church's dying in hopes of participating in its new life. It's a privilege to be alive in a time like this, a privilege to take part in history like the preservation of same-sex marriage in Massachusetts, a privilege to be part of the Church at a time when so many are hearing a call to make it better, richer, more just.

We will benefit, as will those already inside, opening them to a more complete realization of God's love. The Church, after all, is incomplete without us. It is broken. We can enter its imperfection.

Many, of course, are already there. At the Shrine, for example, my predecessor on the Lay Ministry Committee was an out gay man. He and his husband (another Scott!) were civilly unionized in Vermont on their twenty-fifth anniversary and subsequently civilly married in Massachusetts. (One of their friends quipped, "You guys have been married more times than Elizabeth Taylor!")

The cantor was gay. A half-dozen eucharistic ministers were gay. The friars . . . well, not exactly breaking news. But there was indeed a whole shadow world I had managed to overlook in my time there.

"Why are you still Catholic?" I asked a gay father of three.

"Entirely aside from my spiritual life and my promise to the good priests and nuns that were here when my children were christened, I also feel a political responsibility not to leave but instead to sit my gay ass in the pew and not to be budged by people who don't want me there," he said. "It's the Rosa Parks thing. I'm just not moving. It's my Church, too, as much as theirs. If I want to leave, I will, but I won't leave because somebody else wants me to leave or because it makes somebody else uncomfortable. I just won't do it. I won't do it for myself and I won't do it for people who are not yet born, who will have the same struggle. That's . . . my very quiet of saying, 'We're here, we're queer, and I'm proud of it.' I'm there, and [my husband] is there, and I'm proud we're there. If it were appropriate to raise my middle finger, that's what I am doing — in a polite, kiss-of-peace kind of way."

Pucker those lips and raise that finger high. Blessed, of course, are the meek and the poor in spirit. Blessed are the Hale Marys and the Myrons and the Mama Bears. But also give me Catholics like the gay father of three, Bear-Daddy, Ann Franczyk, Thelma and Louise — Catholics who are ribald and frothing and furious, irrepressible, lusty, pigheaded men and women who like to get dirty and yell and drink grog and eat without worrying about their cholesterol, men and women who howl at the moon, for whom a few conversational bruises is par for the course, who weren't beaten up in the schoolyard but maybe a few times since then, who kick down doors and run their heads into walls, who laugh and cheer, break bones and skin, who carry their brothers and sisters, who savor the vast silences, jubilate with the noise, and who listen well.

Give me a God unafraid of a few bruises, jostling elbows, hickies, a God with a sense of humor and a sense of mission.

Give me fellow Catholics who understand that this book is an act of love.

We have too many advantages, too many graces, to act solely from resentment. Act instead from joy. As Cardinal O'Malley once said, "I often use humor in my talks. . . . It helps to focus people. Our religion should bring us joy, and it also keeps us from taking ourselves too seriously." Impiety and irreverence have always been my puny defense against this all-consuming faith and love that make me feel naked and vulnerable as the day I was born. As I wrote in the beginning, I never intended this book to be an attack on the Church.

I'm no saint. No one is going to cut out my heart when I die — at least not as an act of veneration, anyway. Since my last confession, I've sucked cock, written porn, cheated on my Church by flirting with gay-friendly Protestant alternatives, insulted Mama Bear, failed to walk old ladies across the street, fantasized about murdering my brother, YouTubed for schadenfreude's sake, littered my parts in the streets, felt superior to Ye Olde Piety Show, failed fully to forgive the snitches, and stalked Cardinal Seán.

And I'm not as sorry as I could be.

XVIII

Last Chance for Love

You are no longer to pray for vocations. Stop right now. We have so many voca-
tions, it's unbelievable. We have married men, we have former priests, we have
women who have been trained theologically who are ready to go. Your prayer
shouldn't be for more vocations, but that the Church have the courage to recognize
the vocations among us.

— Father Walter Cuenin

Meanwhile, Back at the Shrine

O MARK THE ANNIVERSARY of September 11, Father
Bear-Daddy set up a five-thousand-pound Bell of
Remembrance in the street outside the Shrine. The
names of the victims appeared on a sixty-five-foot-
long banner strung from one end of the Shrine to
the other. He rang the bell at 8:46 A.M., when the first plane struck the
Twin Towers, and again and again for each successive crash and the
collapse of the towers.

The massive bell tolled throughout downtown Boston, and I
thought immediately: *There is something real in this ritual, something*
substantial. You can feel it in your gut.

It turned out that Father Bear-Daddy had a personal stake in the
September 11 memorial. Father Mychal Judge — the openly gay
Franciscan chaplain of the Fire Department of New York City who
died at the foot of the Twin Towers — was a close personal friend.[†]

[†] "Close personal friend" is not a euphemism for "gay lover." That would be a "particular friend," as many priests know.

"[Father Judge] had the ability to heal and bring people closer together. Along with his sense of humor, that is what I will miss most about him, and what I was reflecting on today as I heard the bells and looked back," Father Bear-Daddy said. "He could always help people, and everyone loved him."

Prior to his 9/11 heroics, Father Judge had founded Saint Francis AIDS Ministry, one of the first Catholic AIDS organizations in New York. According to a former Marist brother who worked with him in this ministry, Father Judge had been a member of Dignity. He also had a keen appreciation for gorgeous men, exclaiming, "Isn't God wonderful!" when he came upon a group of them one night.

"Was he a gay saint?" I asked Father Bear-Daddy.

"Not a gay saint, no," Father Bear-Daddy said. "In fact, if he had died of natural causes, no one would be talking about him being a saint. And knowing Mychal, you are getting half of it — not even — if you take just the gay part. But he was a phenomenal man, the epitome of the word *charism*."

According to Father Bear-Daddy, Judge was a this-worldly priest — practical, pastoral, and with a great sense of humor. "I don't know exactly how Mychal died. You hear all kinds of pious stuff — he was giving last rites, he was helping someone out from the rubble. But I do know what kind of guy he was, and what would be typical of Mychal."

After Father Bear-Daddy's ordination, Father Judge took him out to dinner and solemnly said, "You, Bear-Daddy, were ordained in one Church, and I was ordained in another." Father Judge had been ordained before Vatican II, and Father Bear-Daddy after. "It's a whole different Church," Father Judge said. "Don't let anyone tell you any different."

Father Judge then slid a box across the table, saying, "This is for you." The box contained a commemorative gold coin from the Second Vatican Conference.

"Wear this medal," Father Judge said. "It's a symbol of the priesthood that you are going to lead. Whenever you look at this medal, I want you to think of me and what your priesthood means."

Choked up, Father Bear-Daddy solemnly agreed he would.

Then Father Judge grinned. "But if you ever get in trouble, Bear-Daddy, hock the damn thing. It's worth a fortune."

Why Catholic? (Part 3)

"I am sixty-two years old, and I'm only in it for the paycheck," a priest confessed.

Said his confessor: "Good, you're finally doing something for yourself. No shame in that."

Last Chance for Love

The final Mass at Boston's "gay church" brought back hundreds of those who had fallen or moved away — the old homosexual Jesuits, the musical directors, the unchurched, and the otherly churched. They fondly recalled the old days. Out flowed tears, laughter, and fond reminisces about the *Boston* magazine article that identified the JUC as the hottest spot to pick up men. At the doughnut social, everyone joked that the closing hymn ought to have been "Last Dance, Last Chance for Love," the famous anthem that marks closing time at gay clubs everywhere.

The humor masked a real sense of loss. For almost thirty years, the JUC served as a haven. One longtime member of the community told me,

> Several guys have major life-threatening diseases, a number are active in AA, other people feel more comfortable than being in bars. The sermons gave them something to feed on during the week. They would find something to challenge or support or encourage them. There are a number of parents of gay children, especially those who have lost kids, and [the JUC] has helped them to reconnect with a Church that was hurting their kids. A lot of people really do love the traditions and values of the Church and feel chopped off from Church life. They can come here and be who they are and not be chopped at.

For many, the JUC was a last stop on the Catholic line, including for those who had left the seminaries and orders and had not again found such a deep community of men. The members bitterly complained that the Jesuits had pulled the plug on the JUC so abruptly. They were angry that the Jesuits made no effort to continue the ministry in a cheaper location. They were upset that *The Pilot*, the Diocesan newspaper, made no mention of gays and lesbians in its article covering the closing.

The absence of Jesuit leadership on the future of the community forced the members to take action. Mama Bear and a handful of other men formed a steering committee to hunt for a new home. Seventeen sites, about half of them Catholic churches, opened their doors.

Even the chancery got into the act. The archdiocese's new COO, Vicar General Father Richard Erickson, pledged to help find the JUC a home in a church in the archdiocese.

Mama Bear and the boys greeted the offer with skepticism. "Can we trust you?" they asked. "You know we are all gay?"

The vicar general assured them that the chancery valued the JUC community. He found an underutilized diocesan church nearby where the JUC could move intact, keep its own liturgy, music, and — above all — its doughnut social. Some members of the JUC preferred Saint Cecilia's, a welcoming parish in the South End with a friendly pastor, mostly straight congregation, and huge student population. Either place, Erickson assured them, was fine with the archdiocese.

I asked Erickson, "Does O'Malley know about what you're doing to help the JUC? Won't he accuse you of wrongfully leasing a car or something if he finds out?"

"Everything I do, I'm doing on behalf of the cardinal," Erickson assured me. Father Kick-Me also confirmed that the cardinal knew all that was being done in the name of the archdiocese.

Love Thy Neighbor

The Vatican apparently failed to make Father Erickson aware of the Satanic conspiracy that homosexuals had launched to seduce priests. News of the conspiracy first surfaced in October 2007, when Vatican high-honcho Monsignor Tommaso Stenico lured a hot young man to his office, where they had X-rated discussions, and the good monsignor opined that the sin that cries out to heaven for vengeance was A-OK in his book, the sooner the better. After video of this colloquy broadcast nationally, Stenico explained that he was conducting research into the above-mentioned conspiracy. Even the Vatican laughed. But me, I understood perfectly. Like my trying to score a kiss from Cardinal Seán, Stenico was just trying to get to know the enemy better. No shame in that.

Other signs of post-marriage-debate redemption surfaced:

- Reverend Erickson started making pilgrimages to the gay-lesbian outreach ministries of some of Boston's Jesuit and Paulist churches to start a dialogue.
- O'Malley gave a much closer advisory role to the Rev. Brian Hehir, a man widely viewed as insufficiently conservative by the snitches.
- O'Malley appointed a woman as Hehir's replacement at Catholic Charities; she was the first woman ever to head the organization.
- Reverend Kick-Me assured me that Cardinal Seán now stood firmly against using the Eucharist as a battleground, and wouldn't ban anyone from receiving it.
- On the Brown Bag blog, Seán graciously included a photograph from a talk he gave at an Irish pub that shows a six-inch sliver of my bald pate sticking out among the heads of the more pious.

I no longer needed His Eminence's approbation, but I tried to keep my heart open to his conversion. To paraphrase Father Bear-Daddy's instructions to the recalcitrant lay ministers, Seán is not dead yet; he can still learn new tricks. Perhaps these signs, small as they were, signaled a first step. If so, it was still worth meeting with Seán, to worship with him, and to witness to him. I imagined our colloquy might go like this:

We kneel next to one another in the pew. We are exhausted, pock-marked, worn, our dark nights of the soul kept at bay with alcohol, Xanax, and masturbation, YouTubing and CardinalCasting. Our fingers ply rosary beads; I've stolen Sherwin's for the occasion. We have a deck of prayer cards, but we're each playing a losing hand. We are silent, intent, listening. Mentally squirting calicos with plastic water pistols.

Seán is thinking, perhaps, of the pastoral days at the Centro Católico in Washington, D.C., before he acquired the cocked red hat that made a mockery of his simple brown robe. He is remembering perhaps the first Mass he said at the monastery of the Poor Sisters of Saint Clare in Cleveland. He may be thinking, Lord have mercy. We're not in Cleveland anymore.

I, perhaps, am recalling the moment of Mikaela's baptism, the lie I told my pastor at age fifteen when I said I was ready for my confirmation, the Hispanic guy with the broken accent at the Shrine's legal center who was the only client I could say for sure I had truly helped, or a hug from Father Bear-Daddy that lifted me off my feet.

Cardinal Seán might break the silence to say something I once heard Father Myron say: "The problem with beautiful Catholic imagery is that we can easily convince ourselves we see God when we do not see God. No one has seen God, so we have to content ourselves with seeing Him in others. And the most contented people I know are those who have success in this."

I might respond, "Here I am, Seán," because I can think of no more powerful or destabilizing argument.

"How can a porn-writing sodomite consider himself a real Catholic?" Seán might ask.

"How can a cat-squirting goldfish-murderer consider himself a true Franciscan?" I might reply.

Sure, I might concede that maybe writing porn is not the highest use of what few gifts God gave me. But then, neither is using the pulpit of the archdiocese to achieve strictly political ends the highest use of that grace, particularly when you are dishonest about your arguments.

I therefore add, "I'll make you a deal, Your Eminence. I'll give up writing porn if you give up the political campaign against gay marriage and the uncharitable broadsides against gay parents and goldfish. How about that?"

Maybe Cardinal Seán nods solemnly and takes the offer under advisement. Dialogue, after all, is not the cardinal's strength.

That's when I throw in the kicker: "Tell you what, Seán. As an added incentive, I'll even throw in the towel on the YouTube habit. Gratis."

"*Done!*" Seán might say, and shake my hand.

Or maybe he'll just Donald Trump me without a second thought: "You're excommunicated!"

Why Catholic? (Part 4)

Asked why he is still Catholic, Father Butterballino said:

> I recognize that I have made a compromise. People ask, 'Do you believe in all that stuff?' And I say, I believe in all the stuff in the Gospel, and I believe what we do in this parish. That's important enough for me to stay with this. . . . Sometimes I picture a straight couple, and their kids are all grown up and married, and what had held them together is now gone, and the guy looks across the breakfast table at his wife and asks, 'What keeps me here now?' And he realizes he spent most of his life with her. Well, I spent a chunk of my life with the Church, and I did a good job. So I'm trying to find new ways to be in love with her. To love her in a different way. To continue that image, I am not going to divorce her, because I spent most of my life with her, and it was good.

And So What?

If O'Malley — through his graciously pleasant secretary Reverend Kick-Me — told Father Bear-Daddy that he was no longer to permit me to lector, take communion, volunteer at the legal clinic, or advise the human services providers or the liturgy committee, I would certainly miss offering my gifts — mean as they are, gay as they may be. Let's face it: those ministries are the only good work I do all week. I am, after all, a lawyer. My vocation offers few moral satisfactions. I can't fix cars, or build bridges, or heal wounds.

But if they took my ministries from me, there would be nothing tragic or shameful about sitting behind the remaining Hale Marys rather than beside them. In fact, I think I would feel an embarrassing sort of undeserved richness: for continuing health, a boyfriend who loves me, a family and godchildren who nurture me, a G-L Spirituality Group full of wounded heroes and heroines, forebears like Dignity, ministries like Always Our Children, priests like Lewandowski and Cuenin, wise scholars like Keenan, and friars and lay ministers who bury babies, welcome lonely seniors, visit Mary with her broken hip, fill kids' backpacks with school supplies, push Chewbacca back to his place at his bulletin delivery ministry, and create a Broadway liturgy that really pulls you out of the drama of which you are the center, first through words that pry free your moorings, then through music that tosses you about, and finally through shared, familiar prayer.

I would find some other saving, secular ministries. I would support my lectors. If they let me, I'd continue to teach them on the sly. If a lector asked, I'd be glad to give private advice.

I don't think I would feel lost or betrayed. I'd be able to forgive them for taking from me. After all, Seán and I are each rich if you have eyes to see us that way — if, for example, you see God in us. His Eminence often speaks of the schizophrenic, deinstitutionalized stranger who thinks he is Jesus Christ, and, in a disturbing, challenging manifestation, that stranger is indeed Jesus.

For now, I treat each lector training like the last. I am extra careful and extra solicitous, and I always try to make sure that a G-L Spirituality Group member sits among the volunteers. Lector ninjas must carry on after Seán throws me out so that, on any given day at any given mass, someone wonderful will proclaim the Word.

The ministry, after all, is not about me.

Epilogue

AY PEOPLE CONTINUE TO MOVE out of the South End, and they put their spare housewares out for sale on the brick sidewalks: a 1950s vintage ice bucket shaped like a green apple complete with stem, leopard-skin pillows, a snakeskin belt, and alligator shoes. But my eye fell again and again on the authentic kneeler covered with light blue cloth, a cross carved into the wood frame. I kneeled.

"Let's buy it!" I said to Scott. "It'll look great in the living room next to the pew." The kneeler would assuage the intellectual guilt of watching *Desperate Housewives*.

"A kneeler?" Standing in front of me, his crotch at face level, he deadpanned, "I think it would be better in the bedroom, don't you?"

Amen. Makeup sex is always best. We all have rubrics we religiously follow that bring normalcy to our day and maybe supply the illusion of control and a measure of timelessness. We all have our own private rituals of reconciliation.

Scott and I form a tiny congregation, he and I sitting side by side on our pew. I reach out with that tentative, postfight touch. My fingertips brush his shoulder, and he flinches as if scalded. Then he takes a deep breath, and I gather him in, his head to my shoulder and our arms wrapped around each other, waiting for deliverance on the hardest pew known to man.

Talk about a goddamn leftover miracle. I'd be lying if I told you that I completely understand.

Acknowledgments

OZENS OF PEOPLE ASSISTED ME in ways large and small in writing this book. In particular, my special thanks to those who shared their stories or introduced me to people who shared stories, including Sherwin Aguilar, Marek Bozek, Gary Buseck, Chuck Colbert, David Convertino, Gary Convertino, Walter Cuenin, Don Currier, Fred Daley, Eileen DiFranco, Marianne Duddy, Austin Fleming, Ann Franczyk, Holly Gunner, Ellen Grund, Joan Houk, Richard Iandoli, Robert Kickham, Richard Lewandowski, Casey Lopata, Jim Lopata, Mary Ellen Lopata, Gregory Maguire, Jean Marchant, Charles G. Martel, Myron McCormick, Frank McHugh, Brian McNaught, Andy Newman, Jim Nickoloff, Ray Niro, Michael Parisi, Robert Quinan, Joan Rosazza, Victoria Rue, Sal Sapienza, Jon Schum, Diane Sidorowicz, Brian Smail, Rene Sontag, Jackie Stewart, Ray Struble, John Sullivan, Kathy Vandenburg, Peter Weston, Claire Wilcox, and a host of people who requested that they not be named here for fear of retaliation from the Church hierarchy.

Special thanks also to past and present members of the G-L Spirituality Group, the Hale Marys, and the friars. In different ways, their faith was and is the beacon I follow.

Love and thanks to my mother and father, my three siblings (even those who voted for Bush in 2004), my three godchildren, Gram, Rory, Jezebel, and the rest of the Whittier clan. Their love helps me understand what it means to be loved by God. I am the luckiest person in the world.

To the folks at Gay and Lesbian Advocates and Defenders, Mass Equality, the General Court of the Commonwealth of Massachusetts, and all the other heroes of the same-sex marriage fight, I'd like to eat your hearts.

For editing above and beyond the call of duty despite a tragic nasal accident, I owe a huge debt to James Jayo at Arcade. Many thanks!

For their faith in this project and diligence in bringing it to publication, thanks to Ike Williams and Melissa Grella at Kneerim & Williams.

Finally, to my boyfriend, Scott Whittier, for patience and love far beyond the call of duty: I thank you and love you, Koala Bear.

Notes

HE EVENTS DESCRIBED HERE are generally true, but in many cases I have changed names, identifying details, topics of discussion, and the timing of events in order to protect confidentiality and/or for narrative convenience. Friars, priests, lay ministers, and G-L Spirituality Group members are all composites drawn from real people.

Prologue

The quotes from Pastor Bob and Ruben Israel come from "Signs of War at the State House," *Boston Globe*, March 12, 2004.

Chapter I

The quotation attributed to B16 is from the *Catholic New Times*, October 9, 2005.

Chapter II

The quote at the beginning of the chapter is from Seamus Heaney, *District and Circle* (New York: Farrar Straus & Giroux, 2006).

Chapter III

The quote from Gabriele Amorth and much of the material on the Vatican condemnation of Harry Potter comes from Lifesitenews.com, March 1, 2006, and from the *New York Times*, January 1, 2002. A similar account appeared in other news media, including the *Daily Mail* in the United Kingdom and *The Age* in Australia.

In addition to Abraham, some of the material on the history of lay ministry came from Kenan B. Osbourne, *Ministry* (Mahwah, N.J.: Paulist Press, 1993), 215–16, 219.

Chapter IV

The quote from Jim Naughton appeared in *The New Yorker*, April 17, 2006.

The quote from the friar concerning O'Malley came from the *Boston Herald*, July 2, 2003.

The smut I imagined Myron reading comes from Scott Pomfret and Scott Whittier, *Hot Sauce* (New York: Warner Books, 2005).

The quotes from the Baltimore Catechism are actually from *A Catechism of the Catholic Religion* (New York: Schwartz, Kirwin & Fauss, 1878).

The quotation regarding pornography comes from the *Catechism of Catholic Church* (Ligouri, Mo.: Ligouri Publications, 1994).

The quote from the Congregation for the Doctrine of the Faith is from its letter, "On the Pastoral Care of Homosexual Persons," October 1, 1986.

The statements attributed to the USCCB come from their document, "Ministry to Persons with a Homosexual Inclination: Guide to Pastoral Care," November 14, 2006.

The 1992 Congregation of Doctrine of Faith statement was reported in the *National Catholic Reporter*, October 14, 2005.

Statements attributed to Cardinal O'Malley concerning gay marriage come from the Web site of the Massachusetts Catholic Conference (www.macathconf.org), unless otherwise indicated.

Chapter V

Alban Butler, *Butler's Lives of the Saints*, edited by Herbert Thurston and Donald Attwater (New York: P. J. Kennedy & Sons, 1956).

The quote regarding "KKK without sheets" comes from the *South Florida Sun-Sentinel*, October 17, 2002.

The story regarding O'Malley's disinviting a judge came from the *Boston Globe*, October 1, 2000.

The quote regarding Jefferson Davis and the associated discussion derives in part from the religioustolerance.org Web site.

Chapter VI

The book by Trebor Healey that I reference is *Sweet Son of Pan* (San Francisco: Suspect Thoughts Press, 2006).

The quote under the "Rainbow Church" heading is from Mark Jordan, *The Silence of Sodom* (Chicago: University of Chicago Press, 2000).

The source for Fr. Arpin's coming-out is Bill Zajac, "Gay Priests in Barely Closed Closet," *Springfield Republican*, February 29, 2004.

The source for Fr. Danyluk's coming-out story is Matthai Chakko Kuruvila, "Gay Priest Leaves Parish He Loves," *San Francisco Chronicle*, June 23, 2007.

The source for Fr. Morrison's coming-out is "Gay Priest Comes Out to Parish," 365gay.com, January 8, 2006. Fr. Morrison did not respond to a request for an interview.

The source for Fr. Kurylowicz's coming-out is Charles Honey, "Gay Priest 'Comes Out' after New Ways Symposium," *Grand Rapids Press*, March 29, 1997.

Chapter VII

The quote from Bishop Gregory comes from David France, "Gays and the Seminary," MSNBC, May 20, 2002.

Chapter IX

"Sucksluts Anonymous" was published in *Lust for Life* (Montreal: Vehicule Press, 2006) and *Best Gay Erotica 2007* (San Francisco: Cleis Press, 2006).

The statistics regarding the good works of the Archdiocese of Boston derive from its Web site, www.rcab.org.

The quote from Bishop Vigneron is from Robert J. Johansen, "Homosexuality and the Seminaries: How to Read the New Vatican Instruction," *Crisis*, February–March 2006.

The Rat's threat to world peace is found on the Vatican Web site and dated December 11, 2007: "Everything that serves to weaken the family based on the marriage of a man and a woman, everything that directly or indirectly stands in the way of its openness to the responsible acceptance of a new life, everything that obstructs its right to be primarily responsible for the education of its children, constitutes an objective obstacle on the road to peace."

The quote from Bishop Raul Vera is from *Newsweek*, September 17, 2007.

The quote from the papal envoy to Spain was reported in the *Guardian* (London), May 5, 2004.

The source for Pope Gregory's views on railroads is Charles R. Morris, *American Catholic* (New York: Vintage Books, 1997), 67.

The letter to the editor of the *San Francisco Chronicle* was published on July 28, 2007.

The quote from Nancy Wilson appeared in *Boston Spirit*, December 2006.

The hierarchy of truths quote derives from the Decree on Ecumenism Unitatis Redintegratio, UR#11.

I borrowed the slavery argument from Luke Timothy Johnson, "Homosexuality & the Church: Experience & Scripture," *Commonweal*, June 15, 2007.

Chapter X

Parts of the short history of excommunication derive from a National Public Radio report on Father Ned Reidy, available at www.npr.org/templates/story/story.php?storyId=5074599.

The Pope Pius X quote was reported in the *Catholic New Times*, October 9, 2005.

The Pope John XXIII quote appeared in a letter to the editor, *America*, June 21, 2004.

Fr. Cachia's story appeared in, among other media, *Catholic New Times*, October 9, 2005, and *Globe and Mail*, October 22, 2005.

Material regarding Fr. Bozek's experience came from *St. Louis* magazine, April 2006, and several stories in the *Chicago Tribune* and the *Springfield News-Leader*, in addition to a written interview with me.

The story of the lesbian couple denied communion appeared in the *Gilette News-Record*, March 10, 2007, and in an Associated Press story published in various media in March and April 2007.

The *Boston Globe*, July 27, 2003, is the source for the story about Shirley Gomes.

Chapter XI

The quote from Andrew Sullivan was from a speech he gave at Stonehill College, April 17, 2007.

The quotes from Fr. Hennessey and the other priest come from the *Boston Globe*, October 4, 2006.

Quotes and information concerning relics, including Cardinal O' Malley's Padre Pio relic, derive from the *Boston Globe*, January 14, 2007.

Chapter XII

The short history of marriage is loosely based on an open letter from Father Steven Schloesser, S. J., History Department, Boston College, to Senator Marian Walsh, West Roxbury, Massachusetts, February 19, 2004.

The financial report of the Archdiocese of Boston is the source for the information concerning spending. It is available at the archdiocese's Web site, www.rcab.org.

The letter from the papal nuncio was reported in the *Boston Herald*, December 7, 2005.

The quote from Cardinal George appeared in *U.S. Catholic* 69, no. 11 (November 2004).

The Vatican II quote is from Lumen Gentium #35.

The list of rebel saints is taken from James Martin, "Saints That Weren't," *New York Times,* November 1, 2006.

The quote from B16 comes from a commentary on Gaudium et Spes ("The Church in the Modern World") in Herbert Vorgrimler, ed., *Commentary on the Documents of Vatican II* (London: Burns and Oats, 1969), 134.

I am indebted to Father Rich Lewandowski for the idea of the archdiocese attacking divorce with the vigor with which it opposed gay marriage.

Chapter XIII

The source for Protestant condemnations of Boston's Irish Catholics is Thomas H. O'Connor, *The Boston Irish* (Boston: Back Bay Books, 1995), pp. 15-16, 43-45, 64, 67, 77.

The story of the goldfish trapped in the closed school came from the *New York Times*, June 11, 2005. O'Malley ultimately allowed a parent to rescue the fish three days after the closure.

The story of the legal clinic client has been changed to preserve confidentiality.

Chapter XIV

Names of participants and details of their lives and conversation have been changed to protect the confidentiality of the meeting, except for quotations from Father John, who agreed to be interviewed.

The quotes from Bishops Skylstad and Clark appeared in the *New York Times*, November 23, 2005.

Chapter XV

The source for the facts suggesting O'Connell's homosexuality is Charles R. Morris, *American Catholic* (New York: Vintage Books, 1997), 121–22.

The priest who related the AIDS story to me is Father Jim Callan, now excommunicated.

Holly Gunner related the story involving Representative Chris Fallon.

The statement of the Worcestor bishop appears on the Massachusetts Catholic Conference's Web site, www.macathconf.org.

The statement attacking the renegade priests is also from the Web site of the Massachusetts Catholic Conference.

Holly Gunner provided the quotes attributable to Marian Walsh. Walsh did not respond to requests for an interview.

Representative Paul Kujawski's story was reported in the *Worcester Telegram and Gazette*, June 16, 2007.

Representative Canavan's story was in *Baywindows*, June 21, 2007.

Chapter XVI

The quote from Fr. Boyle appeared in the *New York Times Magazine*, December 24, 2006.

The quote attributed to Fr. Ahern appeared in *Innewsweekly*, October 6, 2005.

Chapter XVII

Alison's quote comes from his *Faith Beyond Resentment: Fragments Catholic and Gay* (NY: Crossroad Publishing, 2001), 142.

Representative Paul Kujawski's story was reported in the *Worcester Telegram and Gazette*, June 16, 2007 and *Baywindows*, June 21, 2007.

Paul Loscocco refused to be interviewed to confirm the account of his switch.

The polling data is from a Center for Applied Research in the Apostolate at Georgetown University news release, January 12, 2005.

The *Boston Globe*, October 25, 2007, reported the banning of Harry Potter from a Catholic school in Wakefield, Massachusetts.

O'Malley's fishbowl quote is from the *National Catholic Reporter*, November 4, 2005.

The "listening before speaking" quotation comes from Richard R. Gaillardetz, *By What Authority? A Primer on Scripture, the Magisterium, and the Sense of the Faithful* (Collegeville, Minn.: Liturgical Press, 2003), 118.

Chapter XVIII

The stories and quotes concerning Mychal Judge derive from personal interviews and the *Boston Pilot*, September 15, 2006.

The story regarding Monsignor Stenico was widely reported, including in the *Toronto Star*, October 15, 2007.